"Few tasks are as important in th.                    In this new book, Phil Newton teaches pastors how to disciple leaders and how to shepherd a congregation that values investing in future leadership. As Newton reminds us in this book, bringing up future leaders isn't just the job of the pastor, but of the whole congregation. This is an urgently needed book in churches today."

—R. Albert Mohler Jr., President of the Southern Baptist Theological Seminary

"The question for Christians today is not if they are called to leverage their lives for the Great Commission; it's only a matter of where and how. And who better to train our people to seize those opportunities than the local church? As we often say at the Summit, "Discipleship happens in relationships." This book gets at the heart of discipleship—intentional, strategic, biblical relationships that equip people and send them out into God's mission."

—J. D. Greear, pastor, author, and theologian

"Pastors everywhere struggle to train leaders. We know we need to do it, but we don't know where to begin. *The Mentoring Church* combines biblical truth and historical insight with contemporary examples of churches that are raising up leaders for the future. Pastor, read this book! You'll be glad you did. Better yet, study it with your leadership team. No other book covers this topic so completely. I'm glad Phil Newton shared his wisdom with the rest of us. May God use this book to raise up a new generation of leaders for the cause of Christ."

—Dr. Ray Pritchard, President, Keep Believing Ministries

"Phil Newton's *The Mentoring Church* is essential reading for Christians interested in mentoring or being mentored. Newton shows the absolute centrality of the local church for spiritual mentorship, constructs a practical mentorship template for churches, and provides contemporary examples that will help pastors envision spiritual mentorship in their own unique contexts. Highly recommended."

—Bruce Riley Ashford, Provost and Dean of the Faculty,
Southeastern Baptist Theological Seminary

"This call for pastors to give themselves to mentoring the next generation of church leaders is rooted in Scripture and illustrated from church history as well as different contemporary church models. This book encourages us to keep focused on this vital work for the health of local churches and ongoing spread of the gospel of our Lord Jesus Christ."
—Paul Rees, Lead Pastor, Charlotte Chapel, Edinburgh

"Phil Newton loves the church of Jesus Christ and is passionate about its spiritual health and growth. It is this passion that drives this book about the making, mentoring, and maturing of godly and effective leaders in Christ's church for his glory."
—Liam Goligher, Senior Minister, Tenth Presbyterian Church, Philadelphia

PHIL A. NEWTON

# THE
# MENTORING
# CHURCH

## HOW PASTORS AND CONGREGATIONS
## CULTIVATE LEADERS

**KREGEL**
MINISTRY

*The Mentoring Church: How Pastors and Congregations Cultivate Leaders*

© 2017 by Phil A. Newton

Published by Kregel Publications, a division of Kregel, Inc., 2450 Oak Industrial Dr. NE, Grand Rapids, MI 49505-6020.

ISBN 978-0-8254-4464-7

*Printed in the United States of America*

This book is dedicated to the
church planters, missionaries, pastors, elders,
and church leaders mentored over the past thirty years at the
South Woods Baptist Church, Memphis, Tennessee

and

to the congregation that has so faithfully loved, served, challenged, shaped, prayed for, and encouraged them.

# CONTENTS

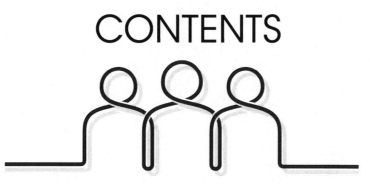

# FOREWORD

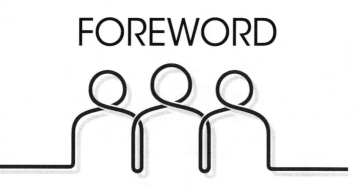

Phil Newton has blessed congregations and congregational leaders with a thoughtful and carefully designed proposal to help develop a new generation of pastors and leaders for the churches. Drawing on Scripture, healthy models from church history, and his own pastoral ministry experience, Newton has provided a gift for congregations and their leaders.

This vision for mentoring a new generation of church leaders will require well-prepared and gifted ministers, as well as willing congregations and other ministry partners, in order for implementation of this work to take place. The proposal found in this extremely helpful volume is informed by the deep realities of the Great Commandment (Matt. 22:37–39) and grounded in the commission of Jesus Christ himself who commissioned the church to make disciples of all the nations (Matt. 28:19–20). In Ephesians 4:11–16, the apostle Paul identifies the goals for an effort such as this one, which involves building up the church, guiding it to maturity in faith, and leading it to unity. Those first-century goals continue to be the focus for mentoring and developing leaders for our day as well. This work calls for mature leaders to invest themselves in younger God-called minsters, in a manner that follows Paul's pattern with Timothy and Titus. What Timothy and Titus had heard from Paul, they were to pass along to faithful leaders who could teach others also (2 Tim. 2:2). Newton's proposal envisions the replication of these practices in a similar way.

The picture with which we are presented in the book that you hold in your hands does not eschew the important work of Christian colleges, theological seminaries, or other specialized parachurch ministries. Instead, this proposal calls for cooperation and collaboration with these entities—a both/and perspective rather than either/or. Recognizing that academic institutions need congregations and that congregations can benefit from other institutions or agencies, Newton has put forward an encouraging model for partnership that should be both welcomed and encouraged by all who are called to prepare the next generation of ministers.

Church leaders have been entrusted with the Christian faith, the body of truth "once for all delivered to the saints" (Titus 1:9; Jude 3). The Christian faith is not just faith in faith—some subjective, amorphous feeling—but is, in an objective sense, a body of beliefs, which in the Pastoral Epistles is called the teaching, the deposit, the faith, and the truth. This pattern of Christian truth is now available to mentors and mentees, to churches and church leaders, in the New Testament. One of the first responsibilities in the development of young, God-called and Spirit-enabled ministers includes instruction in the basics of these Christian beliefs about the Trinitarian God (Father, Son, and Holy Spirit), Scripture, humanity, sin, salvation, the Christian life, the church, the kingdom of God, eternal life, as well as Christian ethics.

Mentors and congregations also have the responsibility to prepare young ministers for the issues and expectations that they will encounter in their churches. The vision for mentoring must be holistic, preparing head, heart, and hands. Congregations need ministers who are well informed, but who also are Christianly formed and prepared for the various responsibilities of ministry.

Mentoring helps mentees learn to see the world from a biblical perspective, to respond scripturally to the issues of life, and to shape Christian motivations and strategies for ministry. The importance of connecting mentoring with the life of congregations is vital for this effort. Newton has provided well-researched models for his readers, showing how Zwingli, Calvin, Spener, Gano, Spurgeon, Bonhoeffer, and others invested in this important work during their time and in their contexts. Thus, we are invited to learn not only from Scripture itself, but, also, from the wisdom of those who have gone before us.

Newton's vision for a partnership between ministry leaders, congregations, and theological institutions recognizes that theological education has its roots in the churches. In the apostolic and post-apostolic period, pastors and church leaders were called to ongoing study (2 Tim. 2:15) in order to provide oversight for the ministry of the Word of God in the midst of worship services, as well as to train and disciple new converts (2 Thess. 2:15; Titus 1:9). Such an approach recognizes that theology is best done in, with, and for the church.

Scripturally centered mentoring recognizes the Bible as an inspired and authoritative source for understanding life, worship, and ministry; as a wellspring for preaching, teaching, and liturgy; as a primary source for the formulation of theology; as a model for pastoral care; and as a foundation for spiritual and worldview formation. Church leaders and congregations must create a community context—including relational connections—where young ministers and mentees will be able to learn best practices regarding the interpretation of the Bible, the study of Christian theology, and the application of these truths for the practical administration of church and church leadership, as well as for preaching, worshiping, and ministry. Mentoring practices may also include the strengthening of one's understanding of denominational distinctives, as well as specialized ministry callings, in addition to the essential work associated with funerals, weddings, pastoral counseling, the administration of the ordinances, global missions, racial reconciliation, and intercultural competencies.

Ultimately, Newton's vision for mentoring focuses on the building up of the people of God and the advancement of the gospel mission. In embodying that mission, the church is called to be faithful to discern, interpret, and proclaim the gospel of Jesus Christ as the transforming power for the world. Such mentoring practices help to eliminate the scholar vs. practitioner/academy vs. church dichotomy that exists in some portions of the Christian community.

Young ministers who have been prepared for church ministry through faithful mentoring will be prepared to understand what the church has believed through the ages, to proclaim the good news of the gospel, to lead others in the worship of our majestic God, to recover a true understanding of church health, and to provide genuine significance and security for the living of these days. Mentoring pastors and congregations will help the next generation of church leaders to be prepared to serve with conviction, giftedness, and humility—serving together with other brothers and sisters in Christ to extend the shared work of the gospel around the world, advancing the kingdom of God. Such young ministers will learn to relate to one another in love and humility, bringing about true fellowship and community in orthodoxy as well as in orthopraxy before a watching world.

We join with Phil Newton in praying that God will raise up a new generation of faithful, well-prepared, convictional, and compassionate church leaders who are prepared for the ever-changing and ever-expanding challenges of the twenty-first century and who will accept the responsibility for investing in the lives and ministries of those called to serve the next generation. We join together to ask the Lord to expand and renew our vision for ministry and leadership, for discipleship and churchmanship. We trust that the next generation of church leaders will manifest a stronger and deeper dedication to the work of church and ministry, giving thanksgiving for and learning from the many who have gone before us.

The vision that has been proposed in this volume for effective and faithful mentoring is informed and shaped by the best practices of church history, enabling us to bring together an understanding and knowledge of the past that will keep church leaders from confusing what is merely a contemporary expression or fad from those things that are enduringly relevant. Shaping these truths and ministry practices in the context of Christian history offers insight for today and guidance for the future.

We pray for pastors and church that will seek to implement this vision as they serve together to help prepare the next generation of ministers and leaders for ministry and leadership in the churches of the Lord Jesus Christ. The work of mentoring and developing young church leaders is indeed a distinctive and important calling. Let us pray for God's blessings and favor to rest upon those who accept the challenge of this calling—for the good of the churches, for the advancement of the gospel message, and for the glory of our great God.

David S. Dockery
President, Trinity Evangelical Divinity School/Trinity International University

# ACKNOWLEDGMENTS

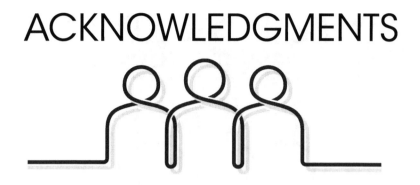

B ooks grow in community. They evolve and take shape through the sharpening and honing of brothers and sisters living life together in Christ. My life continues to be enriched and affected by this kind of fellowship with the body. These relationships contribute, knowingly and unknowingly, to the process of putting words on a page. For that reason, I must call the reader's attention to just a few who made this book possible.

South Woods Baptist Church in Memphis, Tennessee, has given me the opportunity to serve them for thirty-years. In this time, they've supported and encouraged me to mentor for ministry. My fellow elders—Tom, Dan, Jim, Tommy, Chris, Drew, and Matt—have joined me in mentoring. Those in our congregation that we've mentored together, along with others already engaged in ministry, have contributed to our joy in mentoring. You brothers have given us far more than we've given to you.

Special thanks goes to those who've offered suggestions for improving this work: John Hammett, Alvin Reid, Matt Sliger, Bruce Ashford, Chris Spano, Ray Pritchard, Jonathan Leeman, Matt McCullough, Jordan Thomas, and Raymond Johnson. I'm thankful for Debbie Jones' assistance with a load of details. David Dockery exemplifies the scholar-churchman faithful in training the next generation. I appreciate his encouraging Foreword to this book. Once again I'm grateful to work with the excellent team at Kregel Publications. Thanks to all of you!

Karen, the love of my life, has moved this project forward in countless ways by her support, encouragement, listening ear, prayers, and always good counsel.

May Jesus Christ who trained his disciples to preach the gospel receive all glory!

# SIXTEEN, CALLED, AND CLUELESS

A long with hundreds of other communities, the sweep of the Jesus Movement in the late 1960s and early 1970s brought the message of the gospel
to my small town in Alabama. Our church's pastor had no clue of what to do
with teenagers and young adults professing faith in Christ, sharing testimonies,
witnessing in the community, and meeting several nights a week for fellowship.
So he ignored us. Along with that, he punted on involvement with several of us
who sensed God's call to ministry. Out of that atmosphere, as a sixteen-year-old
who knew nothing about ministry, I began to pursue gospel ministry.

While several hundred people attended our county seat First Baptist Church,
most seemed contented to just act nicely, attend the dry worship services, toler-
ate gospelless sermons, and maintain the façade of Christianity. Yet the invasion
of God's Spirit in regenerating power in the lives of my friends and me left us
hungering for more.

We saw through the disunity on the church staff, the popularity contests to
elect church deacons, and the superficial talk about missions. Spending three-
fourths of our Sunday school hour discussing Friday night's football game, with a
quick fifteen-minute read through the packaged lesson, did nothing to stimulate
Bible study or satisfy our spiritual hunger. That was not the ideal setting to prepare
for gospel ministry.

Despite spending three years in that church after announcing my call to
ministry, the pastor never talked to me about spiritual disciplines, a daily quiet
time, Scripture memory, Bible study, or good books to read. Twice he gave me the
opportunity to preach, where I muddled through poor attempts at expounding
my chosen texts, with hardly a clue on what to do, and with no guidance from

him. No feedback followed to help steer me toward better exegesis and clearer homiletics. Nothing. No encouragement, no correction, and no guidance—just silence, with the expectation that whenever I completed college and attended seminary, then I would get what I needed to prepare for gospel ministry. That seemed to be the ethos for most in the church as they looked from a distance at the "preacher boys."

Thankfully, a few couples invested their time and spiritual nurturing in helping my friends and me. They opened their homes, taught us the Scripture, prayed with us, listened to our endless questions, and modeled satisfaction in Christ. That small band of church members, without realizing it, started the process of preparing me for gospel ministry. They mentored me for living as a Christian and serving in ministry.

Fortunately, my time in college helped, with my first sustained exposure to men seeking to expound the Scripture. My heart raced at hearing the Word opened and applied. I wanted to do the same, but how?

Eager to jump into ministry, I accepted a church's offer to serve on their staff. This small church in the city where I attended college had little to offer the members or me. We endured repetitive sermons that lacked gospel clarity, followed by extended pleas and coaxing for decisions. Again, yet another pastor never engaged me to give direction, mentor, or teach the details of ministry. The church seemed to be gasping for its last breath. The best lesson that I learned was that I did not want to emulate that pastor or have a church so unhealthy.

My next staff position provided many more opportunities to learn but the pastor, while warm and caring toward me, had himself never been mentored in a healthy congregational setting. He typically followed denominational protocol without much thought to developing a strong, Christ-centered church. Although I did not understand at the time, he seemed to grasp little about shepherding the church toward spiritual health. His preaching scarcely followed the dynamics of biblical exposition. So when I preached on the short notice that he usually gave me, other than maybe telling me, "Good job," he never took me aside to correct and hone my preaching. I needed lots of honing! But no one had mentored him in the details of pastoral shepherding, so he had no direction in mentoring me to shepherd the church. Thankfully, as I sought to disciple a group of young adults, we banded together to grow in spiritual disciplines and gospel witness. Without realizing it, the questions, interactions, and accountability from that small part of the church helped to mentor me for ministry. The time with them in active Christian community shaped my future pastoral work more than anything.

During my last year of master of divinity work, I began pastoring a small, rural church a couple hours north of my seminary. I committed to preach expositionally and consequently, received some excellent training in biblical preaching through one of my professors. But I still understood little about shepherding a congregation, the dynamics of a healthy church, or the functions of a Great Commission church. I knew how to craft biblical sermons but not how to shepherd God's flock. Patiently, that little church endured my many mistakes and gave me a chance to begin to learn a few lessons in pastoral ministry. More lessons would follow in other churches that I served. But so would mistakes. Time after time I reached for the telephone to call a brother in ministry for advice on what to do next or how to walk through a dicey membership problem. Apart from the patient counsel of those brothers, I'm sure that I would not have made much progress in ministry. And I might not have lasted long. They mentored me, whether they realized it or not.

You might have noticed a theme running through my personal narrative. Those preparing for ministry need mentoring. Such mentoring certainly calls for the wise guidance of a seasoned pastor or elder. But just as critical to the process, the kind of mentoring that prepares future pastors, missionaries, Christian workers, and church planters best takes place with the involvement of a healthy congregation. *The most effective mentoring teams together pastors and congregations to help shape those who will serve Christ's churches.*

That's what this book is about. I seek to consider the biblical and theological foundation for local churches and pastoral leaders training those that the Lord raises up from among them for gospel ministry. To do that, we will take a look at mentoring models in Luke, Acts, and the Pastoral Epistles. The details that we will consider lay groundwork for contemporary churches.

But it's also important for us to see how others built on the biblical models through the centuries. Since historical examples help us to navigate the process of training for ministry, we'll consider some from five centuries, with well-known and lesser-known pastors. Perhaps even more applicable, visualizing current examples of church-centered mentoring helps to better frame how we can do the same in our churches. So we will look at four local churches that range in size, vary in leadership, and approach mentoring from different angles. Then we will identify a workable church/pastoral leader template that will be useful in embarking on training up gospel workers, regardless of the church's size. So let's journey on!

# ABBREVIATIONS

| | |
|---|---|
| *ANF* | *Ante-Nicene Fathers* |
| BDAG | A Greek-English Lexicon of the New Testament |
| BECNT | *Baker Exegetical Commentary on the New Testament* |
| BGC | Billy Graham Center |
| BST | Bible Speaks Today |
| DBW | Dietrich Bonhoeffer Works |
| *EBC* | *Expositor's Bible Commentary* |
| EKK | Evangelisch-Katholischer Kommentar zum Neuen Testament |
| *EMQ* | *Evangelical Missions Quarterly* |
| HNT | Handbuch zum Neuen Testament |
| *ISBE* | *International Standard Bible Encyclopedia* |
| JSNTSup | Journal for the Study of the New Testament, Supplement Series |
| LCC | Library of Christian Classics |
| LNTS | Library of Second Temple Studies |
| NAC | New American Commentary |
| NASB | New American Standard Bible |
| NICNT | New International Commentary on the New Testament |
| NIGTC | New International Greek Testament Commentary |
| NSBT | New Studies in Biblical Theology |
| NTC | New Testament Commentary |
| PNTC | Pillar New Testament Commentary |
| SBL | Society of Biblical Literature |
| SBLDS | SBL Dissertation Series |
| SNTSMS | Society for New Testament Studies Monograph Series |
| WBC | Word Biblical Commentary |
| ZECNT | Zondervan Exegetical Commentary on the New Testament |

# CHAPTER 1

# HEALTHY CHURCHES NEED HEALTHY LEADERS

While ministering in Brazil, a pastor invited me to preach in his evening worship service. It happened to be "pastor appreciation day," so I witnessed what seemed to be genuine affection for the pastor. Lively music, songs by the children's choir, and a presentation preceded my sermon. But I knew that I was in trouble when I stood to expound the Scriptures and noticed that my translator did not have a Bible with him. After borrowing a Portuguese Bible, I asked him to turn to Titus so that he could read the text before I began the sermon. Although a faithful church member, he couldn't find Titus. I knew enough Portuguese to help out and ease his embarrassment. I noticed that many in the congregation sitting in the straight-backed pews had as much trouble as my translator finding Titus. Some searched for it in the Old Testament. Grieved, I realized that this pastor and church neglected biblical exposition and Bible learning. While they were lively, they were not healthy. Noise and movement do not equate to church health.

Yet that's not a problem localized in Brazil or in other countries. I've witnessed similar experiences, without quite the liveliness, in the United States. Some pastors react to the unhealthy congregations by making a decision to plant a church. I know that personally, since I did the same after nine years of pastoring unhealthy churches.

No casual observer of the state of Christianity in North America would squabble over the need for new churches. Yet merely *multiplying* churches fails to answer the need for *effective* Great Commission churches (Matt. 28:18–20). Missionary leader David Platt points out that far too many churches simply assume knowledge of the gospel without admitting that many of their adherents have never understood and believed the gospel.[1] Ed Stetzer, a leading church planter and strategist, echoes Platt's concern by warning that evidence of genuine discipleship seems unnecessary for many churches to call someone a Christ-follower.[2] We need more than just new churches.

While the need for church multiplication rises, so does the need for churches to maintain gospel-centered focus and faithfulness.[3] Apart from such focus and faithfulness, a church remains unhealthy. So then, what is a healthy church? Washington DC pastor Mark Dever explains, "A healthy church is a congregation that increasingly reflects God's character as his character has been revealed in his Word."[4] Healthy churches should be normal, yet far too often churches confuse busy activity—like that church in Brazil—with the spiritual health that grows in corporate Christian character. Unfortunately, sometime pastoral leaders seem paralyzed at shepherding ailing congregations toward robust health.

While assessing North America as a mission field, theologian Jeff Iorg admits that many churches "have lost their mission, identity, focus, and in some cases, their credibility." He wisely reflects, "But do not dismiss the Church too quickly. God will sustain the Church and churches, both universally and locally (Rev. 5:9–10)."[5] Great Commission churches must be different from those that have slipped into unhealthy patterns and practices. They will need to return, Iorg asserts, to proclaim the biblical gospel, raise membership standards, practice church discipline, maintain doctrinal fidelity, embrace a missional mindset, and model Christian community. Additionally, they will need to show creativity in adapting to the cultural context of their communities.[6] Pastoral service in churches that take seriously the call of Jesus in the Great Commission requires a deliberate approach to training and equipping the leaders who serve them.

In considering the global front, David Platt explains his desire as leader of Southern Baptist's International Mission Board: "We're working and pleading with

---

1 Lillian Kwon, "Is the Church Dying in America's Bible Belt?" *Christianity Today*, April 28, 2010, n.p. [cited 24 January 2012], accessed January 24, 2012, http://www.christiantoday.com/article/is.the.church.dying.in.americas.bible.belt/25802.htm.

2 Ibid.

3 See Joseph Hellerman, *When the Church Was a Family: Recapturing Jesus's Vision for Authentic Christian Community* (Nashville: B&H Academic, 2009), 120–181; Timothy Keller, *Center Church: Doing Balanced, Gospel-Centered Ministry in Your City* (Grand Rapids: Zondervan, 2012), 13–84.

4 Mark Dever, *What Is a Healthy Church?* 9Marks (Wheaton, IL: Crossway Books, 2005), 40.

5 Jeff Iorg, "North America as a Mission Field: The Great Commission on Our Continent," in *The Great Commission Resurgence: Fulfilling God's Mandate in Our Time*, eds. Chuck Lawless and Adam W. Greenway (Nashville: B&H Academic, 2010), 228.

6 Ibid.

God to raise up multitudes of workers," so that they might be funneled through the denomination's mission agency. While mission leaders can troll colleges and seminaries for potential workers, the *multiplication* of future missionaries will only take place through healthy churches developing and training potential missionaries.[7]

## ORGANIC LEADERSHIP DEVELOPMENT

The development of leaders for the early church took place *organically* rather than institutionally. The orientation of the church with small beginnings in Jerusalem and gradually expanding into Judea, Samaria, and the rest of the world, shows an intentional thrust in fulfilling the Great Commission (Acts 1:8). Jesus *prepared* his disciples to proclaim the gospel, and to establish communities of believers throughout the Roman Empire that would continue to do the same.

Clearly, as North Carolina pastor J. D. Greear explains the early practice, "God's strategy for fulfilling the commission of Acts 1:8 was the planting of Acts 2:42–47 style churches in every city of the world."[8] We admire the way that the early church "devoted themselves to the apostles' teaching and the fellowship, to the breaking of bread and the prayers." The simplicity of community, generosity, service, table fellowship, and gratitude distinguished believers from their neighbors and heightened their gospel witness. The Lord raised up leaders to serve the expanding network of churches from that kind of lively discipling community atmosphere, as we will see in the next three chapters.

Does that approach seem too far-fetched for the sophisticated churches and strategies of the twenty-first century? While we have better organizational structures to help with developing pastoral leaders, we cannot improve upon the strength of healthy congregations birthing healthy leaders through a combination of pastoral oversight, congregational mentoring, and making the best use of academic training.

## MENTORING NEW LEADERS

Although the vocabulary that explains mentors and trainees has expanded in our generation, for twenty centuries Christian workers have been mentored and trained to start new congregations and to serve as catalysts for reviving others. Those who would lead in pastoring churches—locally or globally—need to be

---

7  Tess Rivers, "Trustees: IMB's Platt Unfolds Five-Point Strategy" [cited 4 December 2014], http://www.bpnews.net/43691/trustees-imbs-platt-unfolds-fivepoint-strategy.

8  J. D. Greear, "Great Commission Multiplication: Church Planting and Community Ministry," in *The Great Commission Resurgence*, 342.

trained, at minimum, in apostolic doctrine, biblical theology, proclamation, ec-clesiology, missiology, and spiritual leadership. We most often turn to the acad-emy to provide this sort of intensive training. Yet, the New Testament demon-strates that the kind of training necessary for healthy pastoral leaders in any setting finds added effectiveness when rooted in the context of healthy models of community. As one regularly involved in training Christian leaders, Manhat-tan pastor Tim Keller's explanation of the importance of community makes the connection between the local church and ministry training.

> Community shapes the nature of our witness and engagement in mission . . . shapes the development of our character . . . shapes our ethics and the spoken and unspoken rules that guide our behavior . . . is the key to true spirituality as we grow to know God by learning to know one another in relationships . . . [and] is perhaps the main way that we bear witness to the world, form Christ-like character, practice a distinctly Christian style of life, and know God personally.[9]

The practice of forming new communities of disciples, baptizing, and continu-ing to teach the disciples *in community* implies the need for effective leadership in these Great Commission tasks (Matt. 28:19–20).[10] Paul spoke of the pastoral and leadership gifts of Christ to the church (Eph. 4:10–16), "as [Jesus] supplies the church with everything necessary to promote the growth of the body until it matches his own fullness," as F. F. Bruce explained.[11] These gifts need cultivating and maturing in their use.[12] Jesus set the pattern: *Spiritual leaders working through community train leaders who will shepherd, plant, and revitalize discipling com-munities, who replicate the same work.*

How will new leaders prepare for the challenges of their ministry? Quite often, the training will take place in an academic setting. However, British author Stuart Murray, in discussing training church planters, points out the gaps that exist in theological education due to an emphasis on theory rather than application in theology. Then he makes a useful point that "perhaps *partnerships between local churches, networks, and training institutes* can provide leadership training which

---

9  Keller, *Center Church*, 311–314; see also 311–320 for more detailed explanation.
10  Ibid., 355–365.
11  F. F. Bruce, *The Epistles to the Colossians to Philemon and to the Ephesians*, NICNT, F. F. Bruce, ed. (Grand Rapids: Eerdmans, 1984), 344–345.
12  See Colin Marshall, *Passing the Baton: A Handbook for Ministry Apprenticeship* (Kingsford, Australia: Matthias Media, 2007), 15–17, 34–39, for helpful examples.

will equip church planters with theological insights, spiritual resources, and practical skills to plant churches with solid foundations and the potential for creative
reproduction."[13] His observation goes beyond church planters to include the broad
scope of pastoral and missionary leadership. If church leaders are to be trained
for their global tasks, then the training must eclipse the theoretical to embrace
the experiential. It is not that the theoretical has no place in training—it does. Yet,
while the academy normally appears best suited to expand on the theoretical, the
local church brings theory into application and experience.

While preparing for ministry as a college student, my involvement in local
churches shaped me spiritually, provided much-needed accountability, and gave
me regular outlets for exercising my gifts in the body. Unfortunately, when I moved
away to begin theological studies, my pattern lacked this same level of involvement.
While my wife and I regularly attended church, we made lots of weekend trips
to visit with family and friends, delaying settled involvement in the rhythm of a
congregation. I failed to realize at the time how necessary the church was for our
personal growth as well as our preparation for ministry. And yet, I was preparing
to pastor! The emphasis on seminary without the intensity of congregational life
diminished my theological and pastoral preparation.

I realize that many seminaries seek to bring the practical, experiential aspects
of training into the curriculum. For instance, Southeastern Baptist Theological
Seminary (SBC) in Wake Forest, North Carolina does this through their Equip
Network, as they combine an academic approach with local church pastoral
mentoring. Reformed Theological Seminary has eight campuses strategically
located, so that many students can attend seminary while continuing training
in their home churches. Seminaries and Bible colleges hold special importance
in ministry training. They address necessary subjects such as biblical languages,
theology, hermeneutics, and homiletics. Yet the academy is not the church—the
sphere in which those aspects of training will be most exercised. The partnership
between academy *and* church both doing what they do best to train leaders, as
proposed by Murray, presents an effective training model for equipping leaders.

## JESUS'S EXAMPLE

In his classic work, *The Training of the Twelve*, A. B. Bruce, a nineteenth-century Scottish pastor and theology professor, asserted that Jesus's statement in
John 17:6, "I have manifested Your name to the men whom You gave Me out

---

13  Stuart Murray, *Church Planting: Laying Foundations* (Scottsdale, PA: Herald Press, 2001), 227
     (italics added).

of the world," implied that "the principal part of His own earthly ministry" involved training those who would carry on the work he had initiated.[14] Bruce made two important points that define what is meant by *leadership training*. These points serve as a helpful platform for exploring pastors and congregations mentoring leaders.

First, as a trainer, Jesus not only wanted disciples around him but also wanted them close and attentive to him. In that way, he might train them to make disciples as they replicated what they had intimately witnessed in his life. *Effective mentors seek to replicate their own lives and ministries with those they train.* Much of the replication happens in the full-orbed relationships of community, where real-life issues bring to surface the full application of the gospel to life. Only by life in community do trainees see the depth of genuineness in their mentor's life.

During my college days, two local pastors who were about the same age served two of the city's strongest churches. The first pastor spent an enormous amount of time investing in young men preparing for ministry. He kept them close, met with them for discussion, invited them along at special events, and made himself accessible to them. He made sure that they were woven into the fabric of the congregation. Even with his large church, he knew them all by name. Forty years later, I often run into men whom he mentored and shaped for ministry and missions.

The other pastor provided a superb example from the pulpit for biblical exposition but his rigid schedule seemed to have little time for young men preparing for ministry. While he gained more notoriety for his pulpit skills than the former pastor and spoke in many large churches, the former impacted a virtual army of pastors, missionaries, church planters, and Christian leaders. The latter eventually pastored one of the largest churches in the country, but the former multiplied his ministry exponentially by the time spent mentoring men for ministry. Effective mentors give priority to replicating their lives and ministries in those they train.

Second, Bruce described the work of the mentor as finely polishing the mirrors of the trainees so that they might "reflect the image of Christ."[15] Mentors polish the mirrors by speaking into the lives of their protégés so that they might better reflect the image of Jesus Christ in life and ministry. Polishing removes the rough edges, sharpens the focus, and brings out the strengths of trainees. *Yet mentors do not stand alone in polishing* (1 Thess. 1:6). The hands of a healthy congregation join him in smoothing and refining trainees who aspire to ministry. That has been my observation in three decades of mentoring for ministry. Only when trainees are

---

14  A. B. Bruce, *The Training of the Twelve* (Grand Rapids: Kregel, 1971 reprint from 1894), 13.
15  Ibid.

immersed into the life of the community, so that Christians sharpen Christians, are they properly honed and prepared for leading others.

One of our older ladies would regularly have younger couples in her home. While munching on her homemade sugar cookies and sipping coffee, she asked questions that led to fruitful, Christ-shaping conversation. Just over a month after this woman's death, my wife and I traveled to another country where we sat in the family room of a couple from our congregation who serve an unreached people group. As we talked, this dear saint's name came up, as did details of how she helped them to understand gospel application for their own lives. From her, they learned about living in the hope of Christ. While I taught them missiology and church planting, she taught them to rest each day in Christ. That's what I mean by mentors not standing alone in polishing their trainees. The congregation gets involved.

Bruce explained Jesus's training model as "a regular apprenticeship for the great office of apostleship, in the course of which they were to learn, in the privacy of an intimate daily fellowship with their Master, what they should *be*, *do*, *believe*, and *teach*, as His witnesses and ambassadors to the world."[16] Jesus set the stage for developing healthy Christian leaders in every generation by establishing the goal and the method for training them. This basic approach to training can be followed and replicated in every generation.

*First, the goal for trainees involves being, doing, believing, and teaching.* (1) *Being* concerns spiritual formation. Unless the trainee develops in spiritual maturity, he may possess great gifts but these gifts alone will not suffice for kingdom work. Furthermore, *being* does not take place in isolation. It happens in community. Life together in community reveals the strengths and weaknesses in his spiritual formation. The way that he lives in relationship to others tests the genuineness of his spiritual maturity.

The community helps as well, by praying for one another, wrestling together with biblical texts, discussing good books that strengthen devotion to Christ, and fellowshipping together in the gospel. We do not mentor to develop cloistered monks but spiritual leaders, who will be immersed in shepherding God's flock. Spiritual formation taking place in the body deepens relationship toward God and one another.

(2) *Doing* refers to the actions or kingdom work that involves the whole gamut of living out the Christian life. *Doing* does not happen in isolation but with the community. Here, quite naturally, spiritual gifts develop in service to the body of Christ, as members get involved in serving one another. Relationships grow and find the challenge to love, forgive, accept, encourage, and serve. Until a trainee learns to

---

16  Ibid. (italics added).

serve others in the body, he remains unprepared for pastoral ministry or mission work or church leadership. I've found that the collegial atmosphere of the training cohort helps each member to better recognize and sharpen his gifts for ministry.

(3) *Believing* focuses on doctrine, insisting that the trainees will not do their work robotically, but rather out of an understanding of and reliance upon the doctrinal foundation established in Scripture. Believing becomes the motivation for perseverance in the work of ministry. Mentors set the stage for their trainees in grasping this theological reality as they demonstrate the practical application of doctrine to daily life. As the congregation that the trainees are part of lives out its understanding of Christian truth, trainees find intensive reinforcement to their faith.

(4) *Teaching* became the primary pastoral work carried on by Jesus's protégés, for as they taught, they set the content and application of the gospel at the heart of their ministries. So, too, those trained in a congregational setting should establish a priority on biblical teaching. Jesus gradually entrusted responsibilities to his disciples, step by step turning over the reins of ministry to them after his ascension. His disciples became the teachers of the first congregation in Jerusalem, as well as future congregations in the Roman world. Teaching remains foundational for the church's existence. That's why Jesus not only set the example in teaching, but also trained his disciples to go and do likewise.

At this point, mentors must hone the teaching and preaching gifts of trainees by providing opportunities to teach and preach, to discuss preparation, and to critique afterward. I've watched the steady progress of young men involved in our pastoral training ministry by trusting them with teaching and preaching, and then following up to shape them for the future. Several of our elders join me in this honing process. Those we've sent out to serve in pastoral or mission settings repeatedly thank us for the process that allowed them to learn to teach and preach with a "safety net." That aspect of our ministry continues to bear fruit today, with other congregations profiting from this investment in pastoral training.

*Second, following the pattern of Jesus, the method used by mentors for their protégés involves doctrine, praxis, and sending.* (1) As we will investigate more fully in the historical mentoring models, *doctrine* must stand at the heart of training pastors, church planters, church leaders, and missionaries. Doctrine must never be presumed with trainees. I've found it normal that some pastoral trainees lack doctrinal clarity in a number of areas. Sometimes it shows up in their preaching; other times in discussion. It will certainly be reflected in the way that they shepherd the flock. So mentors must press doctrinal precision, since it affects the whole of gospel ministry.

(2) *Praxis* refers to the actual experience of ministry rather than just talking about it in a sterile environment. Trainees engage in pastoral and mission work,

often under the direct supervision of a mentor, in order to test and hone their gifts, to learn to develop precision in various pastoral roles, and to give evidence of readiness to be involved in ministry. Both the historical and contemporary models that we'll consider in subsequent chapters will offer ways to bring praxis to the forefront in leadership training.

(3) The ultimate purpose for mentoring and training involves *sending* into ministry. Pastors and congregations join to prepare their trainees to embark upon places of ministry, maintaining ongoing encouragement, prayer, counsel, and support, as their protégés serve Christ's kingdom locally and globally.

## THE WAY FORWARD

Despite no use of contemporary mentoring terminology, Jesus obviously mentored the Twelve and the Seventy (Luke 9–10) who engaged in mission work and church planting. Some of these, in turn, mentored others who followed in their steps. For example, New Testament scholar Richard Bauckham offers convincing evidence that the church father Papias (c. 70–163) learned the message of the gospel and its application from a firsthand hearing by either the Apostle John (called "John the Elder") or another John who had apostolic training.[17] Mentoring took place, though not likely in a formal sense so popular today, by sitting at the feet of those who knew the Lord, remembered his teaching, and understood the shape of how the gospel would be planted through communities of believers. This same mentoring pattern, although sometimes with more structure, has continued through the centuries.

The way forward in training Christian leaders cannot be left to perusing manuals or books. Missiologist D. Michael Crow observes, "We find that materials-without-mentoring tends to inoculate people. They think they've 'got it' when they really haven't."[18] Just as Jesus engaged in life-on-life relationships with his disciples in the sphere of community, who then planted congregations and expanded mission work, even so contemporary church leaders find a replicable paradigm in Jesus and his disciples for mentoring those who will serve and establish churches. *The life-on-life relationship of mentors with trainees centered in local communities of Christ-followers remains the best way to shape a new generation of healthy Christian leaders.*

---

17  Richard Bauckham, *Jesus and the Eyewitnesses: The Gospels as Eyewitness Testimony* (Grand Rapids: Eerdmans, 2006), 12–38.
18  D. Michael Crow, "Multiplying Jesus Mentors: Designing a Reproducible Mentoring System—a Case Study," *Missiology: An International Review* XXXVI.1 (January 2008): 106.

CHAPTER 2

# JESUS ON MENTORING

When we hear the term *disciple*, we might conjure images of a Zen master with his pupil or a diet guru with hunger craved followers. We might think of a financial wizard with his acolytes or a successful football coach with loyal assistants. Each would appropriately convey disciples in their context.

Ancient disciples among Jewish rabbis and Greek philosophers attached to their masters so that they might learn the repetitive teaching from their traditions. The disciples broke from their worlds to follow after the teaching and life of wisdom found in their masters.[1]

*Jesus did the reverse.* He called disciples to himself, demanding the radical following after him in which all other relationships became secondary. Jesus's disciples heard and accepted his call to a new life of obedience to his Lordship. "The center of this new life was Jesus himself," not a philosophy or only a teaching, explains Michael Wilkins, "because his disciples gained new life through him (John 10:7–10), they followed him (Mark 1:16–20), they were to hear and obey his teachings (Matt. 5:1–2), and they were to share Jesus's mission by going into all of the world, preaching the gospel of the kingdom and calling all people to become Jesus's disciples (Luke 24:47; Matt. 28:19–20)."[2] By contrast, his disciples would not just teach, as common among rabbinic and philosophical disciples; they were called to "fish people," gathering and recruiting more followers of Jesus.[3] That sets the stage for how Jesus mentored his followers.

---

1 Martin Hengel, *The Charismatic Leader and His Followers* (Eugene, OR: Wipf & Stock, 1968), 27–33. In some ways, the repetitive teaching produced robotic followers rather than lively disciples.

2 Michael J. Wilkins, "Disciple, Discipleship," in *Evangelical Dictionary of World Missions*, eds. A. Scott Moreau, Harold Netland, and Charles Van Engen (Grand Rapids: Baker, 2000), 278–279.

3 Eckhard J. Schnabel, *Early Christian Mission: Jesus and the Twelve*, 2 vols. (Downers Grove, IL: IVP, 2004), 1:276–277.

Darrell Bock explains Christian disciples as those "learning the basics" of what it meant to follow Jesus, including "mission, commitment, love for God, love for one's neighbor, devotion to Jesus and his teaching, and prayer (Luke 9:51–11:13)."[4] Disciples, in the truest sense, were those personally attached to Jesus so that he shaped their lives.[5] They were "learners." *The process of shaping disciples equates to contemporary mentoring.* Jesus mentored the Twelve as he shaped them for future ministry.

Luke's gospel and Acts reveal both the ethnic and geographical progression of the gospel beyond the people of Israel and its borders.[6] The disciples were not naturally ready for this progression. As Eckhard Schnabel points out, the short-term mission work of the disciples served "as a paradigm for their later missionary work that would last longer and would take place in a different context."[7] What Jesus did with the disciples in preparing them for future ministry becomes a framework for disciple making, church planting, and missions throughout the centuries, including training and mentoring as Jesus did the disciples.

D. M. Crow shows the future effects of Jesus's training and commissioning of his disciples. "He commanded the disciples to make disciples who would make disciples who would make disciples. Jesus envisioned leadership reproducibility and multiplication."[8] This kind of disciple multiplication did not focus merely on individuals but on developing communities of Christ-followers throughout the Roman Empire. Luke sets the stage for this in the narratives on the Twelve and the Seventy, expanding it in Acts.

Jesus's call to his disciples to become fishers of men (Mark 1:16–20) is foundational to the expansion of gospel witness and consequent planting of churches throughout the Roman Empire—and paradigmatic for those that follow after them. Churches left in the wake of their mission dotted the empire by the end of the first century. Did the apostles—the Twelve—personally plant each church? Obviously not, but their forward movement, direction, teaching,

---

4  Darrell L. Bock, *Luke 1:1–9:50*, BECNT, Moisés Silva, ed. (Grand Rapids: Baker, 1994), 24.

5  K. H. Rengstorf, *Theological Dictionary of the New Testament*, 10 vols., Gerhard Kittel and Gerhard Friedrich, eds.; Geoffrey W. Bromiley, trans. (Grand Rapids: Eerdmans, 1964–1976), 4:441.

6  Bock, *Luke 1:1–9:50*, 28–29, 41; e.g. tax collectors (Luke 7:18–30; 19:1–10) and various races (Luke 7:1–10; 8:26–56; 17:11–19).

7  Schnabel, *Early Christian Mission*, 1:292; he cites D. A. Carson, *Matthew 1–12* (EBC; Grand Rapids: Zondervan, 1995), 242, who states: "In this sense the Twelve become a paradigm for other disciples in their post-Pentecost witness, a point Matthew understands (cf. 28:18–20); and in this sense he intends that Matthew 10 should also speak to his readers."

8  D. Michael Crow, "Multiplying Jesus Mentors: Designing a Reproducible Mentoring System—a Case Study," *Missiology: An International Review* XXXVI.I (January 2008): 92.

training others, and mission consciousness led to church plants. They also extended concern for the stability and ongoing health of the churches, including correct doctrine and faithful leadership.[9]

To help us visualize how Jesus trained leaders, we turn to Luke's gospel as a reliable framework for contemporary leaders involved in mentoring pastors, church planters, and missionaries.

## THE TRAINING OF JESUS'S DISCIPLES

Since Luke concerned himself with Jesus's saving mission in both his gospel and Acts, his inclusion of the training and sending of the Twelve *and* the Seventy[10] bears attention for those who now carry the mantle of gospel extension.[11] Our focus will be on the two narratives of the Twelve and the Seventy in Luke's gospel.

### *The Training of the Twelve*

The disciples learned from observing Jesus as the fulfillment of the Isaiah 61 prophecy affirmed in Luke 4:16–21. They saw his miraculous works, heard his preaching of the kingdom of God, listened to him pray, and watched how he lived. When he sent them into the villages of Galilee to proclaim the gospel and heal the sick in his name, they went with a consciousness of what they had observed in him.[12] Jesus called the disciples to fish for people (Luke 5:1–11), modeled preaching of the kingdom and calling sinners to repentance (Luke 5:31–32), and taught the distinctions in the new covenant (Luke 5:33–39) *before* he sent the Twelve into ministry. A. B. Bruce observed that the Twelve were only beginners, and yet they were still ahead of those to whom they were sent in their understanding of the call to repentance and kingdom citizen-

---

9  This is particularly evident in the events of Acts 15 and much later in 1 Peter 5:1–5 and 2–3 John. In this sense, revitalization—or bringing to life what has ebbed in fervor—characterized some of the later apostolic work.

10  See Bruce M. Metzger, *A Textual Commentary on the Greek New Testament* (New York: United Bible Societies, 1971), 150–151, who shows the divided argument among textual critics on whether seventy or seventy-two disciples is correct. The United Bible Societies Committee opted to include *duo* in brackets to indicate a level of doubt on its certainty. Craig L. Blomberg, *Jesus and the Gospels: An Introduction and Survey*, 2nd edition (Nashville: B&H Academic, 2009), 338, maintains that the textual evidence is fairly balanced between "seventy" and "seventy-two," but thinks that favor falls on the side of "seventy-two."

11  William J. Larkin Jr., "Mission in Luke," in *Mission in the New Testament: An Evangelical Approach*, American Society of Missiology Series, no. 27, eds. William J. Larkin Jr. and Joel F. Williams (Maryknoll, NY: Orbis Books, 1999), 154–155.

12  A. B. Bruce, *The Training of the Twelve* (Grand Rapids: Kregel, 1971; from 1894 ed.), 99.

ship.[13] Jesus called the Twelve to be "with him" (Mark 3:14), to learn from his teaching and company, so that they would be qualified thereby "for the mission of continuing his mission."[14]

Luke offers a mission-framed understanding of Jesus's appointment of the Twelve as apostles (Luke 6:13). Günther Krallmann calls this relationship "with-ness," that is, the "dynamic process of life-transference" that would take place between Jesus and the Twelve. He developed them as the future leaders of his church while he discipled them as his followers in the basic elements of Christian ministry.[15]

Luke's record of the sending of the Twelve (Luke 9:1–11) identifies at least eight elements in the mission. First, Jesus intentionally called the Twelve together for this task (Luke 9:1). A. B. Bruce explained that Jesus demonstrated a level of trust in the disciples by sending them out even while beginners. Surprisingly, Jesus entrusted them with proclamation at this point. We can be assured, Bruce wrote, that Jesus put "a sound form of words into their mouths" lest they swerve from his purposes. Mentors must be willing to trust their protégés with responsibilities in order to train them.[16]

I've felt the struggle of entrusting my pulpit to a new pastoral trainee in order to give him experience in preaching. Will he communicate the Word? Will he be faithful to the gospel? Will he show theological precision? Will he butcher grammar and mangle homiletical structure? Will he blow the opportunity? Those realistic questions accompany the mentor/trainee relationship, just as Jesus faced the same with his disciples.

Second, Jesus gave them power and authority over demons and for healing diseases (Luke 9:1). Third, he sent them to "proclaim the kingdom of God and to perform healing" (Luke 9:2). Fourth, in order to teach them dependence upon the Father, a lesson that would prepare them well for future ministry, he sent them without staff, bag, bread, money, or an extra tunic (Luke 9:3).[17] Fifth, they were to learn to accept hospitality from whomever it might be offered—a challenge that might shatter some preconceived notions and sensibilities (Luke 9:4). Sixth, they were to shake the dust from their feet as a testimony against those who refused to receive them (Luke 9:5; cf. Acts 13:50–51). Seventh, the apostles were account-

---

13  Ibid., 102–103.
14  Richard Bauckham, *Jesus and the Eyewitnesses: The Gospels as Eyewitness Testimony* (Grand Rapids: Eerdmans, 2006), 95.
15  Günther Krallmann, *Mentoring for Mission: A Handbook on Leadership Principles Exemplified by Jesus Christ* (Waynesboro, GA: Gabriel Publishing, 2002), 13–14.
16  Bruce, *Training of the Twelve*, 102–103.
17  Joel B. Green, *The Gospel of Luke*, NICNT (Grand Rapids: Eerdmans, 1997), 359.

able to Jesus upon their return—a perpetual reality for all sent out on mission by Jesus (Luke 9:10).[18] Finally, Jesus prescribed refreshment by withdrawing from the crowds, although that did not last long (Luke 9:10–11).

Both Matthew and Luke narrate the sending of the Twelve (Matt. 10:1–42), but only Luke narrates the sending of the Seventy. What place did the latter have in Jesus's mission?

### *The Sending of the Seventy*

Although the sending of the Twelve and the Seventy bear resemblance, a few distinctions layer our understanding of how Jesus trained and prepared early disciples for mission. John Nolland rightly suggests that the future ministry of the church may be prefigured in the Seventy[19]—which gives some foreshadowing of future church planting and mission work. The Seventy may include the Twelve or may be in addition to the Twelve, the latter appearing more likely due to the use of *heterous* for "seventy others."[20] Twelve aspects to Jesus's commissioning and training are noted.

First, Jesus sends the Seventy out in pairs as he had done the Twelve (Luke 10:1; Mark 6:7).[21] Second, Jesus prepared and apparently assigned the thirty-five teams to particular locations where he planned to go (Luke 10:1).[22] Third, the disciples were to sense the urgency of their task by praying for the Lord of the harvest to send out more laborers into his harvest—an exhortation that should seem just as urgent in our own era (Luke 10:2). Fourth, Jesus does not send them out under pretense; they will be lambs among wolves (Luke 10:3). One practice that our trainees have found useful is the blunt honesty about the varied issues of ministry. Some ministry situations feel like war zones, others like circuses. Facing reality when entering ministry might keep a young pastor or missionary from succumbing to early discouragement.

---

18  Bock, *Luke 1:1–9:50*, 827, notes Luke's use of *diegesanto* as significant in explaining the recounting of the disciples' experiences to Jesus, since it is the same word Luke used in Luke 1:1–4. It implies a thorough narration of the events in the mission.

19  John Nolland, *Luke 9:21–18:34*, WBC 35B; Ralph Martin, NT ed. (Nashville: Nelson, 1993), 550.

20  Ibid. Nolland suggests that Luke may understand the Twelve "to be involved alongside the Seventy(-two) as a continuation of the role they already have."

21  Robert H. Stein, *Luke*, NAC; E. Ray Clendenen, gen. ed. (Nashville: Broadman, 1992), 304. This includes both practical reason—"mutual support"—and theological reason—two witnesses were necessary in affirming veracity of testimony (Deut. 19:15; Num. 35:30). See Schnabel, *Early Christian Mission*, 1:290.

22  Schnabel, *Early Christian Mission*, 1:321–322, works out a potential strategy of Jesus following the Seventy with six weeks of one-day/night visits in each village. But he acknowledges it to be more plausible that the disciples represent him, taking his place; see Luke 10:16.

Fifth, like the Twelve, the Seventy were to learn dependence upon the Father by not taking extra supplies (Luke 10:4). Sixth, the urgency and focus of the mission was evident in not greeting anyone on the way (Luke 10:4). Seventh, the Seventy were to look for a man of peace for hospitality (Luke 10:5–7), which probably means someone willing to listen and receive the message they spoke.[23] Eighth, they were to learn contentment in the hospitality that the Lord provided (Luke 10:7–8)—discovering, as well, the significance of table fellowship in ministry.[24] Ninth, the disciples were to serve the needy and proclaim the nearness of the kingdom of God (Luke 10:9). Tenth, judgment must also be appropriately leveled against those that reject the kingdom message (Luke 10:10–12). Eleventh, the Seventy disciples were to learn their identity with Jesus as his representatives (Luke 10:16).[25] Finally, the Seventy—and future missionaries following in their steps—were to learn to find their joy in the grace of God shown to them rather than in a particular measure of success (Luke 10:17–20).[26]

While we're only taking a brief look at Jesus's training of the Twelve and the Seventy as noted by Luke, enough evidence remains to offer an appropriate paradigm for contemporary church leaders as they seek to mentor for ministry. The balance of this chapter considers how Jesus's mentoring model should shape our practice.

## JESUS'S MODEL AND YOUR MENTORING PRACTICE

Since the Gospel writers gave only brief explanations of the training of the Twelve and the Seventy, "it is impossible," as Schnabel explains, "to reconstruct or even speculate about the length of this training period."[27] The New Testament narrative indicates that the training with the Twelve exceeded that of the Seventy due to the intimate involvement that the former had with Jesus

---

23 I. Howard Marshall, *The Gospel of Luke*, NIGTC (Carlisle: Paternoster; Grand Rapids: Eerdmans, 1978), 419–420, states that "man of peace" is a frequent idiom in Classical and Hellenistic Greek and in the Semitic language, meaning not one who is already a disciple "but to offering salvation to those who are willing to receive it." In other words, they were to look for those who were open to hearing and receiving their message. This best suits the context.

24 Marshall, *Luke*, 421. Table fellowship may have been a significant point of gospel communication. Derek Tidball, *Ministry by the Book: New Testament Patterns for Pastoral Leadership* (Downers Grove, IL: IVP Academic, 2008), 61, offers a valid assertion: "So much of Jesus's most important teaching takes place over the meal table ([Luke] 5:27–32; 7:36–50; 10:38–42; 14:1–24; 19:1–9; 22:7–38; 24:13–35)."

25 Stein, *Luke*, 307, rightly expresses this as "the corporate solidarity of the messenger and the Lord," an important truth for future generations of missionaries and church planters to keep in mind.

26 Bruce, *Training*, 107, calls this "a timely caution against elation and vanity."

27 Schnabel, *Early Christian Mission*, 1:290.

during his earthly ministry. When local church leaders plan a mentoring strategy for those preparing for ministry, they certainly should view the work that
Jesus did with the disciples as a model for their own considerations.[28] What is
involved in this model?

### *The Impact of Mentoring*

Mentoring takes place in close association or "consociation," as Krallmann puts
it. He notes that Jesus saw "consociation with him as the most fertile soil for his
disciples' growth relative to character, understanding and skill. Hence he made
the experience of his with-ness the pivot of their training."[29] Crow concurs, adding that the limitation of *content*-driven training such as found in seminary class-
rooms, lectures, or conferences, calls for *mentoring*-driven training that adds
the personal dimension to shape the trainees. He recommends building training
curriculum around the mentoring relationships just as Jesus did.[30] "Jesus mentored in ways tailored to each individual."[31] The local church provides the most
consistent atmosphere for this kind of tailored approach in mentoring since, as
happened with the Twelve and the Seventy, it includes mentoring in the context
of community. This approach does not disparage intense academic training but
rather puts it into perspective by insisting on the local church's ability to more
effectively shape ministers for the practical demands of ministry.[32] Seminaries
and Bible colleges supplement *in partnership* with the local church, where the
church may lack the capacity to offer a thorough theological education.

Through contact with Jesus, E. F. Harrison explains, the Twelve "almost
unconsciously absorbed from him. They must have learned something about
the art of meeting people and handling situations as they witnessed their
Master threading his way through life with its maze of difficult circumstances
occasioned by the public character of his work."[33] The best way to maintain this
similar strategy of Jesus with those preparing for ministry is for faithful pastors
to bring them into a mentoring relationship in a local church context. As with

---

28  Ibid., 1:292; see Carson, *Matthew*, 241–242, who concluded that the training did not stop
     with the sending of the Twelve. More training appeared necessary. He notes, "In this sense the
     Twelve become a paradigm for other disciples in their post-Pentecost witness."
29  Krallmann, *Mentoring for Mission*, 53.
30  Crow, "Multiplying Jesus Mentors," 93.
31  Ibid., 92.
32  Warren Bird, "Churches Taking Back the Task of Theological Education," *Leadership Network*
     [cited 12 Jan 2013]: n.p., leadnet.org//resources/advance/churches_taking_back_the_task_
     of_theological_education, discusses Sojourn Church's (Louisville, KY) church-based theolog-
     ical education in partnership with the Southern Baptist Theological Seminary.
33  E. F. Harrison, *A Short Life of Christ* (Grand Rapids: Zondervan, 1968), 143.

Jesus, it costs time and personal involvement; it demands working through the sometime messy nature of relationships, but it yields much fruit in future years. Those mentored *absorb* from their mentors the relational skills, application of doctrine, and insights in handling difficulties by the "with-ness" in the mentoring relationship. Let's consider five replicable aspects of the impact of mentoring from Jesus and his disciples.

*First, Jesus provided an example for mentors to follow.* By contrast, Jewish rabbis expected their disciples to attend to them. Jesus not only declared himself to be among them as one that served (Luke 22:26ff) but he also did it in practice.[34] He washed the disciples' feet (John 13). He fed the multitudes (Luke 9:12–17). He took the weary disciples to secluded places for rest (Mark 7:30–32). He even prepared breakfast for them after his resurrection (John 21:9–14). The disciples also learned about trusting the Father with both livelihood and protection from countless dangers, as they watched the same in Jesus.[35] Jesus even gave them an example of getting beyond the social conventions of the day that were steeped in prejudice.[36]

Contemporary mentors must never minimize the power of example in shaping their protégés. The way that they live out the Christian life, handle difficult situations in the congregation, maintain a healthy marriage, and love the body of Christ presses Christian character and practice for the trainees without ever conducting a class on it. In this case, the mentor's example carries more weight than the classroom.

*Second, Jesus demonstrated the priority of relationships with his trainees.* The framework of discipleship demonstrated this priority, as the intimacy of living in relationship to Jesus *and* the small community of followers shaped lifelong friendships.[37] Krallmann poignantly clarifies: "Yet Jesus did not go about establishing an academy, he went about establishing a fellowship; he first majored on making friends and only later on sending out apostles (cf. Mark 3:14)." He further reminds those involved in mentoring: "A mentoree is not a project but a person. Mentoring implies more than a lecturer-student connection, it is friendship."[38] The tie of friendship between Jesus and the Twelve surpassed the natural support of his family (Luke 22:28; John 17:6).[39] Contemporary mentors will make friendship

---

34  Hengel, *The Charismatic Leader*, 51–52.
35  Harrison, *A Short Life of Christ*, 143.
36  Schnabel, *Early Christian Mission*, 1:278; e.g., relationships with Samaritans, tax collectors, and women.
37  Wilkins, "Disciple, Discipleship," 279.
38  Krallmann, *Mentoring for Mission*, 55.
39  Harrison, *A Short Life of Christ*, 138.

the first order of attachment to trainees. Trainees will ultimately mirror the same love and friendship toward those in their spheres of ministry.[40]

*Third, Jesus modeled love and service in leadership.* Robert Greenleaf's premise that true greatness in leadership begins with service is not missed on Jesus! One must serve before he leads or else once he begins to lead, he must learn to serve.[41] Although Greenleaf approaches leadership from a secular model, he correctly states what we witness modeled in Jesus. As Jesus taught on true greatness when correcting the sons of Zebedee jockeying for lordly positions in the future kingdom, he explained that it is to be found in service: "just as the Son of Man did not come to be served, but to serve, and to give His life a ransom for many" (Matt. 20:20–28). Jesus's life and teaching modeled generosity, forgiveness, service, and humility (Luke 16:1–31; 17:1–10; 18:9–30).[42] His gentleness and engagement with little children demonstrated a remarkable sensitivity and love that needs mirroring in his followers (Matt. 19:13–15). He felt love for the rich young ruler despite the young man's idolatry that kept him from Jesus (Mark 10:21). Mentors must be conscious of modeling service and love with their trainees, for this shapes them to do the same.[43]

*Fourth, Jesus mentored with the cross in view.* Jesus journeyed toward the destiny with the cross where he secured redemption for his people. He regularly pointed toward that destiny as he trained his disciples (Luke 9:22, 43–45; 18:31–34). Likewise, he demonstrated that the terms of following him require a cross (Luke 9:23). This cross may vary in its shape and dimension for each believer but "there is a cross of some shape for all true disciples is clearly implied in the words" of Luke 9:23.[44] Bock asserts the implication, "The disciple's life consists of basic self-denial."[45] Mentors do well to keep their trainees focused on the sufficiency of Christ in his death and resurrection, while also modeling the necessity of dying to selfish desires and embracing adversities, trials, and hardships as the means of throttling the natural tendency toward vanity.

Out of the closeness of mentor and pastoral trainees, I've been able to speak into the lives of some of our young men about their marriages, unbecoming atti-

---

40  Krallmann, *Mentoring for Mission*, 104.
41  Robert K. Greenleaf, *Servant Leadership: A Journey into the Nature of Legitimate Power and Greatness—25th Anniversary Edition*, Larry Spears, ed.; Kindle edition (Mahwah, NJ: Paulist Press/Amazon Digital Services, 2002), loc. 348.
42  Bock, *Luke 1:1–9:50*, 24.
43  Tidball, *Ministry by the Book*, 121, explains that Paul viewed service as "the constant subtext of his understanding of Christian leadership." In Paul's theology, the gospel requires service.
44  Bruce, *The Training of the Twelve*, 183–184.
45  Bock, *Luke 1:1–9:50*, 852.

tudes, prideful ambitions, areas lacking discipline, and rough edges in ministry. Gentle correction sets the trainees on a better path for life and ministry with the cross in view.

*Fifth, Jesus's mentoring included correction.* When John sought to hinder those attempting to cast out demons in Jesus's name, Jesus corrected him (Luke 9:49–50). When James and John wanted to call fire down from heaven because of perceived insult from some Samaritans, Jesus told them, "You do not know what kind of spirit you are of" (Luke 9:51–56). He "exposed and rebuked and corrected" the sins and infirmities of the disciples.[46] Mentors must seek to correct sinful tendencies in their trainees in order to uproot attitudes and rash behavior that would hinder their ministries and distract from the gospel (Gal. 6:1–5). Only the closeness of friendship and service will allow for this kind of openness in correction without bruising the pastoral trainees.

The intimacy of one-on-one and small group mentoring positions local church mentors to impact those under their charge. Their example in relationships, love, service, and dying to self gives future gospel workers a better picture of how to live faithfully as servants of Christ. Mentors not only give an example, but also engage in specific training toward future ministry.

## The Impact of Training in Ministry

Despite lacking knowledge of a specific curriculum used by Jesus in training his disciples, contemporary mentors do well to train their protégés in the broad areas in which Jesus implemented training.[47] Jesus assigned various areas of ministry to his disciples: preaching, exorcising demons, healing diseases, and ministry to the needy.[48] "He taught them how to handle money, receptivity and

---

46  Harrison, *A Short Life of Christ*, 144–145.
47  Robert Coleman, *The Master Plan of Evangelism*, 2nd ed. (Old Tappan, NJ: Revell, 1993), 37, rightly notes that Jesus "was his own school and curriculum."
48  Bock, *Luke*, 999, explains that "acts of healing are signs of the in-breaking of the kingdom (Luke 11:14–23)." Similarly, Carson, *Matthew*, 245, asserts, "The long-awaited kingdom was now 'near' enough . . . to be attested by miracles directed at demonism and malady." Thomas Schreiner, *New Testament Theology: Magnifying God in Christ* (Grand Rapids: Baker Academic, 2008), 47–49, argues cogently that the miraculous healings and exorcising attested the conjunction of new creation and the kingdom's arrival, vividly showing the old order passing away. "Jesus's miracles [so, too, those of the Twelve and the Seventy as immediate agents of the kingdom's arrival], then, are signs of the kingdom manifestations of the new creation" (p. 66). With the kingdom's advent marked by the Holy Spirit's coming at Pentecost (Acts 2:1ff.), the emphasis moves toward gospel proclamation as priority, rather than the miraculous. Consequently, gospel proclamation and disciple making (including church planting) are normative for contemporary church planters rather than focusing on miraculous works.

rejection."[49] The thorough debriefing after the ministries of the Twelve and the Seventy indicate that Jesus offered feedback in coaching his disciples for future ministry (Luke 9:10; 10:17–24).[50] Three areas surface as priority in Jesus's training of the Twelve and Seventy: relationships, proclamation, and focus.

*First, since Christian ministry is relational, Jesus trained his disciples in relationships.* Here the local church setting proves comparable to the close community in which Jesus trained his disciples. The "family-like structure" of Jesus's followers brought them into intimate, regular contact with those from varied backgrounds.[51] This intimate diversity grew, as disciples from various racial backgrounds comprised the early churches.[52] These friendships crystallized as Jesus sent them out by pairs for ministry. Not that tensions never surfaced! Relationships bring fallen beings into close enough proximity so that disagreements may multiply and matters of pride irritate (Luke 9:46; 22:24). Yet this becomes one of the best platforms to validate the power of the gospel (see Eph. 2–3). In the local church mentoring setting, disciples learn the consciousness of being God's fellow workers who engage in teamwork for gospel ministry initiatives.[53]

The closeness of mentoring relationships in the local church also allows for the mentors to better observe the gifts and skills of their trainees.[54] They can discern preaching and teaching gifts, evangelistic and organizational gifts, leadership and mercy gifts. This gives mentors the chance to cultivate gifts and to establish solid teams for church planting or revitalization. With the necessary gifts, they have a better chance of succeeding in their mission. Relationships offer a natural framework for accountability in spiritual walk and gospel ministry. Over the past few years with our pastoral interns, I've watched this pattern play out as the young men grow together while sharpening one another. One strong in preaching learns from another stronger in pastoral skills. One timid in expression learns from another who speaks with passion.

---

49 Crow, "Multiplying Jesus Mentors," 92.

50 Ibid., 99, Crow offers demonstrable evidence of the increased effectiveness of "personalized coach-mentoring methodology" over group lectures.

51 Schnabel, *Early Christian Mission*, 1:274; see also 1:325, where he notes the importance of hospitality. See also Joseph Hellerman, *When Church Was a Family: Recapturing Jesus's Vision for Authentic Christian Community* (Nashville: B&H Academic, 2009), who addresses the family emphasis in the Mediterranean world of the NT, then argues persuasively for rethinking church in terms of family rather than a loosely connected group.

52 Bock, *Luke 1:1–9:50*, 33–35.

53 Stuart Murray, *Church Planting: Laying Foundations* (Scottdale, PA.: Herald Press, 2001), 41; see also Hengel, *The Charismatic Leader*, 83, who offers the example of Paul and Apollos (1 Cor. 3:9; 2 Cor. 5:20) as fellow workers and ambassadors in similar fashion to the sending out of the Twelve and the Seventy.

54 Ibid., 212.

*Second, since mission involves the message of the gospel, Jesus trained his protégés in proclamation.* In Luke, proclamation involved *kerygma* and *didache*—preaching and teaching, with no line drawn between them.[55] The various verbs used to express proclamation in Luke focus on Jesus Christ's crucifixion and resurrection "as God's eschatological act of salvation."[56] "Repent, turn, and faith," consequently, are the responses to the proclamation.[57] Johannes Nissen explains how Scripture and proclamation go together: "It should be noticed that *a re-reading of the Scriptures* was to be the source of mission," as exemplified in Luke 24:13–50.[58] So proclamation has its basis in Scripture—a point mentors must regularly reinforce by teaching and example.

Local church mentors will find that majoring on training protégés in proclamation will produce much fruit in the succeeding years. Whether planting churches, doing mission work, or pastoring, those preparing for ministry must see themselves as both heralds and teachers. As heralds they will continually point their hearers to the death and resurrection of Jesus as the basis of salvation and the central focus of their discipleship.[59] Apart from the gospel message proclaimed there is no eternal hope (Rom.. 10:14–17; 1 Thess. 2:13; 2 Thess. 2:13–15).

Likewise, teaching reinforces through instruction the basic applications of Scripture to the whole of life. Harrison described Jesus's teaching as authoritative, full of wisdom distinct from the scribes and Pharisees, radical enough to build one's life upon, simple by avoiding technical and heavy theological jargon, concrete rather than speculative and theoretical, spontaneous in utilizing the breadth of life to aim at immediate need, and original rather than cluttered with Talmudic casuistry.[60] This provides an excellent challenge for trainees to build into their teaching ministries: authority, wisdom, radical discipling, simplicity, concreteness, spontaneity, and originality.

For this practice that follows Jesus's pattern, the teachers must continually be *learners* themselves, for that is the true heart of being a disciple of Jesus and teaching disciples.[61] Mentors are in a prime position to gauge whether protégés

---

55  Joseph A. Fitzmyer, *The Gospel According to Luke I–IX: A New Translation with Introduction and Commentary*, ABC 28 (New Haven, CT: Yale University Press, 1970), 149.
56  Ibid., 146.
57  Bock, *Luke 1:1–9:50*, 35.
58  Johannes Nissen, *New Testament and Mission: Historical and Hermeneutical Perspectives*, 3rd ed. (Frankfurt: Peter Lang, 2004), 50; italics original.
59  Larkin, "Mission in Luke," 168–169.
60  Harrison, *A Short Life of Christ*, 96–102.
61  Tidball, *Ministry by the Book*, 22–23; Coleman, *Master Plan*, 23–24, shows that despite being impulsive and temperamental, the disciples were teachable. That may be an encouraging lesson for mentors!

display an eagerness to learn or think that they have arrived. The latter prove that they lack the readiness to launch forth in gospel ministry. Just as Jesus challenged the learning process of his disciples, mentors do the same through questions, assignments, accountability, correction, and affirmation. Mentors may find partnership with theological institutions to be co-contributors to trainees' learning and teaching.

Quite often in our pastoral training, I'm challenged to juggle assignments (e.g., reading books, writing reviews, crafting philosophy of ministry papers) that I make with the academic assignments our interns labor under in seminary. I don't want to overburden them so that they lose heart. Nor do I want to go light on them, since Christian ministry constantly stretches us. My goal is to prepare them for real-life ministry. So I ask what kind of classes they are taking, and then, when possible, try to make assignments that will complement their theological studies or will offer some practical issue that should bring satisfaction and joy to their demanding schedules. For this reason, the mentor must get to know his trainees well—to understand how far he can push them, where he needs to exhort them, and how he might help better equip them.

*Third, Jesus kept his disciples on focus for their mission.* Distraction seems to come easily, especially for those in ministry. Multiple demands, aside from personal and family issues, quickly distract attention from the goals of proclaiming Christ and establishing gospel-driven churches. Jesus used care to make sure that the relationship between him and his disciples did not drift into "a lecturer-student connection," and thus lose sight of their *kingdom-focus.*[62] Jesus modeled the outward (missional) focus of mission by his ministry to tax collectors, Gentiles, and sinners of all stripes (Luke 14:1–24; 15:1–32; 19:1–10). While the church develops inwardly, evidenced by the multiplied New Testament "one another" passages, it is also, as Darrell Bock reminds us, "an outwardly reaching group."[63] Just as Jesus did, local church mentors will need to maintain this outward focus in their own lives so that they might model it for their protégés. Jesus's person-oriented rather than task-oriented mentorship offers the appropriate model for mentors to embrace in keeping focus on their mission.[64]

Any effort to keep the focus on mission will inevitably face obstacles. Racial and social prejudices stymie mission focus. Jesus saw this with the disciples and took action, just as contemporary mentors must do. As Luke unfolds Jesus's min-

---

62   Krallmann, *Mentoring for Mission*, 149.
63   Bock, *Luke 1:1–9:50*, 41.
64   Krallmann, *Mentoring for Mission*, 60.

istry through his gospel, he shows how God's saving work in Christ is racially inclusive (e.g. Luke 7:1–10; 8:26–39).[65] Jesus showed no hesitation to cross racial and social barriers in order to communicate the message of the kingdom of God. He asked a Samaritan woman for a drink of water (John 4:7) and a tax collector for food and lodging (Luke 19:5), both reprehensible acts to a self-respecting Jew.[66]

After training and modeling this focus in mission, Jesus left his followers with the certainty that they would take the gospel across every conceivable barrier erected by the prejudices of men (Acts 1:8). Ironically, when he sent out the Twelve he forbade them from entering into the Gentile and Samaritan communities (Matt. 10:5–6), yet later he commanded them to take the gospel to Samaria and to the Gentile world (Acts 1:8). Carson explains this as partly pragmatic since the disciples had shown weak temperament in ministering to Samaritans (Luke 9:52–56), and partly theological because time with the Gentiles would have offended their Jewish audience.[67] Incrementally, Jesus led his disciples in shattering the barriers that could easily have halted their focus on outward mission. He did not expect more of his trainees than he had prepared them to deliver. He layered a kingdom focus that eventually freed them from paralysis in gospel ministry.

That kind of layering doesn't take place in a one-week conference or weekend seminar. It's the life-on-life relationship over time that applies kingdom focus. Likewise, local church mentors, by spending time with their trainees and observing their personalities and gifts, will find an incremental, layering approach useful in divesting their trainees of prejudices, fears, and notions that would hinder their focus on mission and ministry, while building in them a kingdom aim to God's glory.

## CONCLUSION

While the contemporary terms *mentor, mentee, trainer,* and *trainee* cannot be found in the New Testament, their practice pervades the relationship between Jesus and his disciples. Jesus's most important work prior to the death and resurrection, Harrison remarks, "was the selection and training of the men who would represent him in the world in the coming days."[68] Likewise, local church pastors and leaders must mirror Jesus's mentoring practice when they prepare the next generation for gospel ministry. To have served as a pastor but neglect to train up future gospel workers fails at following Jesus's example in ministry training.

---

65  Bock, *Luke 1:1–9:50*, 28.
66  Schnabel, *Early Christian Mission*, 1:278.
67  Carson, *Matthew 1–12*, 244.
68  Harrison, *A Short Life of Christ*, 136.

Jesus's preparing, instructing, and sending out the Twelve and the Seventy on mission provide a paradigm for local church leaders to mentor their protégés in gospel work. Simple lessons from these two training/sending paradigms expand the horizon for contemporary leaders to combine academic training with effective local church mentoring for ministry. This local church model does not replace formal theological training, but stands alongside it as reinforcement for applying theology to all of life and ministry.

Mentoring and training models from the life of Jesus cannot be totally replicated. Yet contemporary leaders must study Jesus and his disciples in order to best understand how to impact those entrusted to them for training. Mentors should remember, "Everything that is done with the few is for the salvation of the multitudes," as Coleman wrote.[69] Keep in mind that the group that Jesus called to himself had leadership, kinship, friendship, fellowship, and with Judas Iscariot, a traitor.[70] Contemporary leaders may expect the same, including the potential of traitors to the gospel. "A disciple is not above his teacher, nor a slave above his master" (Matt. 10:24). Yet no fear of potential problems or even traitors should deter local churches from the God-glorifying task of training a new generation to establish and revive communities of faith. The model of Jesus and his disciples in Luke's gospel offers an appropriate paradigm to embark upon this worthy goal.

---

69  Coleman, *Master Plan*, 35.
70  Harrison, *A Short Life of Christ*, 140–142.

CHAPTER 3

# MENTORING COMMUNITIES

There appears to be a bit of prejudice against the book of Acts. Since it contains a narrative sketch of a few events and personalities in the life of the early church rather than specifically organized teaching, some think it to be less than adequate as a source for validating particular doctrines. Admittedly, Acts does not address the full range of biblical doctrine. While one would not look *only* at Acts for doctrinal bases, it's not a doctrineless work. I faced this prejudice many years ago when writing a doctor of ministry dissertation on church planting. The theological mentor read my extensive use of Acts and pushed back, stating that it was not a good source for the doctrine of church planting. I countered, insisting that since Acts takes the most detailed look at church planting anywhere in the Bible, it has to be at the center of establishing a doctrine of church planting. He accepted my counter.

The same is true when it comes to Acts and a doctrine of spiritual leadership. Luke did not write a book on leadership. But he did show that gospel work and church planting requires faithful leadership. In doing so, he addressed varied angles of leadership by giving ample illustration of what Timothy Laniak calls the "breathtaking choice of God" to use weak, flawed vessels to accomplish his work. He explains, "Biblically, leadership can only be understood in terms of a fully integrated theological vision of God and his work on earth."[1] So, Luke's theological-historical record lays groundwork for understanding leadership development in future generations.

---

1 Timothy S. Laniak, *Shepherds after My Own Heart: Pastoral Traditions and Leadership in the Bible*, NSBT 20; D. A. Carson, ed. (Downers Grove, IL: IVP, 2006), 248–49.

Since the Acts narrative chronicles the emergence of new churches and leaders who planted and shaped them, it gives contours of leadership by *presuming leadership development* rather than explaining it. So while we might develop a theology of leadership from the Pastorals or other books, we find spiritual leadership explained and how it develops by the examples in Acts. While not stated in precept, leadership development for the local church shows up in practice.

Although Peter and Paul served as the primary actors in Luke's narrative, the balance of his story makes clear that these two apostolic giants did not plant and strengthen churches alone. In some cases, Luke identifies additional players in the unfolding mission of the church; in others, he only mentions the work in passing without naming the particular leaders responsible for establishing the new Christian communities (e.g. Acts 9:31; 15:3; 21:3–14). Who were the leaders planting and revitalizing early churches? Who trained them for their responsibilities? What spurred them toward faithful mission in the face of opposition? We will investigate the early signs of leadership training in Acts, the role of the scattered saints in church planting, and the mission of Paul and his partners.

## EARLY SIGNS OF LEADERSHIP TRAINING DEVELOPMENT

Potential leaders had to learn to follow before leading.[2] Yet as they learned to lead they embarked on mission. "The goal of mission," Johannes Nissen explains, "was the formation of a new community in Christ."[3] In obedience to Jesus Christ's command (Matt. 28:19–20), the disciples baptized and instructed new disciples.[4] The atmosphere for training leaders to engage in mission and to strengthen local churches permeated the experience of discipleship. Nurturing in the faith *within the fellowship of the church* prompted a missionary heart in the early church.

### *The Jerusalem Church*

The atmosphere surrounding the Jerusalem church breathes of gospel expansion. The new Christian community's regularity in teaching the apostolic doctrine, fellowship, breaking of bread, and prayer (Acts 2:42) laid groundwork for not only living out the gospel in their cities but also expanding it. Floyd Filson's

---

2  Laniak, *Shepherds*, 22.

3  Johannes Nissen, *New Testament and Mission: Historical and Hermeneutical Perspectives*, 3rd ed. (Frankfurt am Main: Peter Lang, 2004), 111.

4  See D. A. Carson, *Matthew 13–28*, EBC, 2 vols.; Frank E. Gaebelein, ed. (Grand Rapids: Zondervan, 1995), 597, who writes, "The NT can scarcely conceive of a disciple who is not baptized or is not instructed." See Craig Ott and Gene Wilson, *Global Church Planting: Biblical Practices and Best Practices for Multiplication* (Grand Rapids: Baker Academic, 2011), 48, who add, "The incorporation of believers is an integral part of disciplemaking."

significant work on early house churches as the basic unit for Christian community indicates that the rooting of the Christian movement in this structure gave later missionaries, like Paul, a clearer vision for how to plant churches outside Jerusalem.[5] He posits that Paul likely had the objective when entering a city to win a household to Christ so that it "could serve as the nucleus and center of his further work."[6] Since the gospel was central to the instruction in these early Christian communities, the natural desire would be to see it spread.[7] The planting of churches in communities that Luke mentions in passing, e.g., Lydda and Joppa, strongly suggests that those planting the churches were nurtured in pastoral leadership within the framework of the Jerusalem church.[8]

## *The Emergence of Barnabas*

While explaining generosity in the Jerusalem church, in passing, Luke introduces Barnabas, setting the stage for later development of this significant missionary character.[9] His credibility with the Jerusalem church was obvious (Acts 4:36–37).[10] His act of introducing Saul, the former persecutor, as a genuine brother in Christ prepared for the broader expansion of the gospel into the Roman world, although at the time, there may have been little thought of the far-reaching impact Saul's ministry would have in the early church.[11]

Although Barnabas did not initiate gospel work in Antioch, his credibility in pastoral work made him the apostolic choice to verify this expansion of the gospel

---

5   Floyd V. Filson, "The Significance of the Early House Churches," *JBL* (June 1939): LVIII.2:109–111.

6   Ibid., 111.

7   John Stott, *The Spirit, the Church, and the World: The Message of Acts* (Downers Grove, IL: InterVarsity, 1990), 86, perceptively wrote, "The first Jerusalem Christians were not so preoccupied with learning, sharing and worshipping, that they forgot about witnessing. For the Holy Spirit is a missionary Spirit who created a missionary church."

8   Acts 9:32, "the saints who lived at Lydda," and "the disciples" in Acts 9:38, indicate Lukan synonyms for local churches. Who planted these congregations? Luke does not tell us, but every indication would be that the proximity just west of Jerusalem suggests that disciples nurtured in the Jerusalem church expanded the gospel into those communities.

9   Everett F. Harrison, *Interpreting Acts: The Expanding Church* (Grand Rapids: Academie Books, 1986), 99, explains that Luke establishes the background for Barnabas, as a Hellenistic Jewish disciple, leading the mission efforts beyond Palestine. Martin Hengel, *Acts and the Earliest Christianity*, John Bowen, trans. (Philadelphia: Fortress Press, 1979), 101, suggests that Barnabas "seems to have belonged to the earliest community in Jerusalem from the beginning." Martin Hengel and Anna Maria Schwemer, *Paul between Damascus and Antioch: The Unknown Years*, John Bowden, trans. (Louisville: Westminster John Knox, 1997), 205, considered Barnabas as part of the Seventy (Luke 10:1).

10   C. K. Barrett, *Acts*, ICC, 2 vols. (Edinburgh: T & T Clark, 1994), 1:258.

11   Eckhard J. Schnabel, *Acts*, ZECNT, vol. 5; Clinton E. Arnold, gen. ed. (Grand Rapids: Zondervan, 2012), 456–457.

and to establish the Christian community among many Gentiles in that significant Roman city (Acts 11:19ff).[12] Eckhard Schnabel explains that Barnabas was not sent to simply inspect the work, rather, "he was sent as coordinator, missionary leader and theological teacher. The young church continued to grow as a result of Barnabas's work (Acts 11:22–25)."[13] Clearly, the pastoral preparation of Barnabas *in the Jerusalem Christian community* and possibly earlier as part of the Seventy, set the stage for the expansion of the church through planting new congregations in the Gentile world.[14] The community prepared him for ministry.

Although he temporarily floundered when Paul's first missionary journey got underway, John Mark grew to understand the nature of Christian work by the influence of the Jerusalem and Antioch churches and their leaders.[15] The ancient historian Eusebius claimed that John Mark "first established churches at the city of Alexandria."[16] If that's accurate, then Barnabas, Paul, and Peter's mentoring of John Mark *in the framework of the churches in Jerusalem and Antioch*, bore much fruit in the early centuries of the church through his church planting efforts (Acts 12:25; 13:5; 15:37–39; 1 Peter 5:13).

## The Seven and Their Connections

As the apostles juggled teaching, administration, and mercy ministry in the Jerusalem church, they began to realize their limitations due to the demands of shepherding the growing church (Acts 6:1–7). The congregation put forward seven qualified men to handle ministries of mercy, particularly toward the Hellenistic Jewish Christian widows, so that the apostles might concentrate on prayer and the ministry of the Word. The Seven had Greek names, indicating that they were chosen to serve the Hellenistic widows because they were also Hellenists.[17] When persecution erupted, these Hellenist believers scattered from Jerusalem, preaching the gospel that eventually led to establishing new congregations (Acts 8:4–8).

---

12  Harrison, *Acts*, 192, calls Antioch, "the third most important city in the empire," with a cosmopolitan atmosphere of around 25,000 citizens.

13  Eckhard J. Schnabel, *Early Christian Mission*, 2 vols. (Downers Grove, IL: IVP, 2004), 787.

14  Harrison, *Acts*, 193, notes, "For the first time the Christian faith had established itself in one of the major centers of the Roman Empire."

15  Harrison, *Acts*, 203–204, "This young man had many advantages, which ultimately showed up in his character and usefulness (Col. 4:10–11; 2 Tim. 4:11)." Barrett, *Acts*, 1:627, suggests various reasons for John Mark's sudden departure.

16  Eusebius, *Ecclesiastical History*, popular ed.; Christian F. Cruse, trans.; (Grand Rapids: Baker, 1955), 65 (2.16).

17  Jaroslav Pelikan, *Acts*, Brazos Theological Commentary on the Bible; eds. R. R. Reno, R. W. Jenson, R. L. Wilken, E. Radner, M. Root, G. Sumner (Grand Rapids: Brazos, 2005), 93.

Luke's identification of "Nicolas, a proselyte from Antioch" (Acts 6:5), offers the first glimpse at what would later take place in Antioch through Hellenists proclaiming the gospel to that city (Acts 11:19–20).[18] Whether Nicolas had a part in that work, Luke does not say. However, he does make a direct connection with the church planted in Antioch and the persecution that arose against the Hellenistic believers in connection with Stephen (Acts 11:19). Nicolas could have been part of that number.

An important question arises in regard to scattered evangelists and new churches. Who trained these believers to preach and establish churches? We are not told of any programmatic structure for developing preachers or church planters. Luke simply narrates that these scattered believers preached and planted. Their participation in the Jerusalem church with its ongoing doctrinal teaching (Acts 2:42) and involvement with the leaders in the church—the Twelve and the Seven—readied them for the opportunity thrust upon them to preach and plant churches. *They were mentored in community.*

The Hellenists associated with Stephen and Philip would have learned from their gospel ministries. Stephen offered a clearly articulated *apologia* of the faith before his martyrdom (Acts 7). Philip preached the gospel in Samaria and established a new congregation with amazing success (Acts 8:5–24). Their ministries of proclamation, along with that of the unnamed Hellenistic believers who preached Christ as they fled persecution, gives evidence that the *regular ministry of the Jerusalem church prepared them for more than we may realize.*

Was this intentional preparation for evangelism and church planting? At minimum, the Jerusalem church sought to train the congregation to carry on the Great Commission (Acts 28:18–20; Acts 1:8).[19] Although in Jerusalem that may have simply been adding to the already growing church, once the gospel took root outside Jerusalem, churches *had to be planted* in order to fulfill the command to go on teaching the disciples. "The goal of mission," as already noted, "was the formation of a new community in Christ." Churches, as "beachhead of the new creation," inevitably resulted by obedience to Christ's Commission.[20] At the heart of it was the Jerusalem church training the pastoral leaders, who would eventually be thrust beyond Jerusalem into the broader world to proclaim Christ and establish new communities of disciples, who themselves repeated the same process.

---

18 Harrison, *Acts*, 115, adds, "There may also be a hint that Luke himself belonged to Antioch."
19 Ed Stetzer, *Planting Missional Churches: Planting a Church That's Biblically Sound and Reaching People in Culture* (Nashville: B & H Academic, 2006), 38–43.
20 Nissen, *New Testament and Mission*, 111.

## SCATTERED SAINTS—THE CHURCH SPREADS

Logically, when the persecution in connection with Stephen's death began (Acts 7:60–8:4), the scattered saints would have traveled to locations where they had some connection. Rodney Stark explains that the early spread of Christianity followed the lines of social networks, so that disciples connected with relatives or friends of friends, utilizing these relationships for gospel expansion.[21] If Stark is correct, then the Hellenistic saints scattered from Jerusalem due to persecution made their way to Hellenistic communities, such as Antioch, where they networked for the sake of the gospel by establishing new churches. Luke narrates this movement of the gospel in Acts 8–12.[22]

### Philip's Significance

Unlike some of the Jewish background disciples in Jerusalem, Philip's Christology gave him the right attitude in taking the gospel to the Samaritans because he recognized the attitude of Jesus who cared for them (Luke 9:52–56; 10:30–37; 17:11–19; John 4).[23] While Luke does not detail the length of Philip's service to the Hellenistic widows and the broader congregation in Jerusalem, he does show the strong evangelistic gifts that he possessed. How did these gifts develop within the Jerusalem congregation? Luke offers no hint other than he was part of the scattered group that "went about preaching the word" (Acts 8:4), thus "had witnessed, observed and learned in Jerusalem what dynamic evangelistic outreach means," as Schnabel observes.[24] Having been nurtured in sound doctrine and exemplary preaching with the apostles in Jerusalem, and having been entrusted with service responsibilities by the church under the eyes of the apostles, he was equipped to preach Christ and plant churches beyond Jerusalem.[25]

Philip's understanding of ecclesiology intersected with his gospel proclamation. He preached, the Spirit worked, and a new congregation emerged (Acts 8:5–24).[26] Going to an area without established Christian communities

---

21 Rodney Stark, The Triumph of Christianity: How the Jesus Movement Became the World's Largest Religion (New York: Harper One, 2011), 76.

22 Hengel, Acts, 74–75.

23 Ibid., 78. When the apostles heard about the awakening in Samaria, they sent Peter and John to get a firsthand look to verify its authenticity (Acts 8:14–15). John had earlier sought the Lord's permission to command fire from heaven to consume recalcitrant Samaritans (Luke 9:54)!

24 Schnabel, Early Christian Mission, 673.

25 Harrison, Acts, 116, explains that the apostolic laying on of hands of the Seven indicated that the newly appointed men served under apostolic authority. He writes, "Implied also is the pledge of the apostles to stand behind the appointees and support them in every possible way (cf. 13:3)."

26 Dennis Johnson, The Message of Acts in the History of Redemption (Phillipsburg, NJ: P&R, 1997), 141.

*demanded* that the aim in proclamation be to not only seek new disciples but also to form congregations that would baptize, teach, and nurture the new disciples.[27]

After leaving Samaria, and later, the Ethiopian eunuch, Luke comments, "Philip found himself at Azotus, and as he passed through he kept preaching the gospel to all the cities until he came to Caesarea" (Acts 8:40). This remark assumes that he preached in Azotus and then in the villages along the northern coastal route until he reached Caesarea, which likely included Jamnia, Lydda, Joppa, and Antipatris.[28] His pattern would have not been simply to preach and to pass on without regard to Christ's command (Matt. 28:19–20), but rather to preach the gospel, make disciples, and plant churches. He had already demonstrated this pattern in Samaria. While Peter later went to Lydda and Joppa where he met with disciples—Luke's synonym for churches (Acts 9:32–43),[29] it seems likely that either Philip planted the congregations in these communities or he further strengthened the churches that had been previously planted by members of the Jerusalem church.[30] Philip remained in Caesarea where he may have become "a leader in the local church responsible for the proclamation of the gospel" (Acts 21:8).[31] The church in Caesarea may have initiated, under Philip's leadership, extended missionary work in that coastal region (Acts 8:40; 21:8).[32] *His preparation began with faithfulness in the life and nurturing of the Jerusalem church.*

The last mention of Philip is found in Acts 21:8–14, where he is called "Philip the evangelist." One need not think that "the evangelist" retired to Caesarea to let others continue the work without him. Caesarea became Philip's base of operation for advancing the gospel. The fact that "disciples from Caesarea" traveled with Paul and his missionary team to Jerusalem (Acts 21:16) indicates the presence of those in Caesarea intensely concerned with advancing the gospel to other regions. Philip would have been the fitting pastoral leader *to train and develop them for future ministry while nurturing ministry in the Caesarean church community.* Philip led a mentoring church.

---

27  Roland Allen, *Missionary Methods: St. Paul's or Ours?* (Grand Rapids: Eerdmans, 1962, 2002 reprint), 81–84.

28  Yohanan Aharoni and Michael Avi-Yonah, *The MacMillan Bible Atlas* (New York: MacMillan, 1968), 152. See also Barrett, *Acts*, 1:435.

29  Out of twenty-five uses of "disciples" in Acts, twenty-one imply a gathered body of Christ-followers, united together, and identified together, e.g., Acts 6:1–2; 9:19; 11:26; 14:21-22; 18:27; 21:16.

30  Harrison, *Acts*, 153, thinks it likely "that Philip laid the foundation for Peter's ministry in these places." See also Schnabel, *Early Christian Mission*, 691.

31  Schnabel, *Early Christian Mission*, 692.

32  Ibid., 1266.

## Evidence of Churches Established

Peter and John learned about ministry from the Lord Jesus, who always had others about him so that he might mentor them in kingdom life and ministry. It seems likely that Luke mentions Peter and John without specifying others traveling with them, since his usual practice seemed to focus on key characters, e.g., Peter, Barnabas, and Paul. Could there have been a team that traveled with Peter and John in the Samaritan villages (Acts 8:25) that they had mentored for pastoral work in Jerusalem, and who they would have been comfortable leaving with new congregations to continue nurturing them in the faith?[33] By following the pattern that Jesus consistently practiced in training others, it seems logical that Peter and John would have done the same.[34] Potential gospel ministers trained in the Jerusalem church under their tutelage may have become founding pastors of new congregations during this time of ministry.

The Acts 9 narrative recounting Saul of Tarsus' conversion and initial discipling in Damascus gives strong evidence that a church had been earlier planted in that city, particularly noted by "the disciples who were at Damascus" (Acts 9:19). Saul was "with" them, so he congregated with this church that he had earlier intended to persecute. Barrett states that this situation of Christians in Damascus—with a church planted—provides a valuable reminder that Acts does not offer a full record of the early years of the church's expansion, but only a few carefully chosen events.[35] *The quiet expansion of new churches in the early church, though without fanfare, began through disciples trained, mentored, and honed in gospel work through the ministry of existing churches—whether in Jerusalem or in Galilee.*[36] No other explanation of their beginning appears plausible.

Peter traveled to minister the gospel to Gentiles in Caesarea at the home of Cornelius (Acts 10:1–48). Hans Conzelmann explains that the presence of the accompanying disciples of Joppa turned their presence into "an ecclesiastical

---

33  Rudolph Pesch, *Die Apostelgeschichte (Apg 1–12)*, EKK, 2 vols.; Josef Blank, Rudolf Schnackenburg, Eduard Schweizer and Ulrich Wilckens, eds. (Zürich: Benziger Verlag, 1986), 1:318, thinks that Peter later traveled to *all the towns* in Judea, Galilee, and Samaria where Christian communities existed, citing "through all" (*dia panton*) as his reason for this position (Acts 9:31–32).

34  Schnabel, *Early Christian Mission*, 513, "The early Christian missionaries did not travel alone but rather at least in pairs. Possibly they traveled in larger teams on occasions," as Jesus modeled for them. See also Ott and Wilson, *Global Church Planting*, 48–49, who observe, "The use of teams is a clear pattern in Acts. It is rare indeed to find the early apostles engaged in ministry alone."

35  Barrett, *Acts*, 1:447.

36  F. F. Bruce, *The Book of Acts*, NICNT; Ned Stonehouse, gen. ed. (Grand Rapids: Eerdmans, 1954), 199.

action."[37] The witness and agreement with the work of the Spirit through the preaching of the gospel in Caesarea did not simply fall upon Peter's shoulders but upon the involvement of the church at Joppa.

Upon the gift of the Spirit and faith of the new Gentile believers, Peter "ordered them to be baptized in the name of Jesus Christ" (Acts 10:48). This statement suggests at least two important considerations: (1) The new Gentile believers identified with the church at Joppa through their representatives—hence, something of a mother-daughter church relationship appears to be have been established. (2) The representatives from Joppa, consequently, had some leadership role in the founding of this new church. That Peter stayed on a few more days would also imply that the Joppa church leaders did the same, as they continued to disciple the new followers of Christ and strengthen the newly established church.[38] How were these men prepared for this opportunity? The Joppa congregation and its leadership had nurtured them to the point that the church confidently sent them out with Peter, and Peter, likewise, confidently took them along.

### Antioch Church Planting

Ten to twelve years after Saul instigated persecution toward the Hellenistic Jewish Christians in Jerusalem, he found himself as a Christian leader in the Hellenistic community of Antioch, where the church would send him out with Barnabas to spread the gospel (Acts 13:1–4).[39] His time between new convert and church leader, spent primarily in Syria and Cilicia (Gal. 1:21; 2:1), helped to shape him for the missionary work he would enter into with as much fervor as he had earlier in persecuting the church.[40] Paul would work from Antioch as his sending congregation, to plant the gospel and Christian communities in predominantly Gentile regions.

As the Antioch church set apart Barnabas and Paul at the Spirit's calling, the laying on of hands identified the church with the two missionaries—signifying, as Harrison remarks, "that the whole group was going with them in spirit, committed to faithful prayer on their behalf."[41] Neither of the men saw any conflict between the Spirit's call and the church setting them apart—both worked in concert to give them internal and external encouragement in their mission.[42]

---

37 Hans Conzelmann, *Die Apostelgeschichte*, HNT 7 (Tubingen: J. C. B. Mohr [Paul Siebeck], 1963), 63, my translation of "eine kirchliche Aktion."
38 Stott, *The Spirit*, 192, asserts, "The gift of the Spirit was insufficient; they needed human teachers too."
39 Schnabel, *Early Christian Mission*, 1306.
40 Hengel, *Acts*, 103.
41 Harrison, *Acts*, 216.
42 Ibid., 217.

David Peterson notes that the entire church got involved in commissioning them as missionaries.[43] So what part did the Antioch Christian community play in shaping Barnabas and Paul for their mission work? Although both men were leaders in the church, involved in teaching for an entire year, such close discipling relationships are never one-way. Engaging others through teaching and interaction always sharpens one's teaching. *Involvement in the congregation* with all of the typical idiosyncrasies, problems, sin issues, struggles with assurance, cultural baggage, and much more, likely *helped to better prepare the two missionaries for what they would face in the Galatian region church planting.* They learned more about serving Christ and building relationships among Gentiles by their time in the cosmopolitan Christian fellowship at Antioch. Likewise, intense congregational involvement as they experienced continues to bear fruit in future church planters, missionaries, and pastors.

Congregational life changes the view of ministry as a job to a passionate involvement with the church. One man who was a member of another church in our community asked if I would be willing to mentor him. I declined, and then pointed out that the involvement in our fellowship went hand-in-hand with whatever mentoring I might do. In reality, mentoring is not so much about learning a few lessons but experiencing the depths of life in community.

After planting churches in Lystra, Iconium, and Pisidian Antioch, the mission team returned and "appointed elders for them in every church" (Acts 14:23), before returning to their sending church (Acts 14:26–28). They followed the same pattern evident in the Jerusalem church.[44] Schnabel remarks that the appointment of elders had nothing to do with maintaining strong control over the young congregations, but rather with leading the task of nurturing and shepherding the disciples who would surely encounter hardships.[45] If Derek Tidball correctly assesses the pattern of leadership in Acts, then it seems likely that Paul and Barnabas pointed the new elders in the direction of teaching truth, forming new communities of disciples, resolving inevitable conflict, and protecting the integrity of the gospel and the church.[46] Their doctrinal teaching had application

---

43  David G. Peterson, *The Acts of the Apostles*, PNTC; D. A. Carson, ed. (Grand Rapids: Eerdmans, 2009), 375.

44  Peterson, *Acts*, 415; see Acts 11:30; 15:2, 4, 6, 22, 23; 16:4; 21:18. The use of "elder" parallels with "overseer" in Acts 20:28; Phil. 1:1; 1 Tim. 3:2; Titus 1:7. See Benjamin L. Merkle, *The Elder and Overseer: One Office in the Early Church*, SBL 57; Hemchand Gossai, gen. ed. (New York: Peter Lang, 2003), for a convincing discussion of both terms referring to the same office.

45  Schnabel, *Acts*, 614.

46  Derek Tidball, *Ministry by the Book: New Testament Patterns for Pastoral Leadership* (Downers Grove, IL: IVP Academic, 2008), 99–103.

in mission, relationships, and integrity. Obviously, the time to train leaders for such precision would have been brief but much would have been "caught" by the careful modeling by the missionaries in living out Christian life and ministry.[47] The small beginning from the Antioch church led to the gospel reaching throughout the Roman Empire through Paul and other Christian workers.

## PAUL'S MISSION AND HIS PARTNERS IN MINISTRY

Johannes Nissen identifies three categories of fellow-workers with Paul. (1) The most intimate circle included Barnabas, Silas, and Timothy. (2) Aquila, Priscilla, and Titus represented "independent co-workers." (3) The last group, local church representatives, put workers at Paul's disposal so that *the churches partnered with him in church planting ministry*.[48] While the first two categories figured most prominently in the New Testament, the last involved considerable numbers of workers and help us to see that local churches invested in mentoring them.

Significantly, Paul's ministry, as Nissen explains, was not hurried proclamation to the nations. "His ministry also had a more pastoral aspect," evident by his letters. He did not simply plant a church and move on to another; he sought to shepherd the new disciples in the faith.[49] Unlike the philosophers of his day that sought to change individuals, Paul sought to form communities of disciples who continued on in the faith—and that could only happen with sufficient leadership.[50] He placed priority on making sure that shepherding leaders continued to teach, mentor, and train churches in the faith (e.g., Acts 17:14–15; 18:24–28; 2 Tim. 4:10–12; Titus 3:12–14).

### Intimate Circle

Considerable attention has already been devoted to Paul's relationship with Barnabas. Additionally, Silas and Timothy maintained an unusually close relationship with Paul throughout most of his missionary career.

**Silas** had been deputed by the Jerusalem church to address the churches of Syria and Cilicia with the Jerusalem Council's message (Acts 15:22–33). Luke

---

47  David Sills, *Reaching and Teaching: A Call to Great Commission Obedience* (Chicago: Moody, 2010), 49–50, recommends the MAWL approach to training, likely similar to what Paul and Barnabas did: model, assist, watch, and leave. See also Daniel Sinclair, *A Vision of the Possible: Pioneer Church Planting in Teams* (Colorado Springs: Authentic, 2005), 233–237.

48  Nissen, *New Testament and Mission*, 110.

49  Ibid.

50  Abraham J. Malherbe, *Paul and the Popular Philosophers* (Minneapolis: Fortress, 1989), 70. See also Steve Walton, *Leadership and Lifestyle: The Portrait of Paul in the Miletus Speech and 1 Thessalonians*, Society for New Testament Studies Monograph Series; Richard Bauckham, gen. ed. (Cambridge: Cambridge University Press, 2000), 134–135, who explains that Luke presents Paul, like Jesus, as one who mentored others in the servant-leadership model.

identified him as one of the "leading men among the brethren" in Jerusalem (Acts 15:22). As a Roman citizen (Acts 15:37), he had the political capacity to move freely about the Empire. As a Jewish believer, he was well schooled in the Scriptures, demonstrating this reality through his gifting as a prophet (Acts 16:32). His fluency in Greek is also noted by serving as Peter's amanuensis for his first epistle (1 Peter 5:12).[51]

That the church in Jerusalem recognized his giftedness as a good representative of the faith indicates that Silas spent considerable time *involved with the Jerusalem congregation*. The "whole church," along with the apostles and elders, chose him as a representative to the Gentile believers (Acts 15:22). The church had ample opportunity to attest to his character, servant leadership, knowledge of Scripture, and preaching ability. They sent him on no small task! *Silas's involvement in the Jerusalem church shaped and prepared him for future ministry, to the point that his congregation happily commended him to this epochal ministry to the Gentile church.*

Silas proved to be a capable crosscultural preacher (Acts 15:32). The opportunities granted earlier to Silas by the Jerusalem church gave them confidence to send him on this vital and sensitive mission of the early church. The Jerusalem church's leaders and congregation left its mark on Silas's ministry as he joined Paul's missionary team (Acts 15:36–41).

*Timothy*, notably, held the place as Paul's most intimate associate.[52] Paul called him "my beloved and faithful child in the Lord" (1 Cor. 4:17), "my true child in the faith" (1 Tim. 1:2), and "my beloved son" (2 Tim. 1:2). Luke called him a "disciple" who "was well spoken of by the brethren who were in Lystra and Iconium" (Acts 16:1–2). Curtis Vaughan commented that Timothy was converted on the first missionary journey, noted particularly by Paul's endearing father-son language used later in the epistles.[53] Although still a young man, eighteen to twenty years old by various reckonings,[54] the evidence of his call to ministry and gifts to serve, prompted the Lystran and Iconium elders to set him apart for gospel preaching and teaching (1 Tim. 1:18; 4:14; 2 Tim. 1:6–7).[55] Significantly, his reputation went

51  Harrison, *Acts*, 260. Harrison, 252, also thinks Silas could have been a Hellenistic Jew, while Judas was a Hebrew (Acts 15:22–32).

52  Nissen, *New Testament Mission*, 110.

53  Curtis Vaughan, *Acts*, Founders Study Guide Commentary (Cape Coral, FL: Founders Press, 2009), 111.

54  Vaughan quotes A. T. Robertson, *The Acts of the Apostles*, vol. III in "Word Pictures of the New Testament" (New York: Richard R. Smith, Inc., 1930), 243, as Timothy being eighteen, while Simon Kistemaker, *Acts*, NTC (Grand Rapids: Baker, 1990), 578, counted him as twenty.

55  Kistemaker, *Acts*, 579.

beyond his home church in Lystra to the Iconium church as well.[56] Timothy had likely engaged in some acts of ministry with the latter church so that they could readily affirm his gifts for ministry when sending him out.

Furthermore, Timothy not only received scriptural teaching from his mother and grandmother but *also appropriate mentoring within the Lystra congregation* that proved him ready for training and service with Paul and Silas (Acts 16:1; 2 Tim. 1:5). Otherwise, how could the Lystra and Iconium churches lay hands on him before sending him out (1 Tim. 4:14; 2 Tim. 1:6–7)? Surely, with Paul present, who later cautioned Timothy about hastily laying hands on others for ministry (1 Tim. 5:22), there would have been much seriousness in this ecclesiastical act before sending Timothy out.

What had Timothy learned before joining Paul and Silas for yet more intense lessons in mission and ministry? Obviously, while he learned the Scriptures (2 Tim. 3:14–17), he also learned something of the ministry of elders by observing and receiving from those that Paul and Barnabas had appointed in his church (Acts 14:23). He learned what it meant to model the Christian faith as he observed, and maybe served under, the elders in Lystra and Iconium. By listening to Paul and others ministering in Lystra, he learned about gospel conversations and proclamation. *His home congregation and its leaders mentored him for ministry.*

Timothy had also witnessed courage in ministry, especially after personally knowing the situation of Paul being stoned in his hometown, with elders who continued on in that community setting the example of faithfulness to Christ, despite problems of opposition (Acts 14:19–23). He knew firsthand that those who followed Christ would suffer persecution, as Paul reminded him much later (2 Tim. 3:12). He would need this lesson when Paul and Silas's first venture into Europe led to imprisonment in Philippi, with Timothy left to await their release (Acts 16:23–40). Did he remain with the church in Lydia's home[57] in Philippi while his mentors were jailed? If so, he, along with Luke, had the challenge of encouraging the new followers of Christ in Philppi to continue in the faith despite the opposition. The courage he learned in the congregational setting of Lystra would now bear fruit, as he appeared to take up a leadership role—albeit for only a short period.[58] He would need additional courage when the mission team entered Thessalonica, with some new believers and house

---

56  Harrison, *Acts*, 261.
57  Peterson, *Acts*, 471; Schnabel, *Early Christian Mission*, 1154.
58  Schnabel, *Acts*, 695, points out that the use of the "we passage" at Paul and Silas' departure from Philippi does not resume until eight years later, when Paul travels from Philippi back to Jerusalem, suggesting that Paul left Luke in Philippi (in Acts 20:6, the "we passages" begin again).

church leaders dragged before the local authorities for upsetting the world (Acts 17:1–9).[59]

Paul left Silas and Timothy to continue gospel work with the new church in Berea , while he went to Athens (Acts 17:10–15).[60] The training and opportunities of teaching and discipling that Timothy had learned from the elders and congregation in Lystra were now being put to good use with a new congregation in Berea. What he had incorporated about life in the church would now be passed along to this new community of Christ-followers. Neither Silas nor Timothy could adequately explain Christian community to the Berean church unless they knew something of it through their time in Jerusalem and Lystra, respectively. Such normal influence in Christian community may be unrecognized until the time comes to help shape it in a new circle of believers.

One great challenge for many young pastors and church planters happens when they try to lead a church to health when they've never experienced a healthy church firsthand. No academic training can replace the personal experience of a healthy congregation for those who lead churches toward health. Timothy knew that experience.

Paul sent Timothy to Thessalonica (1 Thess. 3:2), and Silas perhaps went to Philippi, as his representatives before both rejoined the apostle in Corinth (Acts 18:5).[61] On the third missionary journey (Acts 18:23ff), Paul settled into an effective ministry in Ephesus, spending two years "reasoning daily in the school of Tyrannus" (Acts 19:8–10). The Ephesian congregation developed, and in the midst of it, Timothy not only contributed as Paul directed him but also received much from this new fellowship of disciples.

The intimate circle of Barnabas, Silas, and Timothy demonstrate strong, early influence from their sending congregations. Certainly, Paul had a major bearing on each of these fellow workers, mentoring them in study, preaching, teaching, discipline, handling difficulty, suffering, and relationships in the church. Yet they were not church novices before entering into ministry with Paul. Each had been clearly prepared for the challenges of taking the gospel to other people groups through

---

59  Ibid., 707–709, Schnabel states that the charge before the politarchs or senior magistrates, was much more serious than the English translations appear. The opponents portrayed them as criminals, using "the traditional arsenal of polemics, slander, and defamation, while being rooted in some degree in the reality of the effects of Paul's missionary ministry."

60  Peterson, *Acts*, 485, notes that although Timothy has not been mentioned since joining the mission team in Lystra until being left in Berea, Luke commonly focuses on primary rather than secondary figures. Presumably, Timothy remained with Paul the entire time.

61  Harrison, *Acts*, 281; Barrett, *Acts*, 2:827, thinks that Timothy had been sent back to Thessalonica to meet Silas whom Paul had left there, before both joined Paul in Corinth.

the gospel-saturated atmospheres of their home churches. Paul's ministry to them complemented their earlier preparation by continued mentoring in ministry.

## Independent Co-Workers

The independent co-worker did not regularly travel with Paul on his missionary journeys. Aquila and Priscilla served with Paul in both tent making and ministry, most notably in Corinth and Ephesus. Titus, not mentioned by name in Acts, took on assignments from Paul in Corinth, Jerusalem, Dalmatia, and Crete. How were they prepared for ministry?

*Aquila and Priscilla*[62] had significant ministry in Ephesus, where Paul left the couple after their time of service in Corinth (Acts 18:18–19). Paul ministered in Ephesus only briefly before returning on his third missionary journey, but Aquila and Priscilla left no gap in the work initiated, especially by their mentoring efforts with the eloquent Alexandrian believer Apollos (Acts 18:24–28). As they had done in Corinth, the couple opened their home to host a new church in Ephesus,[63] training disciples in that community context, such as Apollos, for fuller gospel ministries. Peterson comments on their leadership in preparing Apollos "for a vigorous and effective ministry in Corinth," with this demonstrating the "interconnection and interdependence of churches in the apostolic period."[64] That they sensitively "took him aside" in order to explain "the way of God more accurately" to him, exemplified wisdom as mentors of a man that would have strong impact for the gospel in the early church.[65]

Luke's narrative during the missionary labors of Paul offers only a small window into the personalities engaged in church planting, as well as those training them. One has no difficulty thinking that Aquila and Priscilla multiplied their discipling and mentoring efforts beyond Apollos, while serving in Corinth and Ephesus (Acts 18), then later back in Rome (Rom. 16:3), and once again back in Ephesus (2 Tim. 4:19). Paul knew them to be dependable, theologically astute, and winsome in relationships—just the right balance needed in training others to preach Christ, plant churches, and build up believers.[66]

---

62  B. R. and P. C. Patten, "Prisca . . . Priscilla," in *ISBE*, 4 vols., Geoffrey Bromiley, gen. ed. (Grand Rapids: Eerdmans, 1986), 3:973. Note Acts 18:18, 26; Rom. 16:3; 2 Tim. 4:19 referring to Prisca or the diminutive form Priscilla, before mention of Aquila.

63  Schnabel, *Early Christian Mission*, 1228.

64  Peterson, *Acts*, 512, fn. 26, 523. When Apollos wanted to go to Corinth to proclaim Christ, Aquila and Priscilla likely used some of their contacts, perhaps even some they had discipled, to gain entry into the fellowship of the church; see Harrison, *Acts*, 304.

65  Ibid., 526.

66  Ott and Wilson, *Global Church Planting*, 10, correctly explain that church planting requires not only spiritual skills but also people skills since "it is also a complex human undertaking." Aquila and Priscilla seemed to hold these tensions well.

Although Luke makes no reference to *Titus*, he was involved in Paul's ministry recorded in Acts. Paul identifies him as a Greek (Gal. 2:3) who accompanied the apostle and Barnabas on a special journey to Jerusalem (Gal. 2:1–10). Assuming that Titus joined Paul and Barnabas on the Acts 11:27–30 famine-relief journey, his association with Paul as a competent representative predated the first missionary journey, indicating him as an early part of the Antioch church.[67]

Titus's understanding of the gospel would have been *honed both in his Gentile Antioch congregation and in his experience with the Jerusalem church leadership.* Obviously, Paul and Barnabas, as well as other leaders in the Antioch church, mentored and trained Titus for future ministry.

Being trustworthy in every way, Titus also received the Corinthian church's collection for the Jerusalem church (2 Cor. 8:6–24), accompanied Paul in church planting work on the island of Crete, served as the apostolic emissary to give leadership and organize the polity of the Cretan churches (Titus 1:4–5),[68] and engaged in mission to Dalmatia along the West Balkan coast (2 Tim. 4:10). Gaps remain in the chronology of Titus, suggesting that he may have done other work of church planting or revitalization when not under particular assignment by Paul. That Paul would send him to Corinth and Crete, two regions of the most difficult churches recorded in the New Testament, indicates the doctrinal fidelity and pastoral skills practiced by Titus throughout his ministry. By every indication, *Titus's early ministry training in the Antioch church under Paul and Barnabas's ministries prepared him to serve Christ's church for many decades.*

Paul called Aquila, Priscilla, and Titus his "fellow workers" (Rom. 16:3; 2 Cor. 8:23), with Titus also called "my partner" among the Corinthian church. Those mentoring them in ministry laid groundwork for strong impact through these Pauline co-workers in the early church.

### *Local Church Representatives*

Paul names upward of forty persons involved in sponsoring his missionary activities.[69] Many more—Jews, Gentiles, women, and slaves—accompanied him

---

67  See Ronald Y. K. Fung, *The Epistle to the Galatians*, NICNT (Grand Rapids: Eerdmans, 1988), 85–86 and Timothy George, *Galatians*, NAC 30 (Nashville: Broadman, 1994), 135–151, on the Galatians 2:1–10 reference corresponding with Acts 11:27–30 rather than Acts 15.

68  G. F. Hawthorne, "Titus," *ISBE*, 864–865. Hawthorne suggests the possibility of two Roman imprisonments for Paul, with Titus accompanying him in church planting on Crete during the window of freedom. However, he cautions against dogmatism on the two-Roman-imprisonment theory.

69  Robert J. Banks, *Paul's Idea of Community: The Early House Churches in Their Cultural Setting*, rev. ed. (Grand Rapids: Baker, 1994), 150–151. Schnabel, *Early Christian Mission*, 1426–

temporarily or permanently on his journeys, participating at various levels of mission work.[70] His practice of involving local church representatives implies an important ecclesiological note: Mission work *is* teamwork.[71] Each disciple involved in proclaiming Christ, planting churches, and nurturing congregations used "their gifts to enrich the church in other places."[72] Although often unnamed, the congregations of the first century sent their finest members to do kingdom work beyond their own communities, giving a model for future generations.

While numerous church representatives went unnamed in Luke's narrative, Acts 19 and 20 identify several, showing that local churches trained and sent out workers to accompany Paul.[73]

**The Acts 19 Representatives:** Along with Timothy, Erastus is identified in Acts 19:22 as one who ministered to Paul during his stint in Ephesus. Paul sent both into Macedonia ahead of his visit. They would have retraced steps from the second missionary journey into Macedonia, likely shoring up weak areas in the churches prior to Paul's arrival. They would have taught, corrected matters of polity, and pastored the Macedonian churches. Toward the end of the apostle's life, he told Timothy that prior to his Roman imprisonment he had left Erastus in Corinth, suggesting that this might have been his home church and the one that sent him out (2 Tim. 4:20).

In Acts 19:29, Luke refers to Gaius and Aristarchus as Paul's traveling companions from Macedonia. While he further pinpoints Aristarchus's home as Thessalonica (Acts 20:4), in this same verse, he mentions Gaius *from Derbe*, a city in the Galatian region, who appears to be a different Gaius than the one from Macedonia.[74] The term *sunekdemoi*, used in Acts 19:29 of Gaius and Aristarchus, and in 2 Corinthians 8:19 of an unnamed traveling colleague with Paul, indicated "trusted and authorized assistants of Paul," according to Barrett.[75] *The authorization came through the churches that equipped and sent them out.*

---

1427, lists thirty-eight coworkers: Barnabas, Timothy, Luke, Aquila, Priscilla, Silas/Silvanus, Titus, Tychicus, Achaicus, Andronicus, Apphia, Apollos, Archippus, Aristarchus, Clemens, Crescens, Demas, Epaphras, Epaphroditus, Erastus, Euodia, Fortunatus, Junia, Jesus Justus, John Mark, Mary, Onesimus, Quartus, Persis, Philemon, Phoebe, Sosthenes, Stephanas, Syntyche, Trophimus, Tryphaena, Tryphosa, and Urbanus.

70  Ibid., 151–155. See also Schnabel, *Early Christian Mission*, 1425ff. for the identity of these fellow workers, along with Paul's designations for them.

71  Ott and Wilson, *Global Church Planting*, 48–49.

72  Peterson, *Acts*, 544.

73  Since Jesus's practice was to travel with several alongside him, it is no surprise that Paul does the same. Nor would it be the least surprising if that were not the common practice with most all mission work in the early church, with Philip's journey in Acts 8 as an exception.

74  Peterson, *Acts*, 547.

75  Barrett, *Acts*, 2:929.

*The Acts 20 Representatives:* After leaving Ephesus, Paul traveled to Macedonia, spending three months in Greece (Acts 20:1–3), and then left for Syria. Sopater of Berea, Aristarchus and Secundus of the Thessalonians, Gaius of Derbe, Timothy, and Tychicus and Trophimus of Asia (or Ephesus) accompanied him (Acts 20:4–5). Who were these partners with Paul in ministry?

After Paul's hasty departure from Berea, Silas and Timothy remained to continue ministering to the newly planted church. Sopater was part of this congregation, which likely means that he had been shaped by Silas and Timothy's ministry in the church.

Aristarchus had already gained reputation for courage as a minister of the gospel (Acts 19:29). Secundus, from the same Thessalonian congregation, joined the group. Gaius came from the church that Paul had planted with Barnabas in Derbe (Acts 14:6, 20; 16:1).[76] Therefore, he would have had a long-time relationship with Paul, indicating Paul as his ministry model.

After mentioning Timothy again, Tychicus and Trophimus of Asia round out the list of Pauline traveling companions. The broad use of Asia probably points to Ephesus as their home.[77] Paul sent Tychicus to Ephesus and Colossae to personally give a report on his behalf (Eph. 6:21–22; Col. 4:7). Paul called him "the beloved brother and faithful minister in the Lord," who had the mission of making everything known about the apostle's imprisonment. He would also offer encouragement and comfort to the Ephesians, who may have been downcast over Paul's prison stay in Rome (Eph. 6:21–22). To the Colossians, Paul called him "beloved brother and faithful servant and fellow bond-servant in the Lord," who brought them information about Paul's status and offered encouragement to them (Col. 4:7–8). Tychicus replaced Timothy in Ephesus during Paul's second Roman imprisonment (2 Tim. 4:12). Either Tychicus or Artemas was sent to Crete to replace Titus so that he might visit with Paul in Nicopolis (Titus 3:12). In both of these regions, Tychicus would have been involved in revitalizing previously established congregations and possibly continuing church planting efforts. *His two-and-a-half years under Paul and Silas's ministry in Ephesus shaped him for his strategic service.* His presence with Paul in the journey to Jerusalem, ministry to Paul in both Roman imprisonments, and willingness to go to difficult places to further gospel work, give evidence of a man well-trained and well-prepared to serve Christ's church. If Ephesians was an encyclical letter, then Tychicus would have spent time with other congregations in Asia Minor, representing the apostle

---

76   "Gaius," *ISBE*, 2:377.
77   Schnabel, *Early Christian Mission*, 1228.

to them.[78] That Paul would call him a "fellow bond-servant in the Lord" (Col. 4:7) shows the respect that the apostle had for Tychicus's gifts in ministry and steadiness in each assignment given to him.[79]

Paul left Trophimus sick in Miletus prior to his second Roman imprisonment (2 Tim. 4:20), indicating that Trophimus traveled and served with Paul during the brief hiatus between the two imprisonments. During that time, Paul had engaged in church planting work with Titus on the island of Crete. Trophimus may have accompanied him in that endeavor, learning about church planting firsthand from Paul. Afterward, traveling to Miletus, Trophimus fell sick and likely had to remain with Christians in the community while Paul continued on. Along with the others named in Acts 20:4, Trophimus teamed to deliver financial gifts from the Gentile churches in Macedonia, Achaia, and Asia to the church in Jerusalem—offering demonstrative proof of the kinship and unity of Gentile and Jewish believers as "one, holy, catholic, apostolic" church.[80]

Paul's investment in the lives of these servants sent from the various churches took on greater preparation by his visit with the Ephesian elders at Miletus (Acts 20: 13ff.). The entourage further spent time with Philip the evangelist in Caesarea, likely hearing stories from this energetic church planter that spurred them to more labor in planting the gospel in other communities (Acts 21:7–16). Some church members from Caesarea ("disciples from Caesarea," Acts 21:16) traveled with Paul and his team to Jerusalem. With no time wasted, it seems apparent that Paul would have utilized the period of travel to continue to train this second generation of Christians in details of Christian ministry. Each being sent out by their respective congregations indicates a level of support for them and Paul's ongoing mission.

## APPLYING MENTORING COMMUNITIES TO YOUR CHURCH

If one tries to locate a manual on developing leadership for church planting, missions, and revitalization in the book of Acts, he may experience a level of frustration. Luke focuses on particular geographical and personal details in his narrative without thought, it seems, for filling in the gaps on leadership development.[81] Who planted the churches in Lydda and Joppa? He does not tell us, so we are left guessing the church planters' identities. Who mentored Philip so that

---

78  C. M. Robeck, Jr., "Tychicus," *ISBE*, 4:930.

79  Eduard Lohse, *Colossians and Philemon*, Hermeneia; Wm. R. Poehlmann and Robert J. Karris, trans.; Helmut Koester, ed. (Philadelphia: Fortress, 1971), 170–172.

80  Schnabel, *Early Christian Mission*, 1229. See Pesch, *Apg*, 2:184–187; Pesch, 187 fn. 13, who wrote about the underlined demonstration of unity with Jewish and Gentile churches through the twelve traveling with Paul who took the collection to Jerusalem.

81  Peterson, *Acts*, 26.

he became an effective church planter? What kind of training regiment did his mentor follow in preparing him to do cross-cultural church planting? How long did Titus travel with Paul; what did the apostle teach him? Again, Luke did not bother to include these matters since his greatest concern centered on selective details to demonstrate the apostolic witness throughout the Roman Empire.[82]

Despite the lack of details on leadership development in Acts, we conclude that in Luke's narrative, wherever people responded to the gospel churches began, gospel witnesses other than the major personalities in Acts also engaged in planting churches; and although Luke mentions no program of training, it appears obvious that *early church planters learned from Christian mentors* the apostolic doctrine, basic elements of ecclesiology, development of relationships, and maintaining the integrity of the gospel and the church.[83] The same essentials remain necessary for those preparing for gospel ministry.

Just as with Jesus, *the early leaders of the church worked in teams* to further the gospel throughout the empire.[84] Younger, less experienced workers, such as Timothy and Titus, profited from "on-the-job-training" under the tutelage of more experienced Christian leaders. That pattern bears repeating in our ministries. As shown with Philip, Barnabas, and Silas, much of this training took place within the fellowship of the local church, so that *the church forged their understanding of the gospel and ecclesiastical application.*[85] Churches planted by Paul, Barnabas, and Silas *developed and sent out workers* to accompany Paul in his missionary efforts. *An unmistakable connection remained with the home church that trained and sent workers into the harvest.* As our congregations train and send out Christian workers, we follow the example of the first-century church.

Mentors like Paul and Silas modeled suffering for the sake of the gospel as a normal part of expanding Christ's kingdom. *Churches networking together, sending out leaders for strategic ministry with Paul, gave a pattern for unified church mission in post-apostolic days.* This same pattern can be noted in the epistles of Ignatius a generation or more later.[86] It's a good plan for our day as well. Both Peter and Paul

---

82  Ibid., 27.

83  See Tidball, *Ministry by the Book*, 99–103.

84  See Ott and Wilson, *Global Church Planting*, 48–49.

85  James G. Samra, *Being Conformed to Christ in Community: A Study of Maturity, Maturation and the Local Church in the Undisputed Pauline Epistles*, LNTS 320; Mark Goodacre, ed. (London: T & T Clark, 2006), 135, explains that Paul considered the local church as essential for believers' maturity. The church facilitates this process of maturity and transformation through five components of the maturation process: (1) identifying with Christ; (2) enduring suffering; (3) experiencing the presence of God; (4) receiving and living out wisdom from God; and (5) imitating a godly example (see 112–132; 152–166; 168–169).

86  See Ignatius, *Pol.* 7; *Smyr.* 11–12 (*ANF* 1).

modeled cross-cultural work for those under their tutelage—a lesson essential for their protégés continuing gospel expansion in the Gentile world.

The details of Luke's Acts, often mentioned briefly, remind twenty-first century churches that the local church still has the responsibility to train and send workers into the gospel harvest. Church planting, missions, and revitalization requires leadership honed and shaped in the local church through faithful mentors.

# CHAPTER 4

# PAUL AS MENTOR

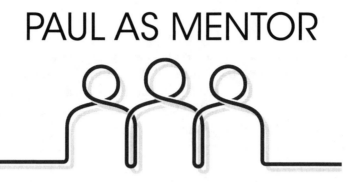

A first-year seminary student might say, "If only I could be mentored by Paul." While that cannot happen, the next best practice would be to learn from the apostle's mentoring approach. That's why we turn to the Pastoral Epistles to consider Paul as mentor.

Paul's letters to Timothy and Titus, commonly referred to since the eighteenth century as the Pastoral Epistles, provides the framework for understanding some details of how Paul mentored his younger associates. Throughout his missionary labors, the apostle regularly worked with associates who shared in the ministry at different levels.[1] Luke called Paul and Barnabas "apostles" (Acts 14:4, 14)—an obviously more elevated position, while Paul called Timothy, "my fellow worker" (Rom. 16:21) and Titus, "my partner and fellow worker" (2 Cor. 8:23). Paul trained them with reference to the gathered community of Christ-followers, rather than in isolation.[2] Their ministries would not be cloistered in monasteries but active in local congregations. Paul mentored them with the church in view.

The Pastorals urge their recipients to a way of life grounded in the revelation of Jesus Christ.[3] Paul taught and modeled multiplication of Christian leaders, since he not only urged Timothy and Titus to follow his example, but also to set the example for others to follow (2 Tim. 1:3–4, 8–14; 2:14–26; 3:10–17; 4:6–8; Titus 3:1–8). Some consider their faith a personal matter, so much so, that they dare not crack the door to allow anyone to take a close look. Yet, as Robert Banks writes, "The gospel is not a purely personal matter. It has a social dimension. It

---

1 Robert J. Banks, *Paul's Idea of Community: The Early House Churches in Their Cultural Setting*, rev. ed. (Grand Rapids: Baker, 1994), 149–151.
2 Ibid., 26.
3 Frances Young, *The Theology of the Pastoral Letters*, New Testament Theology; James D. G. Dunn, gen. ed. (Cambridge: Cambridge University Press, 1994), 74.

is a communal affair."[4] Even when relationships tested and tried Paul's faith, he maintained the social dimension, knowing that his trainees must face the same challenge in their future work.[5]

Perhaps in the back of Paul's mind, as he trained Timothy and Titus, lay the many false teachers who sought to overturn the new communities of disciples. So, while commending instruction to these trainees toward their pastoral charges, he also insisted on their exemplary conduct (1 Tim. 4:12; Titus 2:7). He mentored much more than doctrine; he modeled the way of life in Christ (1 Tim. 4:16).[6]

This chapter on mentorship and training in the Pastoral Epistles will consider the trainees of the pastorals, particular areas of ministry instruction by Paul, and the apostle's approach to mentoring Timothy and Titus. Although the Pastorals cannot give a full picture of Pauline mentorship, they do offer transferable insights useful to contemporary mentors and trainees engaged in ministry.[7]

## THE TRAINEES OF THE PASTORALS

Paul's long connection with Timothy began in Lystra during the second missionary journey. His relationship with Titus started earlier, probably during his ministry in Antioch. As part of strong churches, both young men learned how to walk with Christ and serve the church by the faithful teaching and example of those in the congregation. *Paul built on this congregational mentoring by taking these young men under his tutelage to prepare them for gospel ministry.* The Pastoral Epistles (PE) shed light on the kind of relationship that developed over the years of Paul mentoring Timothy and Titus. The categories in his communication provide a model for pastoral mentors in every generation.

Timothy served under Paul's leadership for much of the apostle's life, at times accompanying him, and other times completing assignments with various congregations as Paul's representative.[8] Part of the training process for his future ministry

---

4  Banks, *Paul's Idea of Community*, 26.

5  See 1 Tim. 1:18–20; 6:20–21; 2 Tim. 1:15–18; 3:10–12; 4:10, 14–18.

6  Young, *Theology of the Pastoral Letters*, 89.

7  Readers will notice some continuation in the Pastoral Epistles of elements from the leadership development modeled by Jesus and in the Acts, e.g., focus on the message of the kingdom (Luke 10:9; Acts 8:4–8; 13:5, 16–41; 2 Tim. 4:1–2; Titus 2:11–14) and the importance of nurturing relationships in the community (Luke 9:3–5; 10:4–8; Acts 11:19–26; 1 Tim. 5:1–16; Titus 2:2–10). The repetition of these elements gives the contemporary church a clearer view of prescriptive elements in leadership training.

8  Philip H. Towner, *The Letters to Timothy and Titus*, NICNT; Ned B. Stonehouse, F. F. Bruce, and Gordon D. Fee, gen. eds. (Grand Rapids: Eerdmans, 2006), 316, uses the term "apostolic delegate" to describe Timothy's role. This implied full representation of what the apostle would say and do were he to be present. See also David C. Verner, *The Household of God: The Social World of the Pastoral Epistles*, SBLDS 71; William Baird, ed. (Chico, CA: Scholars Press, 1983),

involved pastoral assignments by Paul—"on-the-job training." Confidence shown by Paul likely helped Timothy through the more difficult settings. No doubt, the debriefing talks in which they engaged were instructive for Timothy.

Timothy demonstrated well-rounded understanding of pastoral ministry. Records of his work in Thessalonica, Corinth, and Ephesus appear to focus on strengthening existing churches rather than on church planting (although he had church-planting experience in Europe with Paul). In Thessalonica, Corinth, and Ephesus, Timothy dealt with issues of doctrinal fidelity, genuineness in the faith, apostolic authority, moral and spiritual problems, tensions in relationships, reordering the leadership of elders and deacons, structuring an appropriate church response to widows, exposing false teaching, carefully balancing relationships of older and younger men and women, instructing Christian slaves on how to relate to believing masters, and refocusing the worship and polity of the church. He had learned to work through these pastoral issues by close observation and practice in his home church, and then, participation in the diverse settings of mission work under the tutelage of Paul and Silas (and perhaps Luke). Unnamed elders who served as the presbytery that set him apart for ministry likely had substantial involvement in training him, prior to his joining Paul's missionary team (1 Tim. 4:14).

Titus may have predated the first missionary journey by traveling with Paul and Barnabas to Jerusalem, bringing famine relief as a Gentile representative of the Antioch church (Acts 11:27–30; Gal. 2:1–10).[9] It appears likely that Paul led Titus to faith in Christ, indicated by the affectionate phrase, "my true child in the common faith" (Titus 1:4). This journey to Jerusalem suggests that Titus was an early member of the Antioch church, profiting from the gospel-saturated atmosphere of that mission-sending congregation. The diligent and systematic teaching of Barnabas and Paul for an entire year in Antioch shaped his theology (Acts 11:26).

When one considers the influence and training in Antioch, the visit with the church's early leaders in Jerusalem, and the off-and-on contacts/assignments with Paul, Titus had some of the best training of any Pauline associate. Assuming that he was converted in Antioch under Paul's leadership, he would have experienced

---

157–158, who notes Timothy and Titus's roles as special assistants to Paul "rather than as prototypes of the monarchical bishop."

9  Timothy George, *Galatians*, NAC 30; E. Ray Clendenen, gen. ed. (Nashville: B&H, 1994), 134–145, commenting on Galatians 2:1–3, gives a convincing argument to accept the earlier dating of Paul's association with Titus as the Acts 11:27–30 trip to Jerusalem, rather than the majority view of Acts 15 Jerusalem Council visit.

the ups and downs of church planting where the gospel had not been known. He would have learned sound ecclesiology through conversations and observation, as well as grasped essential matters of church polity. In visiting Jerusalem, he would have been involved in weighty theological discussions that clarified the gospel and its implications, shown by Paul's comments in Galatians 2:1–10. Back in Antioch, he would have further grappled with the grace of God in justification by Christ alone when Paul opposed Peter due to his compromise with the Judaizers (Gal. 2:11–21), while simultaneously witnessing the Christian approach to correcting issues that confuse the gospel.[10] Titus's background and association with Paul clearly trained him to effectively pastor, plant, and revitalize churches.[11] It also presents a good picture of the varied hues found in mentoring.

## PAUL'S TRAINING REGIMEN

The richness of the Pastorals for understanding the trainer/trainee relationship cannot be overestimated. Although having already thoroughly trained and mentored Timothy and Titus in pastoral work, the wise mentor continued to bring to remembrance lessons learned, while addressing specific issues pertinent to their ministries. To help mentors get a better picture of the range of areas to address in mentoring, we will consider details of Paul's training regimen in five categories: Doctrine/confessional statements, polity, leadership, relationships, and general pastoral instruction. These same areas of training offer contemporary mentors an appropriate curriculum for their trainees.

### Doctrine/Confessional Statements

Paul explains the right use of the Law with the gospel, contrasting its misuse by false teachers (1 Tim. 1:8–11). His high Christology leads to doxology when offering testimony of the grace of God in his life as a means of encouraging Timothy (1 Tim. 1:12–17). In ordering worship in the church, Paul sets it upon the foundation of God's willingness to save, Jesus as Incarnate Mediator, and the substitutionary work of Christ (1 Tim. 2:1–7). He connects the teaching on women in the church to the fall in Genesis 3 (1 Tim. 2:9–15). William Mounce calls 1

---

10   George, *Galatians*, 169, puts this conflict between Peter and Paul at the end of the first missionary journey, preceding the Jerusalem Council (Acts 14:26–28; Gal. 2:11–14).

11   See R. Bruce Carlton, "Multiplying Leaders on Mission with God," in *Discovering the Mission of God: Best Missional Practices for the 21st Century*, Mike Barnett, ed. (Downers Grove, IL: IVP Academic, 2012): 498–516, who gives current examples of training leaders in a process he calls "pay it forward." He explains, "multiplying leaders involves one's life into the lives of others and possessing a passionate desire to help others become effective leaders and trainers of others" (508). Clearly, we observe this example in Paul with Timothy and Titus.

Timothy 3:14–16, "the heart of the Pastoral corpus . . . which puts the instructions of the corpus into proper perspective."[12] Paul joins the conduct of the church to "the content of Christian theology" summarized as "the mystery of godliness."[13] He weds the church's conduct to its mission, its mission to its theology.[14]

Paul corrects the false teaching and practice of asceticism by the doctrine of creation (1 Tim. 4:1–5). The apostle ties discipline to soteriology (1 Tim. 4:6–10). He exhorts Timothy to "keep the commandment without stain or reproach" in light of a sobering eschatology and the doctrine of God (1 Tim. 6:11–16). Even the instruction to the rich is couched in relationship to the doctrine of last things (1 Tim. 6:17–19).

Second Timothy is no less theologically rich than the first letter. The call to not be ashamed of the gospel soaks with the apostle's passion for Christology and soteriology (2 Tim. 1:8–14). With Paul's plea, "Remember Jesus Christ," John Stott comments on 2 Timothy 2:8–13, "Even so the church has often forgotten Jesus Christ, absorbing itself instead now in barren theological debate, now in purely humanitarian activity, now in its own petty, parochial business."[15] So the apostle anchors his call for endurance and suffering hardship in the doctrine of Christ. The doctrine of the saints' preservation carries the weight of Paul's warning to avoid wrangling over words and worldly chatter (2 Tim. 2:14–19). He explains the believers' perseverance on the foundation of the doctrine of Holy Scripture (2 Tim. 3:10–17). The charge to preach the word is introduced by the solemn reality of the doctrines of God's immanence, judgment, Christ's return, and kingdom (2 Tim. 4:1–5). The doctrine of last things serves as the backdrop of Paul's testimony of fighting the good fight of faith (2 Tim. 4:6–8). Because of opposition to his theology of the believers' security, Paul testified of the Lord's strength for endurance to proclaim the gospel in the face of great opposition (2 Tim. 4:16–18).

Paul's introduction to Titus rides on the doctrine of salvation (Titus 1:1–4). As he instructs the behavior of older and younger men and women and bond-slaves, he bases the rationale for it on adorning the doctrine of God our Savior

---

12  William D. Mounce, *Pastorals Epistles*, WBC 46; Bruce Metzger, ed. (Nashville: Thomas Nelson, 2000), 214. Le P. C. Spicq, *Saint Paul Les Épitres Pastorales*, EBib, 2 vols. (Paris: J. Gabalda, 1969), 1:464, notes, "This is the doctrinal point of culmination of the Epistle and the same key of the Pastorals" (my translation).

13  Mounce, *Pastorals*, 215. This key theological declaration is also considered to be a hymn fragment noted by its structure and rhythm. Mounce, 216, breaks the hymn of 1 Timothy 3:16 into two stanzas: "The first concerned with Christ's life and the second with the world's reception of him."

14  Ibid., 218.

15  John R. W. Stott, *The Message of 2 Timothy: Guard the Gospel*, BST; John Stott, NT ed. (Downers Grove, IL: IVP, 1973), 61.

(Titus 2:1–10). He continues by showing the theological foundation for right practice based on the effects of Jesus's substitutionary death: to redeem and to purify a people for his own possession, who will be zealous for good deeds—the very subject of the exhortation (Titus 2:11–15).[16] So, proper behavior cannot be removed from the theological underpinnings of the doctrines of Christ's person and work. Even the reminder to be subject to God-ordained authorities shows the way by contemplating themes of anthropology, hamartiology, Christology, and soteriology (Titus 3:1–11).

Paul taught and reinforced with his trainees the need for a healthy theological basis for all conduct in the church. The Pastoral Epistles underscore this by joining instruction and exhortation to a doctrinal rationale.

Contemporary mentors should do no less. While culture has changed in the past two thousand years, the nature of God, the gospel, the church, and its mission have not. The Western tendency toward pragmatic methodology for quick results lacks the moorings to sustain Christian leaders and their congregations through the turbulence of life in a fallen world. The standard of confessional statements as the foundation for life and ministry protects the leader and his flock from drifting into doctrinal deviations, and grounds their mission in the world to stand upon the verities of Scripture.[17] Mentors must give priority to our faith's theological underpinnings and how this theology works out in the multiple dimensions of the trainees' life and ministry.

One way that our church reinforces theology for the congregation is through an overview of our doctrinal statement, the 1858 *Abstract of Principles*, during the membership process. We often refer to and cite the *Abstract* as a reminder that we believe theology matters. Our trainees notice. As a number have gone out from our church to serve in other settings, they reinforce the church's confessional statements or introduce one, if they've not had one before.

## *Polity*

The church's polity affects its health. For that reason, Paul addressed the offices and governing structures for the local church in the Pastoral Epistles (1 Tim. 3:1–13; 5:17–22; Titus 1:5–9). David Verner identifies the broad range of author-

---

16  Mounce, *Pastorals*, 420–434.
17  See David Wells, *No Place for Truth; Or Whatever Happened to Evangelical Theology* (Grand Rapids: Eerdmans, 1993), 95–136. See also John Armstrong, ed., *Reforming Pastoral Ministry: Challenges for Ministry in Postmodern Times* (Wheaton, IL: Crossway, 2001), for a series of essays by pastors who are convinced of a strongly confessional Christianity as the foundation for pastoral work.

ity charged to the church's officers in the Pastoral Epistles: pastoral responsibility for membership (1 Tim. 5:1–2), disciplinary authority in the community (1 Tim. 5:19–20), representation to the outside world (1 Tim. 3:7), "preservation, transmission and defense of the teaching," ordering the church's social life, and serving "as the first line of defense against opposition to the teaching" facing the church.[18] Additionally, setting apart elders took place by the laying on of hands, an appointment ritual common in the early church, demonstrating a continuation of apostolic teaching and delegated local church authority.[19] Paul told Timothy not to treat this ritual lightly since it indicates participation with the ones set apart (1 Tim. 5:22). The churches of the Pastoral Epistles would not always have apostles or apostolic delegates present to lead them. The attention that Timothy and Titus gave to establishing the elders would be the foundation for the churches' future.[20]

The practice passed on by Paul, and implemented by Timothy and Titus, for installing elders as the shepherding leaders in the local church establishes the framework for succeeding generations to follow. Training faithful men who will be able to teach and train others ensures that the apostolic faith continues, developing leaders learn to apply the gospel to all areas of life, and the church's mission expands. In this regard, pastors must be intentional with a process that fits their context for developing and recognizing new leaders. This involves mentoring potential leaders in the doctrines of the faith, holding them accountable for the development of Christian character, and entrusting them with ministry responsibilities—mentoring them throughout the process.

## Leadership

Paul's exhortation to "entrust these to faithful men who will be able to teach others also," opens the heart of biblical leadership (2 Tim. 2:2). Steve Walton calls Paul's view of leadership "a feeding leadership which 'oversees' and 'shepherds,' not a domineering leadership."[21] In other words, leadership first centered

---

18  Verner, *Household of God*, 160.

19  Ray Van Neste, *Cohesion and Structure in the Pastoral Epistles*, JSNTSup 280; Mark Goodacre, ed. (London: T & T Clark International, 2004), 61. See Steve Walton, *Leadership and Lifestyle: The Portrait of Paul in the Miletus Speech and 1 Thessalonians*, SNTSMS; Richard Bauckham, gen. ed. (Cambridge: Cambridge University Press, 2000), 196–197, who clearly refutes those who try to establish a *frühkatholisch* ["early catholic"] model of handing down the apostolic office to subordinates, "rather, it is the apostolic teaching which he is to pass on to these 'faithful people.'"

20  Aldred A. Genade, *Persuading the Cretans: A Text-Generated Persuasion Analysis of the Letter to Titus* (Eugene, OR: Wipf & Stock, 2011), 23.

21  Walton, *Leadership and Lifestyle*, 114–115.

on serving the flock by teaching them the Word of God (Acts 20:28).[22] Paul used *didaskalia* (teach) fifteen times in the Pastoral Epistles, while the balance of the NT uses it only six times. Twice, Paul also described himself not only as an apostle but a teacher, further reinforcing the combination of teaching with Paul's understanding of church leadership (1 Tim. 2:7; 2 Tim. 1:11).[23]

Leaders not only teach but also set an example of how the teaching works out in practical behavior. He told Timothy and Titus to be examples of those believing (1 Tim. 4:12; Titus 2:7).[24] Paul had set the example as a mentor to his protégés by strong teaching as he led them, joined by setting an example to follow (2 Tim. 3:10–17). So, as leaders, they were to "give attention to the public reading of Scripture, to exhortation and teaching," while paying "close attention to *yourself* and *your* teaching," persevering in these things to ensure salvation for themselves and those who listened to them (1 Tim. 4:13, 16; italics added). As a Christian leader, Titus must couple purity in doctrine with an example of good deeds (Titus 2:7).

Contemporary leaders who seek to mentor the next generation of pastoral leaders will, like Paul exhorted Timothy, faithfully teach the Word and consistently put truth into practice. This practice means that mentors will major on relationships with trainees as the vehicle for teaching and modeling Christian truth. In other words, anyone with teaching gifts can stand at a podium and offer lectures on biblical doctrines, but only those engaging trainees in *intentional relationships* will model doctrine and life, while consequently shaping their protégés for future ministry. Pastoral mentors can do this in small groups or one-on-one settings. Such practice gives trainees the opportunity to observe, ask questions, and enter into the sphere of the mentor's practical understanding and application of the gospel to the details of marriage, family, community, ministry, and mission.

I've tried to develop an atmosphere in which our pastoral trainees can ask anything that's on their minds. It might have to do with pastoral work; it could be a question on how to strengthen marriage; it might be how to navigate a difficult situation at work; or it could be the consideration of a pastoral or mission charge. If it's a private issue, I maintain strict confidentiality with them. By building relationships and being accessible to the trainees, it opens the door for more intentional focus on training that affects more than just their ministry—it transforms their lives.

---

22  Ibid., 134–136.
23  Young, *Theology of the Pastoral Letters*, 75.
24  Ibid., 76.

### Relationships

Paul sets doctrine as bookends for the instructions on social relationships in the church by the call to speak sound doctrine to the community, thus giving "the theological basis for the instructions" (Titus 2:1, 15).[25] Relationships were not to be built upon merely social dynamics but upon the outworking of the gospel in their lives: as a starting point, "correct behavior (vv. 2–9) is based on correct theology (v. 1)."[26] So the behavior of older and younger men and women and slaves must not dishonor the word of God but adorn the gospel (2 Tim. 2:2–10). With this doctrinal framework for relationships, Paul avoids the ditches of legalism and asceticism common in Judaism and the mystery religions. The gospel shines through the layers of real life. Otherwise, the believer's behavior might confuse the message of the gospel. "Because the heathen cannot see our faith," wrote Martin Luther, "they ought to see our works, then hear our doctrine, and then be converted."[27] What was good for the congregation was good for the one leading it, so Paul inserts a personal exhortation to Titus in the midst of his instructions on social relationships, demonstrating that the gospel minister must "show [himself] to be an example of good deeds" (Titus 2:7–8).[28]

Faced with the predicament of how, as a younger gospel minister, he could correct members of the church at Ephesus, especially as one temporarily in their midst, Paul instructs Timothy, "Do not sharply rebuke an older man, but rather appeal to him as a father, to the younger men as brothers, the older women as mothers, and the younger women as sisters, in all purity" (1 Tim. 5:1–2). Harshness must never accompany church authority. Instead, he must treat them as he would family members of corresponding age.[29] In this regard, pastoral mentors must set an example in exercising wisdom and grace in all relationships. Any mentor's harshness in community relationships will leave trainees confused on genuine gospel application.

At times, difficult relationships arise. In some cases, Paul warns his trainees about some in particular: guarding against Alexander the coppersmith (2 Tim. 4:14–15), silencing those upsetting whole families by their empty talk and deception (Titus 1:10–11), and rejecting a factious man (Titus 3:10–11). In others, he cautions about falling prey to loose speech with those engaging in worldly and empty chatter (2 Tim. 2:14–19) and with those who prefer picking verbal fights to speaking truth

---

25  Mounce, *Pastorals*, 406.
26  Ibid., 408.
27  Ibid., 413, citing *Luther's Works*, ed. J. Pelikan (St. Louis: Concordia, 1966), 29:57.
28  Ibid. Mounce points out that Paul typically embedded personal comments in his discussions.
29  Marshall, *Pastoral Epistles*, 572.

(2 Tim. 2:23). Instead, "The Lord's bond-servant must not be quarrelsome, but be kind to all, able to teach, patient when wronged, with gentleness correcting those who are in opposition, if perhaps God may grant them repentance leading to the knowledge of the truth" (2 Tim. 2:24–25). Such practical advice for those involved in gospel work spans generations. Mentors must detect tendencies in trainees that hurt their relationships and pastoral work by impatient, unkind words that abuse church authority—instructing them, as bond-servants of Christ, in appropriate attitudes and actions toward those seemingly incorrigible members.

One of the most essential relationships for those in ministry is within the circle of the elders. By their faithfulness in governing, preaching, and teaching, some are deemed worthy of appropriate remuneration (1 Tim. 5:17–18). Others, who step outside of the boundary of behavior befitting the office and refuse repentance, must face rebuke in the assembly of the congregation (1 Tim. 5:19–21). But Paul insists on a right balance in this regard. The elder must not be party to frivolous attacks on a fellow elder. He accepts only substantiated charges against an elder, invoking Old Testament practice (Deut. 17:6). Yet when the evidence indicts an elder, regardless of the closeness in friendship, he must be rebuked without bias as a warning to the body of Christ.[30]

A wise practice for pastoral mentors will be to include trainees in elders' meetings, with the exception of occasions requiring executive session. This gives them a clearer picture of iron sharpening iron in ministry leadership. It teaches future ministers the value of plurality and equality in leadership, as they witness how church leaders walk in humility and deference to one another. It also gives mentors an effective framework for developing future church elders who may be sent out to pastor or serve as missionaries, or who may even remain as leaders in their congregation.

### General Pastoral Instructions

The Pastorals contain around seventy imperatives and twenty-five indirect expressions, representing commands or expectations, emphasizing the didactic tone of the letters.[31] Seven times Paul used the verb *manthano*, translated as "to receive instruction" (1 Tim. 2:11) and "to learn" (1 Tim. 5:4, 13; 2 Tim. 3:7, 14 [2x]; Titus 3:14).[32] Much of the three letters focuses on particular instructions in

---

30   Thomas D. Lea and Hayne P. Griffin, *1, 2 Timothy Titus*, NAC 34; David Dockery, ed. (Nash-ville: Broadman Press, 1992), 154–157.

31   Young, *Theology of the Pastoral Letters*, 78.

32   Louw-Nida, 27.12, translates *manthano*, "to acquire information as a result of instruction." See also Young, *Theology of the Pastorals*, 78.

light of current issues in Ephesus and Crete, or on reminding the younger ministers of truths they needed to keep at the forefront of their labors. The general pastoral instructions consider teaching and training, worship, corporate conduct, and widows. Contemporary mentors may vary this list to some degree, but it does serve as a substantial list of critical issues facing new and existing congregations. Discussion between trainers and trainees centered on the doctrinal and practical implications of these issues in church life will serve future ministers and the congregations that they will shepherd.

### Teaching and Training

The training motif is found directly by the Scripture as profitable "for training in righteousness" (2 Tim. 3:16), and metaphorically, by athletic imagery for training in godliness (1 Tim. 4:7–8; 2 Tim. 2:5).[33] As Paul trained his trainees, they were to train others.

Timothy was to remain in Ephesus so that he might engage in instruction (1 Tim. 1:3–4). His instruction, like Paul's, would have the goal of unalloyed love (1 Tim. 1:5). He would entrust to teachable men the things he had learned from Paul so that they might reproduce this teaching in others (2 Tim. 2:2). Paul exhorts him to be a diligent student of Scripture, giving attention to sound hermeneutics (2 Tim. 2:15). This discipline would set the foundation for preaching the Word, with varying applications that "reprove, rebuke, exhort, with great patience and instruction" (2 Tim. 4:2).[34]

Likewise, Titus was to "speak the things which are fitting for sound doctrine," (Titus 2:1) referring both to "an identifiable body of teaching" and "ethical duties which the sound doctrine demands," as John Stott observed.[35] Teaching would do more than increase quantity of knowledge; it would also make specific ethical applications to daily life, relationships, duties, and service. Emphatically, after

---

33 Young, *Pastoral Letters*, 78–79.
34 Mentors will find that reading together and discussing with trainees the following books on preaching will clarify many issues central to a pastoral leader's teaching and preaching ministry: D. Martin Lloyd-Jones, *Preaching and Preachers*, 40th anniversary ed.; contributors Bryan Chapell, Mark Dever, Kevin DeYoung, Ligon Duncan, Tim Keller, and John Piper (Grand Rapids: Zondervan, 2012); J. W. Alexander, *Thoughts on Preaching: Being Contributions to Homiletics* (Edinburgh: Banner of Truth, 1988 from 1864 ed.); John Stott, *Biblical Preaching Today* (Grand Rapids: Eerdmans, 1961, 1982); John Piper, *The Supremacy of God in Preaching* (Grand Rapids: Baker, 1990).
35 John R. W. Stott, *Guard the Truth: The Message of 1 Timothy & Titus* (Downers Grove, IL: IVP, 1996), 185. He added, "For there is an indissoluble connection between Christian doctrine and Christian duty, between theology and ethics," lessons contemporary mentors must inculcate in their trainees (186).

identifying particular ethical duties and their foundation in the gospel, as well as preparing for additional doctrinal and ethical instructions, Paul reiterated: "These things speak and exhort and reprove with all authority. Let no one disregard you" (Titus 2:15).[36] If teaching merely added knowledge, it might not create a stir. But if it calls for an ethical response to the doctrine—evident in Paul's instruction to Titus—strong possibilities of *disregarding* the messenger to avoid the message might take place.[37]

### Worship

Pastoral instruction for corporate worship addressed various facets of prayer (1 Tim. 2:1–2), the universality of the gospel (1 Tim. 2:3–4), the solitary means of salvation through the Mediator's ransom (1 Tim. 2:5–6), and details affecting men and women in corporate worship so that their behavior will not disrupt worship (1 Tim. 2:8–12).[38] While Paul did not establish a formal liturgy for corporate worship, he did preclude issues that distracted from and disrupted the body's gathering to worship.

The church cannot be careless with its public conduct since it is "the household of God, which is the church of the living God, the pillar and support of the truth" (1 Tim. 3:14–15).[39] Paul's use of *dei*, "something which should be done as a result of compulsion,"[40] indicates the seriousness with which he offered his instructions to Timothy and the church. Primary would be the church's corporate witness as "the pillar and the support of the truth," identified by the confessional declaration of 1 Timothy 3:16. As Mounce rightly notes, "It is not the church that is being protected but the gospel that is being protected by the church."[41] The imagery shows the church engaged in "the defense and the confirmation of the gospel,"

---

36  Mounce, *Pastorals*, 432, explains that Paul's summary command looks forward and backward.
37  Ibid., 433. John Piper, *What Jesus Demands from the World* (Wheaton, IL: Crossway, 2006), gives many examples of applying truth through this excursus on the teachings of Jesus Christ.
38  Ibid., 75–77, 104; Mounce points out that Paul's argument likely counters false teachers who espouse "an exclusive gospel that offers salvation only to a select few, and this exclusivism is made clear by their practice of praying for only certain people" (76). Mounce calls 1 Timothy 2:8–15, "the most discussed passage in the PE today" (103). Evidently, angry men and immodest women disrupted the atmosphere of the body gathered for worship, hence Paul's admonitions (see 105–117).
39  The anarthrous use of *oikou theou* ("household of God") shows local congregations rather than the universal church as its subject, Mounce, *Pastorals*, 220–221.
40  Louw-Nida, 71.21.
41  Mounce, *Pastorals*, 222. See David F. Wells, *The Courage to Be Protestant: Truth-lovers, Marketers, and Emergents in the Postmodern World* (Grand Rapids: Eerdmans, 2008), who makes clear what is at stake by the way that the church protects or fails to protect the gospel in their generation.

(Phil. 1:7) while also holding the truth aloft so that its gospel message might be corporately proclaimed to the world.[42]

Corporate gatherings should be times for worship *and* instruction. Timothy needed to solemnly charge the Ephesians *enopoion tou theou*, as though their assembly took place in "the context of a heavenly court (2 Tim. 2:14)."[43] Unseen eyes gazed upon the church gathered in worship, so they were to heed the pointed message addressing their character and practice.[44] The assembled church was to "give attention to the public reading of Scripture, to exhortation and teaching" (1 Tim. 4:13). Justin Martyr (114–165 AD) embraced this instruction as he talked of the weekly worship of the early church. "And on the day called Sunday, all who live in cities or in the country gather together to one place, and the memoirs of the apostles or the writings of the prophets are read, as long as time permits; then, when the reader has ceased, the president verbally instructs, and exhorts to the imitation of these good things."[45] The early church recognized the exposition of Holy Scripture as central to worship.

Conflicts in congregational worship continue to affect the unity and mission of the church. The wise mentor will diligently coach his trainees in both biblical teaching on worship and how to wisely shepherd a congregation in navigating this critical aspect of corporate life and arrive at appropriate changes.[46]

## Corporate Conduct

As already noted, the Pastorals addressed multiple issues of conduct in the congregations of Ephesus and Crete. Women were to quietly receive instruction with an attitude of submission (1 Tim. 2:11). Elders, deacons, and deaconesses (or deacons' wives) were to be above reproach and people of dignity (1 Tim. 3:1–13; Titus 1:6–9). Both elders and deacons were to be good managers of their households (1 Tim. 3:4–5, 12). Paul called upon slaves to relate to their masters in such a way as to bring honor to God and the gospel (1 Tim. 6:1–2; Titus 2:9–10). The rich were to learn contentment and guard against the snare

---

42  Stott, *Guard the Truth*, 105.

43  Marshall, *Pastoral Epistles*, 619.

44  Luke Timothy Johnson, *The First and Second Letters to Timothy: A New Translation with Introduction and Commentary*, ABC 35A; W. F. Albright and David N. Freeman, gen. ed. (New Haven, CT: Yale University Press, 2001), 389.

45  Justin Martyr, "The First Apology of Justin," in *ANF*, 1.67 (186). See also Stott, *Guard the Truth*, 121–122, who insists, "It was taken for granted from the beginning that Christian preaching would be expository preaching, that is, that all Christian instruction and exhortation would be drawn out of the passage which had been read."

46  See Bob Kauflin, *Worship Matters: Leading Others to Encounter the Greatness of God* (Wheaton, IL: Crossway, 2008).

of wealth, while all were to recognize love of money as the root of all kinds of evil (1 Tim. 6:7–10, 17–19).

The exhortations in Titus 2:2–10 demonstrate Paul's discerning analysis of problems befitting the persons' age and gender, with appropriate calls for action. Older men were, as Stott commented, "to exhibit a certain *gravitas*, which is both appropriate to their seniority and expressive of their inner self-control."[47] While avoiding the dangers of malicious gossip and addiction to wine, the older women were to embrace ministry of training the younger women in regard to family duties.[48] Young men were to be sensible.

The Christian community's subjection to governing authorities and readiness for every good deed, would confound those who saw the new religion as problematic (Titus 3:1–2). With false teachers rampant, the church must not jump on board the foolish controversies, spurious genealogies, and wrangling over the Law (Titus 3:9). Instead, they were to "be careful to engage in good deeds" (Titus 3:8). The local congregation must be involved in mission work beyond their community, as they "learn to engage in good deeds to meet pressing needs," a Pauline way of encouraging substantial support for those serving in missionary work (Titus 3:13–14).[49]

The dangers of legalism arising by a misapplication of law and grace, on one hand, and moral laxity shaped by the culture, on the other, confront pastoral leaders of every generation. Mentors must not leave these matters to chance with those they are preparing for ministry. Biblical discussion on Christian conduct will better prepare future ministers for the day that they will be leading congregations in the challenges of appropriate Christian conduct. Including trainees in elders' meetings when discussions on matters of conduct are on the agenda will help them understand how to navigate conduct issues that can tarnish a congregation's testimony in the community or split the church by the lack of decisive action.[50]

---

47  Stott, *Guard the Truth*, 187.

48  Ibid., 188.

49  Paul specifically called on the Cretan congregations to assist Zenas and Apollos, the deliverers of the epistle to Titus, "on their way so that nothing is lacking for them," a clear indication of specific mission support (Titus 3:13). Mounce, *Pastorals*, 458, explains that *propempein*, "diligently help," implies "to help on a journey by supplying food, clothing, etc. . . . and describes the hospitality required of all Christians . . . always in reference to Christian ministry." He further suggests, due to Apollos's association with Alexandria, Egypt, that work in Alexandria might have been their mission goal.

50  See John Murray, *Principles of Conduct: Aspects of Biblical Ethics* (Grand Rapids: Eerdmans, 1957), on applying law and gospel in a congregational setting.

### Widows

Paul devoted considerable attention to widows, indicating that the Ephesian church had numerous widows as members (1 Tim. 5:3–16). Although his specific instructions were new, care for widows was not. The Pentateuch called for widow-care, with remembrance of Israel's suffering in Egypt and the Lord's consequent deliverance, as motivation to extend the same care (Exod. 22:22; Deut. 24:17–18). Part of Job's defense of his conduct referred to having "made the widow's heart sing for joy" (Job 29:13).[51]

Paul showed concern that adult children care for their widowed mothers so that the church could focus on those with genuine needs, whom he called "widows indeed" (1 Tim. 5:3). He further qualified widow support for widows that regularly exercised particular spiritual disciplines (1 Tim. 5:5, 9–10).[52] Younger widows were to be encouraged to remarry, "bear children, keep house, and give the enemy no occasion for reproach" (1 Tim. 5:13–14). Those capable of assisting widows on their own were to do so in order that the church might focus on "widows indeed" (1 Tim. 5:16).[53]

For those serving in pastoral offices in the local church, ministry to the flock loomed large in Paul's understanding of pastoral work, not merely holding titles.[54] Despite the distance and his difficult circumstances, his concern for details of the church's doctrine, polity, leadership, relationships, and varied pastoral duties show the heart of what he communicated to his trainees. Ministry must touch all of life or else it will prove deficient in the pastoral office.

## PUTTING PAUL'S MENTORING MODEL INTO PRACTICE

Having considered the inclinations of Timothy and Titus regarding ministry and Paul's particular areas of ministry instruction in the Pastorals, we will conclude by looking at Paul's multipronged approach to mentoring Timothy and Titus. Contemporary mentors will find each Pauline approach to be readily transferable in their own practice.

(1) *Father-son relationships.* The tenderness in fatherly language that Paul regularly used with Timothy and Titus bears strong evidence that their relationships

---

51  Lea and Griffin, *1, 2 Timothy, Titus*, 146.
52  Ibid.
53  A contemporary pastoral setting may have other congregational needs critical to the church's health, i.e., issues with singles, divorcees, adoption, and aging. Mentors will need to keep current congregational needs in their ongoing discussions and on-the-job training with mentees. See Glen Smith, "Models for Raising Up Church Planters: How Churches Become More Effective through Intentional Leadership Development," *Leadership Network*, 2007; 5–10.
54  Stephen G. Wilson, *Luke and the Pastoral Epistles* (London: SPCK, 1979), 61–63.

went far beyond a lecturer-student setting (1 Tim. 1:2, 18; 2 Tim. 1:2; Titus 1:4). They lived life together. They loved each other. They suffered and served together. Paul found intense satisfaction in the closeness of their relationships.[55] Dietrich Bonhoeffer expressed what should be obvious except for the harried pace in the Western world: "The Christian cannot simply take for granted the privilege of living among other Christians."[56]

(2) *Affirmation, encouragement, and reminders.* The closeness of relationship as a father to his sons puts Paul in the position to affirm his trainees.[57] "In pointing out these things to the brethren, you will be a good servant of Christ Jesus" (1 Tim. 4:6); "For I am mindful of the sincere faith within you" (2 Tim. 1:5); "Now you followed my teaching, conduct, purpose, faith, patience, love ..." (2 Tim. 3:10–17). "If you could do only one thing as a mentor, affirm your protégés," assert Brad Johnson and Charles Ridley.[58] Affirmation by one that walks faithfully with Christ builds strong confidence in trainees heading to the front lines of gospel work.

Paul had been on the receiving end of Barnabas's encouragement (Acts 9:26–30), so he understood how necessary this generous giving of oneself in words, presence, and deeds lifts the spirit of others to persevere under difficulty.[59] When Barnabas sought out Paul to join him in teaching ministry in Antioch, the older believer encouraged Paul in his life work (Acts 11:25–26).[60] Likewise, the apostle showed encouragement to his protégés by giving them difficult assignments and trusting them to do the work faithfully. The tone of his letter breathes an air of encouragement to spur Timothy and Titus forward.[61]

---

55  Mounce, *Pastorals*, 8, notes that Paul's use of *gnesios*, "'true,' conveys both intimacy and authority," referring to 1 Timothy 1:2 and Titus 1:4. See Stott, *2 Timothy*, 28–29, who offers an encouraging note on spiritual friendship.

56  Dietrich Bonhoeffer, *Life Together and Prayer Book of the Bible*, Dietrich Bonhoeffer Works, vol. 5; Gerhard Ludwig Müller, Albrecht Schönherr, Geffrey B. Kelly, eds.; Daniel W. Bloesch and James Burtness, trans. (Minneapolis: Fortress, 2005), 27. Josh Hunt, "Finding Church Planters: Discovering and Discerning Those God Has Called to Start the Next Generation of Churches," *Leadership Network*: 1–17, cited 11 Jan 2013, leadnet.org//docs/CP-2007-JUN-Finding_Church_Planters-Hunt.pdf, explains an important relationship factor related to church planting work. "The more time you invest with a prospective church planter, the more you minimize the chance of surprises" (p. 2).

57  For an excellent work on the power and practice of affirmation, see Sam Crabtree, *Practicing Affirmation: God-centered Praise of Those Who Are Not God* (Wheaton, IL: Crossway, 2011).

58  W. Brad Johnson and Charles R. Ridley, *The Elements of Mentoring* (New York: Palgrave Macmillan, 2004), 10.

59  Michael Pocock, "The Role of Encouragement in Leadership," in *Integrity of Heart, Skillfulness of Hands: Biblical and Leadership Studies in Honor of Donald K. Campbell*, Charles H. Dyer and Roy B. Zuck, eds. (Grand Rapids: Baker, 1994), 301–307.

60  Ibid., 305.

61  Good examples of mentors affirming and encouraging their protégés may be found in a number of collections of correspondence, e.g., Iain Murray, ed., *D. Martyn Lloyd-Jones: Letters 1919–*

Rather than belittling them for what they did not know or were not doing, Paul often simply reminded his trainees of things with which they had already grappled. The use of *anamimnesko* in 2 Timothy 1:6 expresses the idea of causing someone to recall and to think again about something already considered.[62] Because of their experience, mentors hold the capacity to dust off memories in order to bring to the forefront issues that trainees might have overlooked or forgotten. Paul's frequent use of "this is a trustworthy saying," indicates a quoted "saying," according to George Knight,[63] which serves as a reminder of truths readily accessible to the pastoral trainees. Mentors will wisely remind them of important issues in doctrines, relationships, spiritual disciplines, service, humility, and mission in gentle ways, often couched in normal conversation.

(3) *Setting an example to follow.* Many lessons in ministry are better caught than taught. "People watch leaders and learn," writes Walter Wright.[64] Often the examples etched in the trainees' minds remain fresh even when the mentor is no longer around.[65] Paul constantly prayed for his trainees, an example that likely had profound influence on them (2 Tim. 1:3). He set the example of suffering for the gospel without shame or regret (1 Tim. 1:12–14; 2 Tim. 1:8, 15–18; 2:8–10; 3:10–17[66]; 4:6–8). He also demonstrated how to face disappointment (2 Tim. 4:16–18) and how to remain steady at the helm of gospel ministry (Titus 1:1–4). Spending time with protégés is critical to genuinely influence their lives and ministries. One pastor indicated that he mentors by just "hanging out" with his trainees.[67] That's certainly a practice demonstrated by Paul with his protégés!

(4) *Prayer and visits.* The regularity in prayer that Paul showed for his beloved trainees staggers the mind. "I constantly remember you in my prayers night and day, longing to see you, even as I recall your tears, so that I may be filled with joy" (2 Tim. 1:3–4). Whether free or imprisoned, Paul sought visits from them (Titus

---

*1981* (Edinburgh: Banner of Truth, 1994); Jules Bonnet, trans. and ed., *Letters of John Calvin: Compiled from the Original Manuscripts and Edited with Historical Notes*, vol. 2 (Philadelphia: Presbyterian Board of Publication, 1858; no city: Repressed Publishing LLC, 2012 reprint).

62  Louw-Nida, 29.10.

63  George W. Knight III, *Pastoral Epistles*, NIGTC; I. Howard Marshall and W. Ward Gasque, eds. (Grand Rapids: Eerdmans, 1992), 99; see 1 Tim. 1:15; 3:1; 4:9; Titus 3:8; 2 Tim. 2:11.

64  Walter C. Wright, *Relational Leadership: A Biblical Model for Leadership Service* (Carlisle, Cumbria, UK: Paternoster Press, 2000), 34.

65  Ibid.

66  Paul's use of "you followed," *parakolutheo*, implies conforming one's life and "behavior to a particular system of instruction or teaching." In this case, Timothy followed Paul's example too; Louw-Nida, 36.32.

67  See Smith, "Models for Raising Up Church Planters," 9, referring to Pastor Hal Haller, Church of the Highlands, Lakeland, FL.

3:12; 2 Tim. 4:9, 11). The ongoing conversations strengthened the protégés for the continued intensity in pastoral work. It also strengthened Paul. His longing for the fellowship of his younger brothers in Christ taught them to never outgrow the need for fellowship.[68]

(5) *Pastoral/ministry charges.* Due to the closeness of the trainer/trainee relationship, Paul could "charge" his trainees with critical responsibilities that must be exercised in their ministries.[69] He charges Timothy to maintain the principles that he had set forth without bias (1 Tim. 5:21), to keep the commandment without stain or reproach (1 Tim. 6:13), and to preach the word of God (2 Tim. 4:1–2). Paul can tell his protégés to "guard, through the Holy Spirit" (2 Tim. 1:14), to "be strong in the grace that is in Christ Jesus" (2 Tim. 2:1), to "suffer hardship with me" (2 Tim. 2:3), and to "consider what I say" (2 Tim. 2:7). He can tell them to "flee from youthful lusts and pursue righteousness. . . . But refuse foolish and ignorant speculations" (2 Tim. 2:22–23). He can exhort them to "continue in the things you have learned and become convinced of" (2 Tim. 3:14). Despite being in a difficult situation, he speaks into his trainees' lives so that they understand their responsibilities and sense the urgency to continue in them, e.g., "remain on at Ephesus so that you may instruct certain men not to teach strange doctrines" (1 Tim. 1:3);[70] and "I left you in Crete, that you would set in order what remains and appoint elders in every city as I directed you" (Titus 1:5). While he speaks with authority, he does so without heavyhandedness, as a father with his sons.[71]

The reality of friendship need not undermine the authority of mentor with those he trains with reference to correction. The mentor has this responsibility as a shepherd to his flock—including trainees (Acts 20:28).

(6) *Warnings.* Mentors, by virtue of life/ministry experience, recognize stumbling blocks and dangers of which their younger trainees may be unaware. So warnings are appropriate, just as Paul demonstrated. He warned about two men in Ephesus having been shipwrecked regarding their faith (1 Tim. 1:18–20). He warned of those falling away from the faith, giving evidence by paying attention to "doctrines of demons" (1 Tim. 4:1–5). He warned of the danger found in falling prey to substitutes for true godliness (1 Tim. 4:6–10; 6:3–10). He cautions against

---

68  John S. Hammett, personal correspondence, 11 January 2013.

69  Paul used *diamarturomai enopion* (1 Tim. 5:21; 2 Tim. 4:1) in two of his charges, conveying a serious declaration based on presumed personal knowledge, and that, before, *enopion*, the face of God, Louw-Nida 33.223. The use of *paragello enopion* in 1 Timothy 6:13 carries the idea of announcing what must be done, Louw-Nida 33.327. The preposition intensifies both charges (Louw-Nida, 83.33).

70  Towner, *Letters to Timothy and Titus*, 106, calls this a "mandate" feature in the letter.

71  Ibid.

engaging in "worldly and empty chatter" and foolish controversies, as some had already done to their own ruin (2 Tim. 2:16–18; Titus 3:9). Ministry would not be easy, so he warns of difficult times ahead (2 Tim. 3:1–9). Paul offered personal warning concerning individuals that would seek to harm his trainees (2 Tim. 4:14–15). Contemporary mentors, seasoned by various experiences in life and ministry, will find most trainees eager to learn from transparent reflections.

I've found that the gut-level discussions that I've engaged in with our pastoral interns has produced much effect in their grasp of the dangers in ministry. Often, I bring up some mistake that I've made or the way that I misread a conversation or a creeping heresy that I've faced in my years in ministry, in order to help them feel the intensity of dangers lurking in ministry. Pastoral ministry is not for the fainthearted, so such warnings help younger men to better evaluate their propensities for ministry.

(7) *Gospel-centered focus.* If the trainees were to suffer, it was for the gospel (2 Tim. 1:8). If they were to surmount the difficulty of timidity in the faith, they must remember the purpose and effects of the gospel (2 Tim. 1:7–10). Point blank, Paul told Timothy, "Remember Jesus Christ, risen from the dead, descendant of David, according to my gospel," as foundational for suffering hardship as a good soldier of Christ Jesus (2 Tim. 2:8). Here the gospel takes the struggling trainee on the wings of consolation and encouragement.[72] The "hope of eternal life" anchored Paul's proclamation and centers his message to Titus (Titus 1:1–4). The impetus for exhorting the older and younger men, women, and bondslaves are found through *and* for the gospel, just as also the rationale for denying ungodliness and living "sensibly, righteously and godly in the present age" is found in the gospel (Titus 2:1–15). Andreas Köstenberger's *Excellence: The Character of God and the Pursuit of Scholarly Virtues*, although written to the scholarly community, also applies to those involved in ministry. His premise—integrity as a disciple of Jesus Christ must be evident in every aspect of scholarly life—equally speaks to mentors and trainees.[73] Success in future ministry can never replace faithfulness in living out the gospel in the full range of life and ministry.[74]

(8) *Personal requests and advice.* The closeness of the trainer/trainees relationship was such with Paul and Timothy that he could advise him on the delicate matter of personal convictions and a recurring stomach ailment (1 Tim. 5:23).[75]

---

72  Mounce, *Pastorals*, 511.
73  Andreas Köstenberger, *Excellence: The Character of God and the Pursuit of Scholarly Virtues* (Wheaton, IL: Crossway, 2011), 17–29.
74  I'm using "success" in a common way, not as though it opposes faithfulness.
75  Knight, *Pastoral Epistles*, 240.

The end of 2 Timothy contains several personal requests: Bring Mark when Timothy visits Paul; bring the cloak that Paul had left at Troas, along with the books and parchments; greet several friends; "Make every effort to come before winter" (2 Tim. 4:9–21). In more abbreviated fashion, he did the same with Titus, asking him to make every effort to visit him in Nicopolis, presumably before the harsh, forthcoming winter (Titus 3:12).[76] Titus was to also diligently help Apollos and Zenas as they passed through Crete (3:13). Mentors will be involved in the issues of their trainees' lives. Otherwise, a gap will exist in the full scope of mentorship in the Pauline tradition.

While the study in Acts demonstrates that Paul mentored a number of younger ministers in gospel work, the Pastorals give more detailed insights on the relationship he had with Titus and Timothy, as well as some of the focal points of their mentorship. Paul sought to strengthen their doctrinal moorings but also urge them toward the practical application of doctrine in everyday relationships. Pastoral work—whether for planting, revitalizing, or maintaining a local congregation—majors on life and doctrine. Neither can be neglected if the minister would be effective. Paul's mentoring demonstrates this reality.

As we've toured the Pastoral Epistles, we've seen how they provide contemporary mentors with categories for mentoring, along with the doctrinal and ethical points for emphasis with trainees. Although we live in different eras with diverse cultures, Paul's father-son relationship with Timothy and Titus provides a model for those committed to mentoring the next generation for ministry. The emphasis on relationships centered in the gospel offers contemporary trainer/trainees a pattern to emulate. Pastoral mentors will find plenty of guidance on training young ministers as they study and apply Paul's mentoring model in the Pastoral Epistles.

---

76  Towner, *Letters to Timothy and Titus*, 800–801.

CHAPTER 5

# MAGISTERIAL MENTORING —16th CENTURY

W hen we think of the Magisterial Reformers, we might tend to consider great theological minds bent on massive doctrinal corrections, waging written war with the Roman Catholic Church, and affecting the entire religious, political, and social landscape of Europe. And the likes of Martin Luther, Huldrych Zwingli, and John Calvin did just that. But there was much more. Primarily, they were pastors of local congregations who sought to shepherd the flock, train up pastoral leaders, and spread the gospel of Christ beyond their communities. In the way that they conducted their pastoral responsibilities, these reformers modeled what pastors of local churches should do today.

A brief look at two of the great reformers, Zwingli and Calvin, might help us better understand how they mentored pastors, missionaries, and spiritual leaders within the framework of healthy congregational life.

## HULDRYCH ZWINGLI (1484–1531)

"You have offered me not only books," wrote a former mentee to Zwingli, "but yourself also."[1] Another trainee called Zwingli "a tutelary god to us," for his attentiveness in teaching and training the younger men.[2] Zwingli's effectiveness in mentoring relationships exemplifies pastoral mentoring in community.

---

1 Jean Henri Merle d'Aubigné, *For God and His People: Ulrich Zwingli and the Swiss Reformation*, Mark Sidwell, ed.: Henry White, trans. (Greenville, SC: BJU Press, 2000), 14.
2 J. J. Hottinger, *The Life and Times of Ulric Zwingli*, T. C. Porter, trans. (Harrisburg, PA: Theo. F. Scheffer, 1856), 17.

Huldrych Zwingli took his place as one of the magisterial Protestant Reformers during the sixteenth-century Reformation.[3] For the first dozen years of ministry, he served as parish priest in Glarus and Einsiedeln, Switzerland (1506–1518).[4] But the years 1515–1516 marked a shift in this thinking under the guidance of Desiderius Erasmus (1466–1536). Through the humanist scholar's Greek New Testament and visits to Basel, Zwingli radically changed. However, in directions Erasmus did not intend, the change turned him toward areas of biblical reformation.[5]

Zwingli's developing theological model shook his Erasmian views not long after his move to become *the people's priest* at the Grossmünster in Zurich (1518). Historians offer various opinions concerning Zwingli's theological transformation, but as one Zwingli biographer notes, "The banal fact that Zwingli's new insight grew out of his lively relationship with his congregation and community is often overlooked."[6] Zwingli's study, teaching, and training *operated within the orb of the congregation.* By 1522, Zwingli had rejected the traditional Catholic authorities in favor of *sola scriptura* as sole basis for teaching and life, a principle focus he would inculcate in those he trained.[7]

Once Zwingli and his colleagues convinced the Zurich city leaders to reject the Mass and follow the direction of the Reformation, the city council agreed to create a theological school under Zwingli's leadership.[8] This decision laid the foundation for his approach to mentoring and training ministers to serve throughout Europe.[9] The school, called the *Prophezei* or Prophecy, welcomed both clergy and lay people to attend at no cost. Instead of straightforward lectures, Zwingli

---

3   See Timothy George, *Theology of the Reformers* (Nashville: Broadman, 1988), 108–162, for a background sketch and theological appraisal of Zwingli.

4   Denis R. Janz, ed., *A Reformation Reader: Primary Texts with Introductions* (Minneapolis: Fortress Press, 1999), 151.

5   Gottfried W. Locher, *Zwingli's Thought: New Perspectives*, Studies in the History of Christian Thought 25; Heiko A. Oberman, ed. (Leiden: E. J. Brill, 1981), 239. At Erasmus' behest, Zwingli memorized the Pauline Epistles in Greek (239).

6   Ulrich Gäbler, *Huldrych Zwingli: His Life and Work*, Ruth C. L. Gritsch, trans. (Philadelphia: Fortress Press, 1986; from *Huldrych Zwingli: Leben und Werk*; Munich: C. H. Beck, 1983), 45–48. For more reasons for this change, see p. 48.

7   Ibid., 49. Zwingli wrote, "It is my conviction that the word of God must be held by us in the highest esteem (the Word of God being that alone which comes from God's Spirit) and no such credence is to be given to any other word. It is certain and cannot fail us; it is clear and does not let us wander in darkness. It teaches itself, it explains itself and brings the light of full salvation and grace to the human soul," in Zwingli, "Of the Clarity and Certainty of the Word of God (6 September 1522)," Janz, *A Reformation Reader*, 155.

8   Karin Maag, *Seminary or University? The Genevan Academy and Reformed Higher Education, 1560–1620*, St. Andrews Studies in Reformation History; Andrew Pettegree, Bruce Gordon, and John Guy, eds. (Aldershot, Hants, UK: Scolar Press, 1995), 129–130.

9   G. W. Bromiley, ed., *Zwingli and Bullinger*, LCC, Icthus ed. (Philadelphia: Westminster Press, 1953), 97. Bromiley also points out that clergy from the city attended (28). It started in 1525.

and his fellow scholars utilized discussion and debate to instruct their students.[10] They valued the collegial atmosphere to train the young ministers. While giving attention to the expected language and theological studies, in the end, the goal in the *Prophezei* consisted in making good Christians.[11]

The model for study in the *Prophezei* included daily biblical exegesis, starting with an analysis of a Hebrew Old Testament text, followed by Zwingli's Latin interpretation and explanation. A sermon on the text in German proved beneficial to those untrained in Hebrew and Latin. Zwingli or a colleague normally took up a companion Greek New Testament text for further consideration.[12] The students also participated by publicly reading the Latin text under consideration, thus learning to properly read Scripture to the congregation.[13] All of this training occurred in an atmosphere of Christian community.

Aside from the *Prophezei*, Zwingli regularly entertained guests in his home. Pastors, canons, professors, students, and scholars assembled as friends to discuss the issues of the gospel. These times were marked by Zwingli's transparency, as he welcomed corrections in the light of Scripture.[14] Some sought personal reformation through Zwingli's application of Scripture; others sought counsel on how the gospel's proclamation might triumph in their region.[15] The Zurich pastor patiently received these guests and sought to mentor them in gospel work.

Zwingli's correspondence reveals his pastoral heart in training and mentoring others in ministry. Urbanus Regius of Augsburg read Zwingli's letter to John Frosch of the same city, commenting, "I have read Zwingli's letter, and have re-read it, for I felt my soul inspired by it, and kindled to admiration. For the words of this man of God are fire itself, and kindle fire in you."[16] He continued describing the way that Zwingli's passion for the defense of the gospel caused him to realize how

---

10  Maag, *Seminary or University*, 131. Locher, *Zwingli's Thought*, 254, points out that the *Prophezei* became "the germ of the present-day University of Zurich."

11  Bromiley, *Zwingli*, 97–98. Locher, *Zwingli's Thought*, summarizes the three points that run through all of Zwingli's messages, including the teaching in the *Prophezei*: (1) reconciliation; (2) reconciliation that has been accomplished; (3) therefore Christ is Lord over all areas of life (p. 37).

12  Gäbler, *Huldrych Zwingli*, 100–101. See Timothy George, *Reading Scriptures with the Reformers* (Downers Grove, IL: IVP Academic, 2011), 238, who writes, "The greatest contribution of the Zurich reformers to the tradition of preaching was the institution of the 'Prophecy.'" He continues by giving a detailed description of what took place at the Prophecy (238–240).

13  H. Bullinger, "Prophezei," in *Huldrych Zwingli: Documents of Modern History*, G. R. Potter, ed. (London: Edward Arnold, 1978), 64.

14  R. Christoffel, *Zwingli: or The Rise of the Reformation—A Life of the Reformer, with Some Notices of His Time and Contemporaries*, John Cochran, trans. (Edinburgh: T. & T. Clark, 1858), 379–381.

15  Ibid., 381–383.

16  Ibid., 193–194.

slight his own zeal was for the good news. He found renewed determination in faithfulness to Christ through Zwingli's example.[17] According to R. Christoffel, Zwingli's letters and admonitions had strong influence on most of the preachers in south Germany, so that *his life seemed evident in their lives, and the church model in Zurich evident in their ministries.*[18] The DNA of the Zurich pastor and congregation showed up in those mentored and influenced.

How did Zwingli mentor and train young men for ministry? We get a strong idea of it in a letter to Zwingli from Valentine Tschudi, who explained with gratitude how the reformer showed kindness to him, offered his books to him, encouraged him, and offered his assistance and influence with whatever the young man might need. He further indicated that Zwingli did this toward all of his students—which would have been those he mentored in his pastoral work.[19] Personal attention to trainees could not be replaced in Zwingli's approach. Additionally, he sought through the *Prophezei* to recruit "an evangelical ministry" that would be continually engaged in spreading the gospel.[20] His church-rooted training appears regularly, as Gottfried Locher asserts, so that Zwingli did not attempt to stand out or draw attention to himself, but rather "always appears *in community* with his co-workers."[21] In other words, he did not make ministry training about himself but about the whole community's influence.

Through the theological school, Zwingli had ongoing contact with those preparing for ministry and some already involved in pastoral work in the Zurich region. He dialogued with them and modeled biblical exegesis and homiletics through the regular work of the *Prophezei*. Even his ultimate successor, Heinrich Bullinger, after returning from his studies in Germany, sought out Zwingli in Zurich, determining to follow the reformer's example. Zwingli welcomed him and continued the relationship of influence with Bullinger.[22]

---

17  Ibid.
18  Ibid., 194. Christoffel notes that Christian brethren from Germany fleeing persecution found refuge with Zwingli in Zurich, who nurtured and cared for them (202–203). Christoffel also mentions Zwingli's engagement in correspondence with those seeking to proclaim the gospel in France and Italy, in order to encourage them in the face of suffering, reassuring them of the power of the gospel and its promised fruitfulness (pp. 203–208).
19  Hottinger, *Life and Times of Zwingli*, 17. Bromiley, *Zwingli*, 16, notes that the reformer had obtained a considerable library, probably through his papal pension.
20  Bromiley, *Zwingli*, 28.
21  Gottfried Locher, "The Message and Impact of Huldrych Zwingli: The Significance for His Time," in *Prophet, Pastor, Protestant: The Work of Huldrych Zwingli after Five Hundred Years*, E. J. Furcha and H. Wayne Pipkin, eds. (Eugene, OR: Pickwick Publications, 1984), 110, italics added.
22  J. H. M. D'Aubigné, *For God and His People: Ulrich Zwingli and the Swiss Reformation*, Mark Sidwell, ed.; Henry White, trans. (Greenville, SC: BJU Press, 2000), 68.

Berthold Haller (1492–1536), several years Zwingli's junior, had taken up responsibilities at Berne when he was twenty-one. Due to his gifts, he had been named canon and later preacher of Berne's cathedral. However, he had yet to grasp the gospel until he came under the broadening sway of Zwingli and those whom the Reformer had taught. Through this influence, Haller came to faith in Christ and considered Zwingli his father in the faith. When the trials and opposition were so strong against him that Haller decided to resign his position and return to his home in Basel to take up the life of a scholar, Zwingli exhorted him to take courage and boldly stand for Christ in Berne.[23] "My soul has been awakened from its slumber," he responded to Zwingli. "I must preach the gospel, Jesus Christ must be restored to this city, whence He has been so long exiled."[24] Until his death in 1531 at the second battle of Kappel, Zwingli continued to give of his time and energies to shape the rising generation to persevere in the work of reformation in Switzerland and surrounding nations.

## JOHN CALVIN (1509–1564)

After evaluating the effects of the *schola publica* of Geneva's Academy that began in 1559, Karin Maag commented that in the years leading up to John Calvin's death, "Geneva's main export was ministers, principally heading for France."[25] This unusual *commodity* exported to surrounding regions came out of a burden that Calvin sensed when he recognized the paucity of trained pastors to serve evangelical congregations and begin new ones in Switzerland and beyond.[26] As he considered his own training and evaluated the need for congregational understanding and application of Scripture, he determined to train pastors who would, in turn, teach their congregations the Word of God. With his strong view of the local church,[27] he believed that each member should develop the skills to

---

23 G. R. Potter, ed., *Huldrych Zwingli: Documents of Modern History* (London: Edward Arnold, 1978), 77, notes that Zwingli, in a letter to Haller on 29 December 1521, counseled, "Such wild beasts need to be stroked gently and their growls tolerated for a space until, convinced by the constancy and depth of our perseverance, they are tamed by patience."

24 Ibid., 65–66.

25 Maag, *Seminary or University*, 23. The Genevan Academy had two schools. The first, *schola privata*, had seven classes or levels that began with basics of Latin and French languages, gradually moving toward study in Latin and Greek authors. Upon finishing the *schola privata* curricula, students could enroll in the *schola publica*, an advanced twenty-seven-lecture course with curricula that focused on Hebrew, Greek, exegetical studies, and the art. See Wulfert de Greef, *The Writings of John Calvin: An Introductory Guide*, Lyle D. Bierma, trans. (Grand Rapids: Baker, 1993), 53–54, for a detailed look at the Academy's structure.

26 Randall C. Zachman, *John Calvin as Teacher, Pastor, and Theologian: The Shape of His Writings and Thought* (Grand Rapids: Baker Academic, 2006), 58.

27 Most of Book IV in John Calvin, *Institutes of the Christian Religion*, LCC 20–21; John T. McNeill, ed.; Ford Lewis Battles, trans. (Philadelphia: Westminster Press, 1960), addresses ec-

be able to read, interpret, and apply the Scripture to daily life.[28] Calvin believed the way to church revitalization took place when congregations regularly heard the Word expounded and pastorally applied to the multifaceted needs of life, so that they learned to profit by personally reading and applying the Word.[29] Yet this had to start with well-trained pastoral leadership in local congregations.

Calvin had the benefit of Martin Bucer (1491–1551) of Strassburg mentoring him after his exile from Geneva. Bucer came to Reformation convictions after hearing Martin Luther preach in 1518. Consequently, he led his city in embracing the Protestant faith.[30]

Bucer recognized Calvin's gifts, cultivating them by asking him to pastor a French-speaking congregation in Strassburg. Calvin found Bucer's polity of church offices and practice in worship to be models that he later incorporated in the Geneva church. Bucer also spoke into Calvin's life, correcting attitudes and behavior unbefitting to ministers of Christ.[31] That pattern bore fruit in Calvin's later ministry in those he trained for ministry.

Persecution of Protestants in France at the behest of King Frances I (1494–1547) stymied the growth of the church. Calvin understood this firsthand, having fled the persecution in 1534, to live in Basel under an assumed name.[32] Upon Calvin's return to Geneva in 1541, after a three-year exile in Strassburg, Geneva began to slowly turn toward intentional mission work in France. By 1555, Geneva provided a regular stream of pastors and publications to counter persecution and restore stability to the French Protestant churches.[33] Since the Lutheran state-model for establishing Protestantism would not work in France, the model developed by Calvin in Geneva, learned from his mentor Bucer, adapted well to the French circumstances.[34] Convinced of his ecclesiological model, Calvin dis-

---

clesiology. Calvin's focus on the local church is unequivocal: "he who voluntarily deserts the outward communion of the church (where the Word of God is preached and the sacraments are administered) is without excuse," 21:1033 (4.1.19).

28  Zachman, *Calvin*, 148.

29  Ibid.

30  W. Robert Godfrey, *John Calvin: Pilgrim and Pastor* (Wheaton, IL: Crossway, 2009), 43.

31  Ibid., 43–45. Calvin sought advice from Jean Sturm, the Rector of the Strassburg Academy, as well, honing his plans for a Geneva Academy based on Sturm's model. See Greef, *Writings*, 36–38.

32  Robert L. Reymond, *John Calvin: His Life & Influence* (Fearn, Ross-shire, UK: Christian Focus, 2004), 44–46. This inflamed persecution led Calvin to publish the first edition of his *Institutes of the Christian Religion* prematurely in 1536 (p. 46).

33  C. Scott Dixon, *Protestants: A History from Wittenberg to Pennsylvania 1517–1740* (West Sussex, UK: Wiley-Blackwell, 2010), 56–57.

34  Ibid., 57. This required an ecclesiology independent of government. Calvin's "presbyterial-synodal system," as Dixon calls it, provided oversight for the French congregations who would be led by

couraged churches forming, according to Williston Walker, "until the close-knit congregation after the Genevan model could be had."[35] In other words, mentoring encompassed the influence of the congregation that would follow in the newly formed churches. Scores of churches with pastors, elders, and deacons started each year in France, with the Company of Pastors in Geneva sending 120 pastors to French churches between 1555 and 1566 for this purpose.[36]

Calvin viewed the work of ministry as, "the chief sinew by which believers are held together in one body."[37] Consequently, the church's spiritual well-being depended upon the faithful teaching and application of Scripture in both public gatherings and meetings with individuals in the church.[38] In light of this need, in 1541, Calvin set forth in the *Ecclesiastical Ordinances* a proposal for developing a church-based college to instruct young men for the ministry and civic service, "so that the Church is not left desolate to our children."[39] It took another eighteen years, due to the nature of Genevan politics, before the college opened its doors.[40] In the succeeding years after his proposal, skilled Latin and Greek teachers taught the students of Geneva. Calvin labored at preaching, teaching, lectures, and writing commentaries, while taking the congregation through verse-by-verse study of Scripture. Yet he realized that to change the values of the city, establishing the Academy for training, coupled with the work of ministers and magistrates, had to take place.[41]

The Geneva Academy enrolled students in 1559, with the largest percentage in its first five years coming from France.[42] Calvin recruited young men for the Academy so that he might train them and then, send them to plant new churches

   pastors and elders. This structure was prominent in reformed congregations throughout "the provinces of Dauphiné, Languedoc, Gascony, and Poitou."

35  Williston Walker, *John Calvin: Revolutionary, Theologian, Pastor* (Fern, Tain, Ross-shire, UK: Christian Focus, 2005; from 1906 ed.), 297.

36  Ibid.

37  Calvin, *Institutes*, 21:1055 (4.3.2).

38  Scott M. Manetsch, *Calvin's Company of Pastors: Pastoral Care and the Emerging Reformed Church, 1536–1609*, Oxford Studies in Historical Theology; David C. Steinmetz, ed. (New York: Oxford University Press, 2013), 71.

39  Philip E. Hughes, ed. and trans., *The Register of the Company of Pastors of Geneva in the Time of Calvin* (Grand Rapids: Eerdmans, 1966), 41.

40  Gillian Lewis, "The Geneva Academy," in *Calvinism in Europe 1540–1620*, Andrew Pettegree, Alastair Duke, and Gillian Lewis, eds. (Cambridge: Cambridge University Press, 1994), 36.

41  Ibid., 37. Lewis explains that a change in the balance of power in Genevan politics and a new status accorded French-speaking religious refugees opened the door for starting the Academy. See Maag, *Seminary or University*, 11, for the fascinating explanation of the providential provision of funds for starting the Academy.

42  Maag, *Seminary or University*, 29, stated that the lowest percentage of French students in that period was in 1564, with 61.4 percent, and the highest in 1562 at 86.3 percent.

in France, or to serve in established congregations in Geneva, the surrounding Swiss countryside, and in France. As Calvin sought to develop a qualified faculty for teaching Hebrew, Greek, hermeneutics, and other subjects, he continued to run into obstacles. Then, providentially, conflict between a similar academy in Lausanne, under the leadership of Calvin's longtime friend Pierre Viret, and the government in Berne, led to the wholesale dismissal of the faculty, making choice professors available.[43] Lausanne's Greek professor, Theodore Beza, whom Calvin had recommended for the post, perceived the trouble that eventually erupted in 1558, so he removed to Geneva ahead of the conflict and began as the Academy's first Rector.[44]

Training pastors would occupy much of Calvin and the Company of Pastors' attention due to the unending requests for pastors to be sent from the Geneva church. Calvin organized the Company of Pastors, the *Vénérable Compagnie*, composed of "eight to ten ministers from the city's churches, four professors from the Geneva Academy, and another ten or eleven pastors who served the small parish churches in the surrounding villages under Geneva's jurisdiction," according to Manetsch.[45] They met each Friday morning to discuss theological issues, church business, membership matters, and to examine ministry candidates. Their work involved local and international matters. This model offers a good example of how local networks and associations might partner in ministry training for sending out trained pastors and church planters for kingdom work.

Calvin's process for training included the following: (1) Establishment of the Academy in 1559 gave the pastoral training process an exceptional foundation for providing young men the language and ministry tools for future ministry, coupling "the discipline of theology with the practice of pastoral ministry,"[46] according to Charles Raynall III. Walker called the Academy, "the crown of Calvin's Genevan work."[47] Lewis points out that its aims were "dogmatic . . . evangelical . . . creedal, and it had the Gospel as its *raison d'être*."[48] All of the students subscribed "to a

---

43  See Jean-Marc Berthoud, "La Formation des Pasteurs et la Prèdication de Calvin," *La Revue Rèformée* 201 (Nov 1998): n.p. [cited 17 Jan 2013], http://larevuereformee.net/articlerr/n201/la-formation-des-pasteurs-et-la-predication-de-calvin, who writes, "nearly all of their students [i.e., from the Lausanne Academy under Viret's direction] (near to 1000 in 1558) . . . exiled to Geneva" (my translation from the French).

44  Lewis, "Geneva Academy," 38.

45  Manetsch, *Calvin's Company*, 2.

46  Charles E. Raynall III, "The Place of the Academy in Calvin's Polity," in *John Calvin & the Church: A Prism of Reform*, Timothy George, ed. (Louisville: Westminster/John Knox Press, 1990), 131.

47  Walker, *John Calvin*, 285.

48  Lewis, "Geneva Academy," 48.

lengthy confession of faith—with those in the advanced level, the *schola publica*, further agreeing to doctrinal conformity that eschewed Catholicism and Anabaptism, as well as clarifying a non-Lutheran view of the Lord's Supper.[49] Approximately two-thirds of the Academy students followed careers in ministry.[50]

(2) Similar to Zwingli's *Prophezei*, Calvin and the Company of Pastors sponsored the *congrégations*, a Friday meeting attended by sixty or more, in which intensive biblical instruction, followed by discussion, took place for those called to ministry.[51] Students had opportunity to observe the leaders of Saint Pierre Church dialoging on the interpretation and application of Scripture. This plurality of pastoral leaders shaped the future ministries of the students.

(3) Saturday afternoon expositions required those preparing for ministry to preach before their peers, theological mentors, and various members of the congregation, with critiques following the sermon.[52] The regular gathering gave the trainees an opportunity to hone their preaching skills before being sent out to pastor a church. In the community setting they began to learn the rudiments of pastoral preaching.

(4) In addition to the Saturday afternoon sermons, each month students were to draw up a particular number of theses or positions that they held, in order to defend them before their peers and professors. These were not to be "curious, sophisticated, nor containing false doctrine."[53] This allowed students to interact with their mentors on a variety of doctrinal and practical issues they would potentially face in a congregational setting.

(5) After being sent to plant a church, as was often the case for those returning to France, or beginning pastoral work at an established congregation in or around Geneva, the young ministers still maintained contact with the Company of Pastors. Sometimes they sought counsel. On other occasions, they requested to return to the Academy for further training, with their weaknesses exposed by experience.[54]

---

49  Maag, *Seminary or University,* 16–17. Willem Van't Spijker, *Calvin: A Brief Guide to His Life and Thought,* Lyle D. Bierma, trans. (Louisville: Westminster/John Knox, 2009), 158, points out that Calvin exerted influence on the work of reformation in the Netherlands due to his letters and primarily through instruction at the Academy.

50  Ibid., 29. With the accessibility to theological training in our day, a congregation starting a theological college is not the pressing issue. Instead, training those engaged in theological training must become a priority, as we will expand upon in chapters 8–9.

51  Timothy George, *Reading Scripture with the Reformers* (Downers Grove, IL: IVP Academic, 2011), 248. George points out that the same practice transplanted in England during Queen Elizabeth's reign, became the "pattern of nascent seminary training called the 'prophesyings,'" which prepared future preachers and Puritan leaders (248–249).

52  Lewis, "Geneva Academy," 44, 46–47.

53  Ibid., 44 (my translation from the French citation).

54  Maag, *Seminary or University,* 22–23.

In addition to the Academy, the *congrégations*, Saturday afternoon sermons, theses dialogue, and ongoing contact with the Company of Pastors, those preparing for ministry received attention from Calvin's example and from those the Reformer called, "doctors or teachers."[55] The doctors particularly focused on "educating and training the young for the office of minister or an office in civil service," Wulfert de Greef notes.[56] They taught future pastors and corrected doctrinal damage in the church that might have been done by negligent pastors.[57]

In many ways, Calvin set the pace for young pastors to emulate. His exegetical skills were unrivaled—the fruit of them found in his commentaries on Holy Scripture so that pastors continue to profit from his labors. He spoke God's Word with precision and clarity, addressing complex issues in such a way that the average attender at Saint Pierre could understand. His grasp of Scripture bled through conversations, discussions, and correspondence. Although a remarkable scholar and linguist, he always maintained a pastoral aim in his preaching and teaching, exemplifying to his trainees the application of sermons to their listeners.[58]

Bucer had mentored Calvin during his time in Strassburg. Calvin understood the value of mentoring, which spilled over in the mentor/trainee relationship that he had with Beza. As a mentor to the gifted Beza, Calvin, as Manetsch notes, was "a spiritual father, a theological mentor, a trusted friend, a guide who helped him discover his pastoral vocation."[59] "I would be very cold-hearted," Calvin remarked, "if I did not care deeply for Beza, who loves me more than a brother and honors me more than a father."[60] That picture exemplifies pastoral mentoring. Although the pastoral training process at Geneva might be faulted for failing to give future pastors more practical experience in dealing with church problems before accepting a pastoral call,[61] the training in biblical exegesis, preaching, sound doctrine, church polity, and godly pastoral example more than compensated for any weakness.

---

55  Calvin, *Institutes*, 21:1057 (4.3.4), Calvin considered pastors and teachers in Ephesians 4:11 as constituting two separate offices in the church. He explains, "teachers are not put in charge of discipline, or administering the sacraments, or warnings and exhortations, but only of Scriptural interpretation—to keep doctrine whole and pure among believers. But the pastoral office includes all these functions within itself." This follows the model set forth by Bucer; see de Greef, *Writings of John Calvin*, 132.

56  De Greef, *Writings of John Calvin*, exp. ed., 131.

57  Zachman, *John Calvin*, 61.

58  George, *Reading Scripture*, 244–245.

59  Manetsch, *Calvin's Company*, 38.

60  Ibid.

61  Lewis, "Geneva Academy," 47.

CHAPTER 6

# MODELING MINISTRY —17th & 18th CENTURIES

N arrowing to a few representatives from among models for mentoring in the seventeenth and eighteenth centuries proves challenging. An array of Puritans, such as Richard Sibbes, Thomas Watson, and Thomas Brooks, shaped the generation of ministers who followed their faithful labors. The same could be said for Jonathan Edwards, Andrew Fuller, and John Wesley during the eighteenth century awakenings. This chapter will consider two examples that might be less known than the pastors just mentioned. The German Pietist Philip Spener and the Colonial American Baptist John Gano exercised strong ministries in their day, impacting their respective spheres of influence for the sake of the gospel. Along the way, through their unique approaches, they helped to prepare a new generation of Christian workers, some of whom gained more notoriety than their mentors.

## PHILIP JACOB SPENER (1635–1705)

A common thread runs through the ministries of Moravian mission leader Count Nicolaus von Zinzendorf, Methodist founder John Wesley, Calvinistic Methodist leader George Whitefield, and American revivalist Jonathan Edwards. Each would be involved in training others for ministry, and to some degree, the Pietism of Philip Jacob Spener had affected each one.[1] Spener grew up in Alsace

---

1 See the following books that detail the connections with Spener: Justo González, *The Story of Christianity: The Early Church to the Present Day*, 2 vols. (Peabody, MA: Prince Press, 2001), 207–16; Williston Walker, *A History of the Christian Church* (New York: Charles Scribner's Sons, 1918), 497–508; R. B. Kuiper, *The Church in History* (Grand Rapids: Eerdmans, 1988), 275–279; Bruce Shelley, *Church History in Plain Language*, 2d ed., updated (Dallas: Word, 1995), 326–340; Ian Sellers, "Philipp Jakob Spener and Pietism," in *Great Leaders of the Christian Church*, John D. Woodbridge, gen. ed. (Chicago: Moody, 1988), 280; D. Martyn

under the influence of devout Lutheran parents. Well educated in Strassburg, Wittenburg, and Geneva, during his student years he came under the influence of German mystic Johann Arndt, author of *True Christianity*. Arndt urged experiential Christianity to counter the deadness and formalism of the Lutheran Church. The writings of English Puritans Richard Baxter (*The Necessary Teaching of the Denial of Self*, c. 1650) and Lewis Bayly (*Practice of Piety*, c. 1610), and the preaching of the former Roman Catholic, Reformed Frenchman Jean de La Badie (1610–1674), profoundly impacted Spener, as he moved away from the Lutheran version of scholasticism toward Pietistic views.[2] He found the piety of the Genevan pastors and the structure of the Reformed church, along with the preaching of the Waldensian Antonius Legerus, to further shape his understanding of Christian piety.[3]

After completing his doctorate, Spener began pastoral work in Strassburg, and then moved to Frankfurt am Main (1667). There, his pietistic views came into the broader public arena with the publication of *Pia Desideria* in 1675, which originally served as an introduction to the republication of the sermons of Johann Arndt.[4] The ideas for *Pia Desideria* formed earlier through a 1669 sermon in Frankfurt, where Spener encouraged laymen in their practice of Christianity. He recommended coming together in small groups to read devotional material, read and discuss the Scriptures, and discuss the pastor's sermon. This earliest mention of the small group gatherings, known as *collegia pietatis* (gatherings to foster piety), reflected Spener's adherence to the Reformation emphasis on the priesthood of all believers.[5] In 1670, he had the first *collegia pietatis* or *ecclesiola in ecclesia* (little

---

Lloyd-Jones, *The Puritans—Their Origins and Successors: Addresses Delivered at the Puritan and Westminster Conferences 1959-1978* (Carlisle, PA: Banner of Truth, 1987), 138–140.

2  See Sellers, "Spener," 278–279; Shelley, *Church History*, 326; Walker, *A History*, 496–497. Although pietism as a reaction to scholasticism in the church and academy had taken place at various stages of Christian history, e.g., the rise of Monasticism, Anabaptists, and Roman Catholic mysticism, the Pietism born out of Spener's ministry and writings defined its practice in the seventeenth century and beyond; Walker, *A History*, 496; Sellers, "Spener," 278.

3  Howard Alan Snyder, "Pietism, Moravianism, and Methodism as Renewal Movements: A Comparative and Thematic Study" (PhD diss., University of Notre Dame, 1983), 66.

4  Philip Jacob Spener, *Pia Desideria*, Theodore G. Tappert, trans. and ed. (Minneapolis: Fortress, 1964; Kindle ed.). Tappert writes in his introduction, "John Arndt (1555-1621) had asserted that orthodox doctrine was not enough to produce Christian life and advocated a mysticism which he borrowed largely from the late Middle Ages." In *True Christianity*, Arndt sought to (1) turn preachers and students from focusing on theological controversy; (2) to turn from lifelessness toward Christian fruitfulness; (3) to move from obsession with theory to the practical experience of faith and godliness; (4) to explain what true faith and a true Christian life consists (loc. 151–155).

5  Tappert, "Introduction," *Pia Desideria*, loc. 212–230; see Spener's comments, loc. 1621–1665; Kuiper, *The Church*, 272.

church in the church) meetings. On Sundays and Wednesdays, groups of men and women met in Spener's home, although the sexes were separated and only the men were allowed to speak.[6] The stronger believers were to seek to encourage the weaker—a practice that Spener thought would strengthen his pulpit ministry as well as abate the increase of evil in the community.[7]

The proposals in the *Pia Desideria* were "radical and threatening," notes Howard Snyder.[8] He points out three particular proposals that upset the Lutheran Church. First, Spener called for the laity's role in the church to be upgraded, in light of the priesthood of all believers. Laity would be enlisted "in the reform and pastoral care of the church."[9] This seemed to lay groundwork, whether intended or not, for training future ministers. Second, Spener called for a change in the church's structure with establishment of a council of elders to assist in pastoral oversight of the congregation. For this to happen, new leaders would have to be cultivated through the exercises in the small group gatherings. Third, the confessional would be replaced with the *collegia pietatis*, so that believers would meet in small groups to edify one another.[10] This practice set the stage for developing members of the congregation, as well as nurturing those who would eventually serve the church as ministers.

The publication of the *Pia Desideria* introduced Germany, and later other countries, to the *ecclesiola in ecclesia* (or *collegia pietatis*) in order to bring about reform in the Lutheran Church. Spener began the book by describing the deplorable condition of Germany, its civil affairs, and the church, as well as the poor standing of Lutheran ministers in terms of godly influence. He also spent time addressing the misplaced focus in seminaries that resulted in unprepared (and often, unconverted) ministers leading congregations. He called for his readers to investigate, by the light of God's Spirit, the shortcomings of the church and their personal devotion to Christ, and then to "ponder over the remedies." He then challenged ministers "to introduce what we have found to be beneficial and necessary."[11] He left no group out of the examination in light of Scripture, as he held forth the possibilities of stronger local congregations.

Spener put the greatest burden on ministers and their failure to conduct themselves as men of God.[12] He saw that the root of the problem started with the

---

6   Ibid., loc. 230–234.
7   Snyder, "Pietism," 68.
8   Ibid., 70.
9   Ibid., 70–71.
10   Ibid. 71.
11   Spener, *Pia Desideria*, loc. 649–654.
12   Ibid., loc. 1837.

schools and universities where ministers were supposed to be trained. However, the schools gave attention to tedious scholastic issues but failed to develop the inner lives of the students. He called on the professors to regulate their lives so that they might serve as appropriate examples to the students.[13] Living as Christians would seem obvious for those preparing for ministry, but Spener exposed gross failure at this point. Godly examples would give ministry students the models they needed for cultivating their spiritual lives.

The professors were to embrace the *ecclesiola in ecclesia* with their students, eating together, exhorting them, discussing the Scripture, and talking about hymns and other Christian literature.[14] They could demonstrate that living holy lives held no less consequence than diligent study, adding, "study without piety is worthless."[15] With simplicity, Spener brought his readers to the reality that true Christianity involved deeds as well as words, especially among the spiritual leaders of congregations.

Professors were also to avoid spending their time on theological disputation.[16] They were to prioritize spiritual formation, with Spener commenting, "It would not be a bad thing if all students were required to bring from their universities testimonials concerning their piety as well as their diligence and skill."[17] Instead of a one-size-fits-all approach to theological education, Spener recommended that professors take the time to observe the particular gifts of each student, as well as the context of where the students would serve, so that the professors might make appropriate recommendations of preparation for their future work. He recognized that some students were more skilled in pastoral work, others in teaching, and still others in conducting civil affairs.[18] He further called on the academy to train men in German rather than Latin, so that the students might better communicate with those in their future congregations.[19] "Unless he has somebody to lead him faithfully by the hand," Spener wrote, "a beginning student will hardly know what he needs and what he does not need in these matters."[20] In other words,

---

13   Ibid., loc. 1849–1856. He illustrated what he meant: "Gregory Nazianzen declares in his panegyric on Basil that Basil's speech was like thunder because his life was like lightning" (loc. 1856).
14   As will be noted in chapter 7, Dietrich Bonhoeffer adopted this model in the twentieth century.
15   Ibid., loc. 1861–1865. See also Gerald R. Cragg, *The Church and the Age of Reason 1648–1789*, Pelican History of the Church 4 (Grand Rapids: Eerdmans, 1960), 101.
16   Robert G. Clouse, Richard V. Pierard, Edwin M. Yamauchi, *Two Kingdoms: The Church and Culture through the Ages* (Chicago: Moody, 1993), 353. See Spener, *Pia Desideria*, loc. 1949–1954.
17   Spener, *Pia Desideria*, loc. 1925. This practice would serve to protect congregations the students would eventually serve.
18   Ibid., loc. 1930.
19   Ibid., loc. 1930–1942.
20   Ibid., loc. 1942–1946.

professors could not simply lecture and accomplish what was necessary to train ministers. They had to be involved in the students' lives through mentoring-style relationships. The best framework for this kind of relationship was through the *ecclesiola in ecclesia*, which Spener saw as critical in developing the inner life and healthy community.

While the overall impact of the *ecclesiola in ecclesia* led to some excesses and separation from the established church, the small group/mentoring-style relationships advocated for both congregation and ministry students provided an essential change to the barrenness so prevalent in Lutheran church and academy.[21] The idea of discussion, accountability, transparency, and mentoring by spiritual leaders training up those who would serve Christ in larger spheres, remains an appropriate means in training for ministry. Count von Zinzendorf found the practice useful as he trained up missionaries with the Moravians.[22] So did John Wesley who embraced the *ecclesiola in ecclesia* as a framework for his entire movement, breaking down congregations into societies, classes, and class meetings, where spiritual nurturing took place and lay ministers found their first opportunity to exercise their gifts.[23]

How might contemporary pastoral mentors utilize the *ecclesiola in ecclesia* approach in training young ministers? First, it needs a stated purpose, as Spener had, for spiritual formation and in this case, ministry development. Although Spener addressed professors training students, the same model would work in either seminaries or local churches training students for ministry.[24] Second, from the standpoint of preparing ministers, those participating could utilize the discussion to work through theological issues, biblical interpretation, and the variety of pastoral ministry issues. Selected books could be read and discussed in that setting, while seeking to make application to life and ministry. Assignments could be made so that the trainees receive opportunity to teach their peers, with the pastoral mentor carefully guiding discussion and application.

Third, to avoid a sense of elitism, as Martyn Lloyd-Jones warned,[25] the group will need to practice humility with the congregation and demonstrate servant

---

21  See the critique of the *ecclesiola in ecclesia* in Lloyd-Jones, *The Puritans*, 140–145, who addressed its use among Lutherans, Moravians, Methodists, and other groups.

22  Shelley, *Church History*, 328–329; González, 208–209, who also notes that Spener was godfather to Count von Zinzendorf. Kuiper, *The Church*, 277, writes, "They followed Spener's idea in its deepest import of establishing *ecclesiolae in ecclesia*."

23  Ibid., 339.

24  See Robert J. Banks, *Reenvisioning Theological Education: Exploring a Missional Alternative to Current Models* (Grand Rapids: Eerdmans, 1999), 204–207.

25  Lloyd-Jones, *The Puritans*, 142.

hearts in congregational ministry. Finally, Spener's idea of *ecclesiola in ecclesia* was a reform movement in a dead church. One would assume that contemporary ministry development would start in a healthy, lively church, with the small mentoring gatherings utilized to pray for the congregation's needs and plan areas of service to strengthen the church—normal practices of those serving as pastors in local churches. Otherwise, these groups could become sparks toward local church reformation.

## JOHN GANO (1727–1804)

Just as pastoral mentors helped shape John Gano's expansive ministry, this eighteenth-century Baptist giant gave himself liberally toward helping to mentor the next generation who would pastor, plant, and revitalize churches. Gano mentored Hezekiah Smith, Thomas Ustick, Stephen Gano, and others, accounting for major developments in Baptist churches in that era. His ministry modeled a lifelong concern for making disciples and planting churches. As Gano was mentored, he mentored others.

While preparing for church membership by studying the Westminster Confession, Gano struggled with the infant baptism of his Presbyterian heritage. He delayed membership over this doctrinal issue. Benjamin Miller (1715–1781), one of his mentors, encouraged Gano to profess Christ openly and join a local church. Miller assured Gano "that God's word and spirit would direct" him and remove his doubts. Miller, a prominent colonial era Baptist, added, in Gano's words, "If they [the Word and Spirit] did not make me a Baptist, he did not wish to do it."[26] After much study and prayer, Gano came to credo-baptism convictions.[27]

Gano joined Hopewell (NJ) Baptist Church and soon initiated youth meetings in his town to discuss spiritual matters. Shortly afterward, he began to sense God's call to ministry.[28] Isaac Eaton (1725–1772), the new pastor of Hopewell Baptist Church, took Gano into a mentoring relationship.[29] Many Baptists lacked access to theological education in the eighteenth century due to financial constraints and the lack of theological institutions warm toward Baptist sentiments.[30] So,

---

26  John Gano, *Biographical Memoirs of the Late Rev.. John Gano, of Frankfort, (Kentucky) Former-ly of the City of New-York* (New York: Southwick and Hardcastle, 1806), 22–23. Gano's son, Stephen, edited the *Memoir*.

27  Ibid., 25–27.

28  Lee Sayers Johnson, "An Examination of the Role of John Gano in the Development of Baptist Life in North America, 1750–1804" (PhD diss.; Southwestern Baptist Theological Seminary, 1986), 23.

29  Ibid.

30  Thomas R. McKibbens Jr. & Kenneth Smith, *The Life and Works of Morgan Edwards* (Paris,

Eaton's education from the College of New Jersey (Princeton) and the College of Philadelphia trained him in the classics and also motivated him to make education available to Baptists.[31] Gano profited from his tutoring. He referred to Eaton as, "a judicious and useful minister and friend, who was able to instruct me in the classics, and who was desirous to do it."[32] Eaton not only mentored Gano in his studies but also watched him closely—probing, exhorting, and counseling him toward Christian ministry. At Eaton's urging, although Gano first objected, the Hopewell church examined him for ministry and offered encouragement toward the young man pursuing gospel work.[33]

After a brief matriculation at the College of New Jersey, Benjamin Miller of Scotch Plains (NJ) and John Thomas of Virginia, invited Gano to accompany them on a preaching mission into Virginia at the request of the Philadelphia Baptist Association.[34] Gano never turned back from the work of ministry. The trio of mission partners constituted a new Baptist church in 1752 in Opocken, Virginia. Several of the new members came to faith in Christ through Gano's preaching.[35] Shortly, he began his first pastorate of the new Baptist church at Morristown (NJ) that had been established through the preaching of Miller, Eaton, and Gano.[36]

At Morristown, Gano began mentoring Hezekiah Smith (1737–1805) in the spiritual disciplines and aspects of ministry. He called Smith, "a promising youth."[37]

---

AR: The Baptist Standard Bearer, Inc., 2005), n.p., chap. 1, points out that only seven or eight Baptist pastors in the sixty churches around this period had liberal educations.

31 Johnson, "An Examination," 23–24. Eaton began Hopewell Academy in 1756 as a Latin Grammar School, which "was destined to supply the Baptist denomination with some of her most competent leaders for the remainder of that period [i.e., eighteenth century]."

32 Gano, *Biographical Memoirs*, 28–29.

33 Ibid., 35–36. See Eaton's ordination sermon for Gano in, Isaac Eaton, "A Sermon Preached at the Ordination of the Reverend Mr. John Gano, *Anno Domini*, 1754" (Philadelphia: B. Franklin and D. Hall, 1755) in *The Life and Ministry of John Gano, 1727–1804*, The Philadelphia Association Series; Terry Wolever, ed. (Springfield, MO: Particular Baptist Press, 1998), 1:189–191.

34 Ibid., 39–50; Gano gives interesting details of this time of mentoring and its impact on his ministry. See also David Benedict, *A General History of the Baptist Denomination in North America and Other Parts of the World*, 2 vols. (Boston: Lincoln & Edmands, 1803), 2:309. Gano withdrew from college due to health issues; see Johnson, "An Examination," 25; and Gano, *Memoirs*, 28–39. Andrew M. Sherman, *Historic Morristown, New Jersey: The Story of Its First Century* (Morristown, NJ: The Howard Publishing Co., 1905), 92, tells of Gano's return to preach the dedication of the new meetinghouse in Morristown in 1771. See pp. 78–81 for the early history of the church with the involvement of Isaac Eaton, James Manning, Benjamin Miller, and John Gano. See also Gano, *Memoirs*, 83.

35 Johnson, "An Examination," 26–28; Gano, *Memoirs*, 48–50.

36 Gano, *Memoirs*, 79–80; Johnson, "An Examination," 39–40; see also Thomas S. Griffiths, *A History of Baptists in New Jersey* (Hightown, NJ: Barr Press Publishing Co., 1904), 273–274, for anecdotes on Gano's ministry in Morristown.

37 Gano, *Memoirs*, 80–81.

Smith's conversion came through Gano's regular preaching in his community of nearby Hanover. After his baptism, the church's involvement in shaping Smith appeared evident by their recognition of his gifts; subsequently, they encouraged him toward gospel ministry, including pursuit of education at the College of New Jersey. Gano played a large part in convincing his family to allow Smith this opportunity. He matriculated as a sophomore and sat under the influence of the notable Samuel Davies who was president of the college.[38] Gano maintained a formative influence on Smith's work as the pastor of the Baptist church at Haverhill, evangelist, and church planter, with the two often exchanging pulpits and visiting with one another throughout the years of ministry.[39]

With assistance and influence from Gano's mentor Benjamin Miller and the Scotch Plains church, Gano began serving as the pastor of the First Baptist Church (FBC) of New York City.[40] Excluding the time of chaplaincy during the Revolutionary War when he could not enter the city, his ministry continued for twenty-five years.[41] The lasting mark of his work in New York City was upon the ministers who emerged from his pastoral ministry. First Baptist Church, under Gano's leadership, ordained Isaac Skillman, who was called in 1763 to pastor the Second Baptist Church of Boston, a church born in the midst of the First Great Awakening in 1743.[42] Ebenezer Farris [also, Ferris] was baptized and ordained by Gano at FBC, and later sent out in 1773 to a newly constituted church in Stamford and one at Greenwich.[43] Gano's personal ministry deeply affected both young men and prepared them for their future ministries.

Thomas Ustick showed great seriousness as a Christian and minister, with Gano baptizing him as a fourteen-year-old.[44] At Gano's urging, he received his education at Rhode Island College under the instruction of Gano's brother-in-law, James Manning. Ustick served as a messenger from FBC of New York City to the Philadelphia Association in 1774, while around the same time helping

---

38  John David Broome, *Life, Ministry, and Journals of Hezekiah Smith, 1737–1805: Pastor of the First Baptist Church of Haverhill, Massachusetts and Chaplain in the Revolution* (Springfield, MO: Particular Baptist Press, 2004; reprint of *The Journals of Hezekiah Smith, 1762–1805*, n.d.), 8–11.
39  Ibid., 45, 156–157, 318, 346n, 351–352, 436–437, 439.
40  Joyce D. Goodfriend, "The Baptist Church in Prerevolutionary New York City," *American Baptist Quarterly* 16.3 (September 1997): 220.
41  Benedict, *A General History*, 2:314. While at FBC NYC, Gano maneuvered through three schismatic situations; see Goodfriend, "The Baptist Church," 231–234; Gano, *Memoirs*, 88–90.
42  Goodfriend, "The Baptist Church," 226; Isaac Backus, *A History of New England with Particular Reference to the Denomination of Christians called Baptists*, 2 vols. (Newton, MA: The Backus Historical Society, 1871), 2:422–423.
43  Backus, *History of New England*, 2:170.
44  Gano, *Memoirs*, 91.

with the start of a new Baptist church in Ashford.[45] He later began a long, distinguished pastorate at the historic First Baptist Church of Philadelphia in 1781. Ustick demonstrated the same character, grace, doctrinal soundness, and indefatigable work ethic as his mentor, John Gano, handling difficulties with a heretical former pastor and serving alongside Dr. Benjamin Rush during the 1797 yellow fever outbreak.[46]

Stephen Gano, John Gano's son, studied medicine before entering the Revolutionary War as a surgeon. Converted and called to ministry after the War, according to David Benedict, he was ordained by FBC of NYC in 1786 and then served "successively at Hudson, Hillsdale, and Nine Partners, until 1792, when, by the call of this ancient church [First Baptist Church, Providence, RI], he removed among them and became their pastor."[47] While at Providence, Stephen Gano and his church were instrumental in spawning "branches" for new congregations, including Smithfield, Gloucester, Scituate, Greenwich, Cranston, and Pawtucket, with his father's church planting spirit evident in his ministry.[48]

Writing toward the end of Gano's life, Isaac Backus stated that Gano traveled more extensively preaching the gospel than anyone in America.[49] In the wake of Gano's influence, hundreds came to faith in Christ, new churches began, new associations birthed, young ministers emerged, and a small Baptist denomination grew exponentially. From New England to South Carolina, eighteenth-century Baptists and others felt the power of John Gano's preaching and godly influence.

Gano traveled extensively, wrote little, and preached widely. He regularly engaged younger or less experienced ministers throughout his travels. His training model, although lacking the structure that we value in contemporary America, demonstrates how a busy pastor, church planter, evangelist, and Christian statesman influenced the rising generation of ministers. Five of Gano's qualities for mentoring stand out as good models for our generation.

(1) *Relationships.* Gano often did personal work late into the night, talking with people about their soul concerns and meeting with ministers in order to

---

45  A. D. Gillette, *Minutes of the Philadelphia Baptist Association A. D. 1707, to A. D. 1807; being the first One Hundred Years of its Existence* (Philadelphia: American Baptist Publication Society, 1851), 138; Backus, *A History of New England*, 2:521.

46  Spencer, *The Early Baptists*, 130, 135–136, 153; Goodfriend, "The Baptist Church," 226–227; Johnson, "An Examination," 141.

47  Benedict, *A General History*, 1:485–486; see also William Cathcart, *The Baptist Encyclopaedia. A Dictionary of Baptist Denomination in all Lands*, 2 vols. (Philadelphia: Louis H. Everts, 1883), 1:434–435.

48  Benedict, *A General History*, 1:485–486.

49  Backus, *History of New England*, 2:494.

tighten loose theology, instructing them in doctrine and polity.[50] Just as Miller, Eaton, and Thomas mentored him in his early ministry, maintaining a strong, ongoing relationship with him, Gano followed the same pattern. He regularly crossed paths with the same men, investing in their spiritual growth and ministry practice. Hezekiah Smith's *Journal* offers ample evidence of this practice.[51] The Philadelphia Association, of which Gano was an active member for most of his ministry, provided grants to help with older pastors apprenticing younger men in the work of gospel ministry. Gano encouraged and engaged in this practice.[52] He built relationships that were fruitful for God's kingdom.[53]

(2) *Partnering in ministry.* Gano took younger ministers along with him to labor in preaching and church planting, giving responsibilities, under his supervision, just as Miller and Thomas had done to him. Gano included Isaac Skillman, Hezekiah Smith, Ebenezer Frances, Thomas Ustick, and Stephen Gano in aspects of his ministry, laying groundwork for each to establish strong ministries of their own.[54] Some of them were responsible for planting multiple churches. Gano's influence lay in the background.

(3) *Example.* Examples of godliness, faithfulness, humility, as well as charity in dealing with difficulties, gave younger ministers a framework for character in ministry by watching Gano. Benedict comments on him, "He had . . . a happy facility in improving every passing occurrence to some useful purpose." Gano's "judgment was good; his wit was sprightly, and always at command." Benedict continues, "his zeal was ardent, but well regulated; his courage undaunted; his knowledge of men was extensive: and to all these accomplishments were added a heart glowing with love to God and men, and a character fair and unimpeachable."[55] He walked in humility, more conscious of answering to the Lord than winning the favor of men. His protégés learned from his consistent example.

(4) *Education.* Gano stood alongside Miller, Eaton, Oliver Hart, and James Manning in forming Rhode Island College (later Brown University), serving as a significant fund-raiser among the association of Baptist churches. His church in New York led the way by collecting above what they had proposed for the college.[56] He regularly encouraged young ministers under his charge to pursue a

---

50   Johnson, "An Examination," 127–134.
51   Benedict, *A General History*, 2:307–309; Broome, *Journals of Hezekiah Smith*, e.g. 295–296, 316–318.
52   Gillette, *Minutes of the Philadelphia Baptist Association*, 246; Johnson, "An Evaluation," 37, 44.
53   Benedict, *A General History*, 2:321.
54   Gano, *Memoirs*, 90–91.
55   Benedict, *A General History*, 2:316–317.
56   Clark, *To Set Them in Order*, 42–43.

strong education as a stewardship in ministry preparation, even intervening with parents to make this happen.

(5) *Networking.* Gano worked diligently to bring Baptist ministers and churches together in associations for mission, fellowship, and doctrinal unity. Gano's regular involvement in the Philadelphia, Warren, Charleston, Elkhorn, and even (to a lesser degree) Sandy Creek associations served as one of the primary ways that he encouraged men in ministry and assisted them toward church planting and revitalization. He either used existing associational networks or labored to form new ones in order to further gospel work.[57] Gano made active use of associations as catalysts for church planting.[58]

While lacking the formal structure for mentoring, Gano used the means that God had entrusted to him for passing the multifaceted ministries of the local church to his younger counterparts. Gano served as a burning light that illuminated and prepared the next generation in the United States for church planting, pastoral ministry, and church revitalization.

---

57 Johnson, "An Examination," 155, 167. See Backus, *History of New England,* 2:408–416, in which Backus gives lengthy praise for the work of the Warren and other associations of uniting churches, maintaining local church autonomy, reproving those lax in doctrine or practice, assisting the weak, guarding doctrine, and promoting the gospel.

58 Johnson, *An Examination,* 141–143, tells of Gano's involvement in helping to plant churches in Staten Island, Coram, Oyster Bay, Peekskill, Bedford, Fishkill, Poughkeepsie, Fredrickstown, Bateman's Precinct, Stanford, and Lyons Farms.

CHAPTER 7

# TRAINING COMMUNITIES —19ᵀᴴ & 20ᵀᴴ CENTURIES

S lightly tweaking a popular aphorism, Todd Bolsinger writes, "It takes a church to raise a Christian."[1] While agreeing with that statement, I would go further: "It takes a church to raise a minister." Christian history bears out the influence of congregations upon the effectiveness of many in ministry. Despite academic institutions receiving major credit for pastoral development, behind the degree lives congregations that pour into those involved in gospel work. Charles Haddon Spurgeon and Dietrich Bonhoeffer understood the necessity for community shaping those they mentored for ministry.

## CHARLES HADDON SPURGEON (1834–1892)

Few pastors can compare to Charles Haddon Spurgeon (1834–1892), nineteenth-century Baptist pastor at London's Metropolitan Tabernacle. If one combined John Chrysostom's oration, Gregory the Great's pastoral application, Martin Luther's prolific writing, John Calvin's pastoral training, John Knox's pulpit boldness, George Whitefield's evangelistic gifts, and John Wesley's ability to organize new congregations, he might better understand Spurgeon's gifts and abilities. Despite years of physical and emotional suffering, he sought to live each day to the fullest—feeding upon Jesus Christ as revealed in the Scriptures while seeking the lost through proclaiming Christ crucified and resurrected.[2] Spurgeon was not content to let the work of ministry live and die

---

1 Tod E. Bolsinger, *It Takes a Church to Raise a Christian: How the Community of God Transforms Lives* (Grand Rapids: Brazos Press, 2004).

2 Tom Nettles, *Living By Revealed Truth: The Life and Pastoral Theology of Charles Haddon Spurgeon* (Fearn, Ross-shire, Scotland: Mentor, 2013), 9–10.

upon him. He intentionally sought to train a host of young men to carry on gospel work.

Pointing back historically, Spurgeon found the example of many—e.g., Geneva's John Calvin, Serampore's William Carey and Joshua Marshman—to be adequate reason for pouring energy and resources into pastoral training.[3] He reinforced his rationale in an address for the college at Cheshunt. "It is nothing but sanctified commonsense that leads the Church to the formation of a college. The Church ought to make the college the first object of its care. Whatever is forgotten in the prayer-meeting, the students of our colleges ought not to be forgotten."[4] His friend and biographer, G. Holden Pike stated that with the dozens of institutions Spurgeon formed, the college proved to be his favorite, and what Spurgeon called, "his first-born and best beloved."[5] Spurgeon often wrote and told supporters that he had no intention of making preachers. Instead, through the training available at the college, he desired to assist those who were already preaching to be better preachers and servants to the church. Consequently, he devoted to the college his best energies.[6] Before he died, Spurgeon had trained almost nine hundred men to plant, revitalize, and pastor churches, with few defecting from the ministry.[7]

Although not quite twenty-three and newly married, Spurgeon began mentoring T. W. Medhurst, a man his age converted under his preaching. Uneducated and uncouth, Medhurst, who had been fruitfully preaching on the streets, told his young pastor, "I must preach, sir; and I shall preach unless you cut off my head."[8] Spurgeon decided to do his best to prepare him for pastoral work. He did so by enlisting another pastor with whom Medhurst would live and study, while meeting for several hours each week with Spurgeon to study theology and pastoral ministry.[9] The training proved so effective, with remarkable improvements in every aspect of Medhurst's life and ministry that another young preacher asked to be mentored and trained. Soon eight more, and then twenty more, desired the same training. Spurgeon enlisted the help of Rev. George Rogers, a paedobaptist, who otherwise held the same theological and methodological views as

---

3   Charles Haddon Spurgeon, *C. H. Spurgeon Autobiography*, 2 vols.; rev. ed. by Susannah Spurgeon and Joseph Harrald (Carlisle, PA: Banner of Truth Trust, 1973; orig. publ. 1897–1900 in 4 vols.), 2:96.

4   G. Holden Pike, *The Life & Work of Charles Haddon Spurgeon*, 5 vols. (Carlisle, PA: Banner of Truth Trust, 1991; orig. publ. London: Cassell & Co, 1894), 4:356.

5   Ibid., 2:232.

6   Ibid., 2:232, 234.

7   Ernest W. Bacon, *Spurgeon Heir of the Puritans* (Arlington Heights, IL: Christian Liberty Press, 1996), 93.

8   Spurgeon, *Autobiography*, 1:388.

9   Ibid., 1:388–389.

Spurgeon, agreeing to join as the director of a new Pastor's College.[10] Initially, Spurgeon had no clearly thought-out plan for what he would do, which should give encouragement to pastors wrestling with how to mentor future ministers. But as the training took shape with Medhurst, and then another, he recognized that he would need to begin the Pastor's College. He did so out of his own resources and a few donations of friends until he presented the concept of the college to the Metropolitan Tabernacle.

In 1861, Spurgeon offered his vision for the Pastor's College to the congregation. He told of the success in the five years that he had been doing this work with the help of Rogers. But the load had grown large, and he needed his church to join in the work of training men for ministry. He further realized that he could enlarge the work to include offering "a common English education" for others during the evenings, preparing business people to be well equipped witnesses, while also training pastors during the day.[11] The key ingredient in the entire training was the congregation at the Metropolitan Tabernacle. Spurgeon wrote, "Through living in the midst of a church which, despite its faults, is a truly living, intensely zealous, working organization, they gain enlarged ideas and form practical habits."[12] By taking part in the breadth of active ministries at the church—involving themselves in the lives of the congregation—students found instruction and inspiration that they would not have had at other ministry schools.[13]

Students at the Pastor's College looked forward to the Friday afternoon meetings with Spurgeon.[14] Sometimes they gathered around an oak tree at the pastor's home for the engaging talks and questions. On other occasions, they met at the Tabernacle and later at the college building, completed in 1874.[15] Spurgeon peppered these times with anecdotes and humor, with the pastor feeling at home with the students as with family.[16] His multivolume *Lectures to My Students* indicates the breadth of pastoral, preaching, ecclesiological, devotional, and practical issues that he addressed with his men on Fridays. He spoke of the call to ministry, the prayer life, choosing a text, the use of the voice, the necessity of the Spirit's power,

---

10  Ibid., 1:385.
11  Ibid., 1:97–98.
12  Ibid., 1:98.
13  Arnold Dallimore, *Spurgeon: A New Biography* (Carlisle, PA: Banner of Truth Trust, 1985), 105. See also Rodney Douglas Earls, "The Evangelistic Strategy of Charles Haddon Spurgeon for the Multiplication of Churches and Implications for Modern Church Extension Theory" (PhD diss.; Southwestern Baptist Theological Seminary, 1989), 97–98.
14  C. H. Spurgeon, *Lectures to My Students*, 4 vols. in one (Pasadena, TX: Pilgrim Publications, 1990; orig. publ. London: Passmore and Alabaster, 1881), 1:iii.
15  Pike, *Life & Work*, 5:115, 135.
16  Spurgeon, *Lectures*, 1:iii.

the call for decision, church planting, open-air preaching, gentle manners with the church, and lengthy explanations in the use of illustrations. He spoke to them on buying books and learning how to choose the best writers so that they might find such resources as water to prime a dry pump.[17]

Since preaching Christ was central to all expositional preaching in Spurgeon's view, he gave much attention to preaching. As a model, the students sat under his weekly preaching ministry. He also taught on all aspects of sermon preparation and delivery, with the students preaching in his presence and receiving his critique. He sought to remove vocal and facial distractions from the men before sending them out on weekly preaching assignments.[18] He took great care in sending the right man into a particular preaching setting, as well as recommending his men to churches in need of pastors.[19] He encouraged many to plant churches when no pastoral opportunities opened.[20]

Spurgeon, Rogers, and other instructors centered the Pastor's College education on biblical theology. Other courses were considered (e.g., mathematics, science, and literature), but they were constellations centered on the glory of Jesus Christ and gospel proclamation.[21] He had no hesitation in describing the theology that the school subscribed to as Calvinistic and Puritan, while steering clear of Hyper-Calvinism and Arminian sentiments.[22]

Although worn out from the toll of preaching, controversies, fundraising, pastoral ministry, multiple institutions that he founded, and his mounting health issues, Spurgeon could tell one of his students that the Friday meetings were like oil to his bones.[23] He regularly engaged his trainees at the college and in his

---

17  Ibid., see the table of contents to learn of the four divisions in *Lectures*. Concerning books, he wrote, "If I can save a poor man from spending his money for that which is not bread, or, by directing a brother to a good book, may enable him to dig deeper into the mines of truth, I shall be well repaid" (4:ii). Spurgeon worked through three to four thousand volumes before commenting on the 1,437 books in *Commenting and Commentaries*.

18  Nettles, *Living*, 135–176, for an excellent description of the details of Spurgeon's view of preaching, his practice, and how he trained his young men to preach expositionally.

19  Pike, *Life & Work*, 3:156. Spurgeon also sent men to plant churches and even had a chapel-building fund set aside to help in lending money without interest for such purpose.

20  Earls, "Evangelistic Strategy," 85, 107–111.

21  Spurgeon, *Autobiography*, 1:384–386; Nettles, *Living*, 167; Bacon, *Spurgeon*, 91; Earls, "Evangelistic Strategy," 93.

22  Ibid., 1:387; see two books by Iain H. Murray that address Spurgeon's conflict with those espousing Hyper-Calvinistic views on one hand, and those that had moved toward Arminian views on the other, *Spurgeon v. Hyper-Calvinism: The Battle for Gospel Preaching* (Carlisle, PA: Banner of Truth Trust, 1995) and *The Forgotten Spurgeon* (Carlisle, PA: Banner of Truth Trust, 1972). The latter book traces his conflict in the diluted gospel, baptismal regeneration, and Down-Grade controversies.

23  Ibid., 2:112.

home, where they would delight in hearing stories, humorous and wise, while being instructed on all aspects of ministry.[24] On other occasions, he would invite students to travel with him—refusing to allow "no" for an answer—where he would mentor them out of his wealth of experience, plus take care of all of their expenses.[25] He regularly corresponded with those in school and those involved in ministry, offering encouragement and instruction to the end of his life.[26]

## DIETRICH BONHOEFFER (1906–1945)

In 1933, early in his pastoral ministry, Dietrich Bonhoeffer came to the conclusion that the approach to theological training for ordinands preparing for Lutheran church ministry was seriously flawed. While focusing on "the cerebral and intellectual side of theological training," the prominent university system practiced by the state church "produced pastors who didn't know how to live as Christians," notes Eric Metaxas in his summary of Bonhoeffer's thought.[27] It was not that Bonhoeffer opposed the cerebral and intellectual, but rather that they had no place in pastoral ministry apart from the warm application of Scripture to the whole of life.

The theologian and pastor did not reach this conclusion overnight. He had gone the route of a liberal education at Tübingen University, the University of Berlin, and Union Theological Seminary (NY).[28] Yet, his experience of discipleship and community at the Abyssinian Baptist Church in Harlem during his brief stay in America, coupled with his own study and meditation on the gospel, transformed the way that he looked at everything, including training young people for local church ministry.[29]

Bonhoeffer's early ventures in teaching theological students proved contrary to the accepted practice. Rather than standing aloof from the students, he engaged them personally, invited them to his home, met them for coffee and theological discussion,

---

24  Pike, *Life & Work*, 5:137–138; Spurgeon, *Autobiography*, 2:108–109.
25  Spurgeon, *Autobiography*, 2:110–111.
26  Ibid., 2:111–116.
27  Eric Metaxas, *Bonhoeffer: Pastor, Martyr, Prophet, Spy—A Righteous Gentile vs. the Third Reich* (Nashville: Thomas Nelson, 2010; Kindle edition), loc. 3955.
28  Ibid., loc. 1097, 1403, 2175.
29  Metaxas, *Bonhoeffer*, loc. 2303–2372; 2584–2598, refers to a retrospective 1936 letter Bonhoeffer sent to Elizabeth Zinn explaining the change that had occurred after his visit to New York in 1931–1932. He described it as a change and transformation: "For the first time I discovered the Bible . . . I had often preached. I had seen a great deal of the Church, and talked and preached about it—but I had not yet become a Christian. . . . Since then everything has changed. I have felt this plainly, and so have other people about me. It was a great liberation. It became clear to me that the life of a servant of Jesus Christ must belong to the Church, and step by step it became plainer to me how far that must go."

and began to press them on concerns about their souls.[30] German theological schools catered to the so-called *brilliant* students preparing for ministry, with attendance at a state-sponsored school compulsory. But Bonhoeffer considered this a waste of time.[31] Providentially, political and religious changes in Germany led to the rise of the Confessing Church and the establishment of "preachers' seminaries."[32] Bonhoeffer had, ironically, found the idea of preachers' seminaries something to avoid; now he delighted to develop the gifts, minds, and hearts of young theologians to prepare them for ministry in difficult times through that institution.[33] His approach covered "all the nuts and bolts of parish life."[34] The Confessing Church, under the auspices of the Old Prussian Council of Brethren, established five regional seminaries that would unite around the theological positions established at the Barmen and Dahlem synods,[35] with Bonhoeffer appointed to direct the one in Pomerania.[36] This began his experiment in *Life Together* at Zingst and Finkenwalde.

In 1935, Bonhoeffer and twenty-three ministry candidates assembled in rustic cabins near the beach in Zingst. The stay proved short as they soon removed to Finkenwalde on the estate of the von Katte family. Formerly a private school disfavored by the Nazis, Bonhoeffer and his students labored to ready the buildings to be livable, including developing a makeshift chapel from an old gymnasium. Bonhoeffer brought his own library to serve the students' needs.[37] Finkenwalde would be much more than the pursuit of academic training. Discipleship in community would become most prominent.[38]

---

30  Ebehard Bethge, *Dietrich Bonhoeffer: Man of Vision, Man of Courage*, Edwin Robertson, ed.; Eric Mosbacher, Peter and Betty Ross, Frank Clarke, William Glen-Doepel, trans. (New York: Harper & Row, 1977 from 1967 German ed.), 156–165.

31  Ibid., 342.

32  Ibid. New laws in 1935 sought to crush the growth of the Confessing Church and to bring all religious activities into conformity with the Nazi state (343–344).

33  Ibid., 341.

34  Charles Marsh, *Strange Glory: A Life of Dietrich Bonhoeffer* (New York: Alfred A. Knopf, 2014), 234. Marsh notes, "practical ministry included instruction on performing baptisms, weddings, and funerals; visiting parishioners in hospitals and at home; as well as administrating church budgets and programs."

35  Bethge, *Bonhoeffer*, 221–223, 300–305. The Barmen and Dahlem synods defined the NT church in such terms as to exclude the Reich Church as a genuine church. See Karl Barth, "Theological Declaration of Barmen" [cited 5 February 2013]: n.p., http://www.sacred-texts.com/chr/barmen.htm. Under the leadership of Martin Niemöller, the Dahlem Synod sought to put into practice the theological confession of *sola scriptura* and *solus Christus* espoused in the Barmen Declaration. It attempted to balance loyalty to the state and separation from the "German Christians" and the Reich Church. See a detailed explanation in Victoria Barnett, *For the Soul of the People: Protestant Protest against Hitler* (New York: Oxford University Press, 1992), 65–68.

36  Bethge, *Bonhoeffer*, 344–346.

37  Ibid., 347–349.

38  See Marsh, *Strange Glory*, 227–262, who called this approach, "a new kind of monasticism."

Bonhoeffer realized that theological studies separated from the intensity of believers living together in community worshiping, serving, confessing, and encouraging one another would fail to prepare ordinands for the realities of pastoral ministry. He chronicled the Finkenwalde experience in his book, *Life Together*.[39] While addressing typical subjects in a theological seminary, he also focused on discipleship centered in the Christian community. As he explained in his book, *Discipleship* (*Nachfolge*), "Whatever the disciples do, they do it within the communal bond of the community of Jesus and as its members."[40] From that angle, he spent the next two-and-a-half years training ordinands in preparation for pastoral ministry. They focused on *community* by which Christians living in the midst of their enemies lived out their mission and work.[41] They approached community as a divine reality rather than an ideal imposed from without. Further, this reality was spiritual, not unspiritual.[42] Practically, love working through faith in Christ built healthy relationships.[43] This would be evident in the way they spent each day together.

Bonhoeffer mapped out each day's worship, work, time alone, and recreation. The community began the day in worship, reading Scripture, singing, and praying together. He particularly focused on learning to pray the Psalms together.[44] Consecutive reading of the Scripture taught the ordinands to listen to God's Word so that they might meditate upon it and apply it to their lives. This practice also involved the students in reading Scripture publicly in such a way as to never draw attention to oneself.[45] He encouraged unison singing as a spiritual exercise.[46] The ordinands

---

39   Dietrich Bonhoeffer, *Life Together/Prayerbook of the Bible*, DBW 5; Gerhard Ludwig Müller, Albrecht Schönherr, and Geffrey B. Kelly, eds.; Daniel W. Bloesch, and James H. Burtness, trans.; Minneapolis: Fortress Press, 2005), 3–9; the editor's introduction offers a good picture of Bonhoeffer's approach at Finkenwalde.

40   Dietrich Bonhoeffer, *Discipleship*, DBW 4; Wayne Whitson Floyd Jr., Geffrey Kelly, and John D. Godsey, eds.; Martin Kuske, Ilse Tödt, Barbara Green, and Reinhard Krauss, trans. (Minneapolis: Fortress Press, 2003), 249. Note, *Discipleship* is the original name of the better known title, *The Cost of Discipleship*. Marsh, *Strange Glory*, 243, writes, "*Discipleship* would evolve into a polemic against the Lutheran tendency to portray faith as a refuge from obedience."

41   Bonhoeffer, *Life Together*, 27. He explained, "Therefore, we may now say that the community of Christians springs solely from the biblical and reformation message of the justification of human beings through grace alone" (32).

42   Ibid., 35. He further noted, "Like the Christian's sanctification, Christian community is a gift of God to which we have no claim" (38).

43   Ibid., 38–47.

44   Ibid., 52–61. See also *Prayerbook of the Bible: An Introduction to the Psalms*, pp. 141ff.

45   Ibid., 61–64. Bonhoeffer wrote, "Proper reading of Scripture is not a technical exercise that can be learned; it is something that grows or diminishes according to my own spiritual condition" (64).

46   Ibid., 66–68.

ate together and then worked—in their case, doing theological studies—as part of their Christian duty, returning to close the day with a common meal and worship.[47]

Beyond the corporate gatherings, Bonhoeffer insisted on time alone for meditation and prayer. He noted, "We recognize, then, that only as we stand within the community can we be alone, and only those who are alone can live in community. Both belong together."[48] The development of one's spiritual life in community and times of silence prepares for service. Here Bonhoeffer modeled what it meant to be a servant leader. On one occasion, a call came for help in the Finkenwalde kitchen. None of the students responded, so Bonhoeffer quietly went to the kitchen, locked the door behind him, and began the work without allowing the sheepish students, who sought entry to the kitchen, to help. When he returned, he never said a word about it. He did not need to since his example spoke volumes.[49]

Bonhoeffer also introduced the students to the practice of confession, a discipline Luther promoted but had long since been abandoned by later followers. He saw it as an act that crushed the root of sin in pride.[50] Confession prepared the community for the Lord's Supper, as "a joyous occasion for the Christian community."[51] Within the life of Christian community, Bonhoeffer sought to combine pure doctrine, the practical outworking of the Sermon on the Mount, and worship as essential preparation for pastoral work.[52]

When the Gestapo shut down the Finkenwalde seminary in 1937, Bonhoeffer initiated the *Collective Pastorates*, in which the remaining students—some had already gone to war—were divided between two sympathetic Confessing Church pastors who took the ordinands under their wings as apprentices. The pastors provided mentoring in pastoral work, while Bonhoeffer traveled between the groups to continue to offer theological instruction, counsel, and leadership.[53]

Even after the ordinands left their *Collective Pastorates* for the front lines in the war or to serve parish churches, Bonhoeffer continued to communicate with them through circular letters as well as personal correspondence.[54] He sought to

---

47   Ibid., 74–80.

48   Ibid., 83.

49   Metaxas, *Bonhoeffer*, loc. 5337–5353.

50   Bonhoeffer, *Life Together*, 111. Luther's *The Large Catechism* states, "Therefore when I urge you to go to confession, I am urging you to be a Christian," a declaration Bonhoeffer embraced (114).

51   Ibid., 116–118.

52   Metaxas, *Bonhoeffer*, loc. 4915, Bonhoeffer wrote to Swiss Reformed pastor Erwin Sutz that he no longer believed in the university approach to training pastors. Rather, it should be "in church cloister-like schools, in which pure doctrine, the Sermon on the Mount, and worship are taken seriously—as they never are (and in present circumstances couldn't be) at the university."

53   Ibid., loc. 5905–5918. See Marsh, *Strange Glory*, 260–262.

54   E.g., see his letters to the Finkenwalde Brothers in Bonhoeffer, *Theological Education Under-*

keep up with the details among his former students, often informing the others of the deaths of their former classmates. Yet even with the sad notes, he turned those occasions to times of encouragement and accountability.[55] In a circular letter of December 20, 1937, Bonhoeffer encouraged the brothers, "to ensure that those among us who are isolated are not left alone."[56] He would also bring the Finkenwalde brothers together for retreats in which they would practice the *Life Together* disciplines, listen to Bonhoeffer's exposition of Scripture, discuss theology, and receive reports on each church represented. The retreats became a springboard for exercising pastoral care toward the former classmates and jointly supported evangelistic efforts.[57]

Many of Bonhoeffer's students died in the war. For those surviving, his impact on their lives remained incalculable. Albrecht Schöenherr, later bishop emeritus for the Regional Church of Berlin-Brandenburg, wrote forty years after Bonhoeffer's death, "Without his influence, I do not know what would have become of me. . . . His thoughts and especially his attitudes have accompanied me ever since [meeting him as a university student in 1932] in *my training of young pastors* and my work in the leadership of the church."[58] Another former student, Gerhard Lehne, explained his apprehensions at sitting under Bonhoeffer's leadership, thinking it would be "the stuffy air of theological bigotry." Instead, he found "accurate theological work on the common ground of fellowship, in which one's own inabilities were never noticed in a hurtful fashion, but rather which turned work into pleasure; true fellowship under the word that united all

---

*ground*, 20–26; 39–41; 47–48; see also Bonhoeffer, *Letters & Papers from Prison*, Eberhard Bethge, ed. (New York: Macmillan, 1972), 302–307.

55  See Tony Reinke, "The Invincible, Irrefutable Joy" [cited 4 February 2013]: 1–4, www.desiringgod.org/blog/posts/the-invincible-irrefutable-joy. Reinke cites an example after Bonhoeffer related the death of their friends: "This joy, which no one shall take from us, belongs not only to those who have been called home but also to us who are alive. We are one with them in this joy, but never in melancholy. How are we going to be able to help those who have become joyless and discouraged if we ourselves are not borne along by courage and joy?" (2), cited from Dietrich Bonhoeffer, *Conspiracy and Imprisonment: 1940–1945*, DBW 16 (Minneapolis: Fortress, 2006), 377–378.

56  Dietrich Bonhoeffer, *Dietrich Bonhoeffer: Theological Education Underground: 1937–1940*, DBW 15; Dirk Schulz and Victoria J. Barnett, eds.; Victoria J. Barnett, Claudia D. Bergmann, Peter Frick, and Scott A. Moore, trans. (Minneapolis: Fortress Press, 2012), 20–21. He offered similar exhortation to aid one another in a March 14, 1938 circular to the Finkenwalde Brothers (39–41).

57  Ibid., 49–52, see anonymous, "Report by One Participant about the Zingst Retreat, June 20–25, 1938."

58  Albrecht Schöenherr, "Dietrich Bonhoeffer: The Message of a Life," in *The Christian Century* (27 Nov 1985): 1090–1094; [cited 4 February 2013] www.religion-online.org/showarticle.asp?title=1928, 1–6. Italics added, showing how the training process continued.

'without respect to person.'"[59] The impact of his influence as a pastoral trainer of pastors bore much fruit in the lives of those under his charge after his death at Flossenbürg Prison in 1945.[60] His personable approach to mentoring, emphasis on adherence to Scripture, exacting scholarship, discipleship in community, and example of perseverance in suffering continue to leave Bonhoeffer's mark on the work of mentoring for ministry.

## OBSERVATIONS

Spurgeon and Bonheoffer, separated by years, denominations, theological convictions, and geography, remained tightly wound in shared passion for training young men for gospel ministry. Spurgeon did so at the height of Victorian Britain, Bonhoeffer during the rise of the Third Reich. Both left the church a legacy in training others for ministry.

*First, both valued personal relationships with their trainees.* Whether Spurgeon taking students on a preaching trip or Bonhoeffer engaging students around the table, they cared deeply about their trainees, demonstrating it in multiple ways. These mentoring relationships continued to bear influence throughout and after their lives.

*Second, both recognized the effect of the Christian community in shaping their trainees.* Spurgeon involved the ministry students in the dozens of ministries shared by members at the Metropolitan Tabernacle. The Pastors College was an arm of the church. Bonhoeffer brought community to an intense level, with the ministry training wrapped into a congregation that lived communally. While his approach takes community to an unlikely communal practice for most of us, the point of involvement in one another's lives must not be missed by the communal emphasis. He sought to show how the church is the believer's necessary community for ongoing discipleship and spiritual maturity.

*Third, they modeled both a seriousness concerning the gospel and Christian ministry, while also showing joy and zest for life in Christ.* None could accuse Spurgeon or Bonhoeffer of dry academic training. They sparked gospel life in their mentees.

*Fourth, both mentored formally and informally.* Lecture and critique times allowed Spurgeon and Bonhoeffer to lay substantial theological and pastoral groundwork in their trainees. The casual atmosphere under Spurgeon's oak tree and Bonhoeffer's Finkenwalde grounds did as much to shape their protégés as the formal training. Their personal letters to those mentored in the years that followed demonstrated ongoing care and influence.

---

59  Bonhoeffer, *Theological Education Underground*, 127–130.
60  Bethge, *Bonhoeffer*, 829–831, movingly recounts Bonhoeffer's last days and death.

*Fifth, both regularly, through their own theological bent, brought the men back to their need to depend upon the Lord.* Spurgeon emphasized the Spirit's power in all of ministry and the necessity of undergirding their ministries through prayer. Bonhoeffer's stress on prayer and meditation intended to cultivate spiritual maturity and dependence upon the Lord. Ministry could not be done without the Lord's power.

Personal relationships, Christian community, zest for life, formal and informal mentoring, and the Lord's power remain effective tools and emphases for preparing the next generation for Christian ministry.

# CHAPTER 8

# A THEOLOGICAL RATIONALE: THE CHURCH IN GOD'S ECONOMY

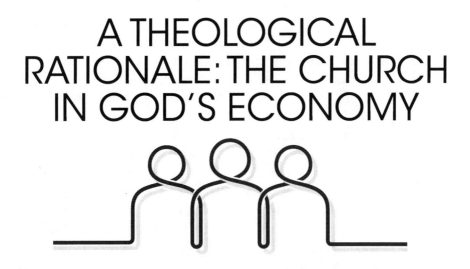

Compared to many of the superb seminaries and energy-charged conferences and training networks available to train for ministry, the local church might come across as boring. Seminaries focus on high-level academics. Conferences address one major theme. But the local church, well, that's another story. When contrasting the daily grind of patiently shepherding diverse people who struggle with various sins and comprise a wide range of personalities, with listening to an engaging speaker who is an expert on a facet of ministry or theology, it's understandable that a church might seem boring. Yet with all of the expertise in seminaries and conferences, nothing can replace the real-life impact of the local church in preparation for ministry.

In this chapter, I have no aim to exclude the practical usefulness of parachurch ministries, including seminaries, to train and influence ministers. They have a vital place in the training process. However, some trainees spend weeks-to-years in ministry-sterile atmospheres that lack the gritty reality of the congregation. So while amassing pertinent information, sharpening theological dialogue, and developing a toolbox of methodologies—all of which may be of later value—they still do not understand how to deal with people or how to work through real-life issues apart from the intense relationships experienced in the congregation. With that in mind, let's consider a theological rationale for why the local church best develops Christian workers by looking at the subject theologically, ecclesiologically, and practically.[1]

---

1 Some pastoral mentors will prefer one trainee at a time. I consider a *training cohort* preferable, since it maximizes the time and efficiency of pastoral mentoring while building strong

## A THEOLOGICAL RATIONALE:
## THE PRIORITY OF THE CHURCH

One of my closest friends and a fellow elder is an internal medicine doctor. Over the years I've asked him countless medical questions and have received his spot-on diagnosis and explanation for a number of pesky health issues. He's a generalist in that he has a wide range of expertise with matters of health. I'm often astounded at just how broad his knowledge is about so many different things. But when my knee recently swelled, I knew that he would shake his head and send me immediately to the orthopedist—a specialist who doesn't bother with sore throats or abdominal pain or bodily discomforts. This specialist only looks at shoulders, knees and elbows—that's it. He's great at what he does but I don't visit him when my throat closes up or with normal health problems. That's when I need the generalist.

Parachurch agencies, as the *specialists*, focus on doing one thing well. They are good at what they do, e.g., how to plant a church or how to preach or how to counsel, etc. They don't face the extra responsibilities common with local congregations, such as pastoral care, discipline, membership issues, polity, benevolence, and an array of ministries to various ages. That necessitates the *generalists*, better known as local church ministers. Pastors, church planters, and missionaries focus on more than one thing. They are not specialists but generalists, since they address the broad range of needs in a local church. If they are only trained by specialists then they might do one thing well, but as pastors they will be involved in multiple issues in local church ministry. We do sometimes need the specialists. But we always need the generalists.

So why claim that the local church and its pastors serve as the best context for developing generalists who will do mission work, pastor, and plant churches? Think of how the church distinguishes itself from every other Christian or parachurch organization. The church alone has its foundation, design, pattern, and mission set forth in the Scriptures. Other Christian organizations can lay claim to following Christ but none hold the solitary position of the church as Christ's bride (Eph. 5:22–33; Rev. 19:7–9; 21:2; 22:7) and the corporate entity for fulfilling the Great Commission (Matt. 28:18–20; Acts 1:8). Since Christ ordained the church (Matt. 16:13–20), died and rose from the dead to secure it (Eph. 5:25–27), and made it to be a kingdom of priests engaged in worship and proclamation (1 Peter 2: 4–10; Rev. 1:5–6; 5:9–10), then *the church* best serves Christ's mission.[2]

---

comradery. This group will ideally be four to eight pastoral trainees serving, learning, and maturing together in preparation for ministry. My subsequent mentioning of a training cohort has these parameters in mind.

2   This assertion does not mean that parachurch groups have no validity. Rick Warren, *The Purpose Driven Church: Growth without Compromising Your Message & Mission* (Grand Rapids:

One primary way that the church serves Christ's mission is through training and equipping pastors and missionaries to be sent into the world. Other Christian organizations such as theological institutions and mission agencies offer useful expertise in training and equipping; they are specialists that focus primarily on one purpose. On the other hand, the church is called "the pillar and support of the truth" (1 Tim. 3:15), "God's household" (Eph. 2:19), and "a dwelling of God in the Spirit" (Eph. 2:22)—so the church has biblical/theological, family/household, and doxological/missiological purposes. This broad range sets the church apart to uniquely shape those who engage in Christ's mission regarding the extension and health of his church.

The Great Commission (Matt. 28:18–20) that Jesus gave to the Eleven, D. A. Carson explains, came "in their role as disciples," adding, "Therefore they are paradigms for all disciples." He further notes that Jesus's commission "is binding on *all* Jesus's disciples to make others what they themselves are—disciples of Jesus Christ."[3] The most natural means for disciple making takes place through the church, especially since Christ's commission to make disciples called for baptism and ongoing teaching, which are distinct responsibilities for the church.[4]

Following the narrative of Paul and Barnabas, after being sent out on mission by the Antioch church, exemplifies the organic relationship between missionaries and the local church. Once the team completed their first missionary journey, they returned to Antioch to offer a firsthand report—demonstrating accountability to the church (Acts 14:26–28). After a brief respite with these brothers and sisters, the Antioch church sent the missionary team to Jerusalem, serving as representatives of their church (Acts 15:1–4). The Antioch church further sent out two missionary teams after the Jerusalem Council (Acts 15:36–41), particularly evident in Paul's accountability by reporting to the Antioch congregation after the second missionary journey (Acts 18:22–23). Rather than an early version of parachurch versus local church, Paul and Barnabas were sent out to represent the congregation with whom they had covenanted.[5] While acknowledging the superb contributions made by

---

Zondervan, 1995), 126–127, points out that parachurch organizations best help the church when they "focus on a single purpose." In this way, they "have greater impact on the church" (126). They are specialists while churches are generalists. By exercising their specialty, the parachurch organizations *assist* the church.

3  D. A. Carson, *Matthew 13–28*, EBC; Frank E. Gaebelein, gen. ed. (Grand Rapids: Zondervan, 1995), 596; italics original.

4  Ibid., 597. Baptism identifies the new disciple with a particular community of believers with whom he/she enters into covenant in Christ. See also John S. Hammett, *Biblical Foundations for Baptist Churches: A Contemporary Ecclesiology* (Grand Rapids: Kregel, 2005), 263–267.

5  Acts 13:3 explains that the church "sent" Paul and Barnabas; *apelusan*, Louw-Nida, 15.66, "to cause someone to depart for a particular purpose—to send." In other words, they were

many parachurch missionary organizations, those organizations do not constitute the church, but rather, at their best, are a "servant-partner" with the church.[6] As long as parachurch groups recognize this *partnership*, rather than attempting to become a *substitute* for the church, they maintain a vital role in kingdom work.

The early centuries of the church recognized the unique role of the church in God's plan for the ages. As an example, the Nicene Creed (325) affirmed some concrete identities of the church. These classic marks of the church, known as the *notae ecclesiae*, distinguish the church from parachurch organizations. They also demonstrate that the church, as *apostolic*, holds responsibility for proclaiming the gospel in mission.[7]

Church traditions from wide perspectives agree that the four *notae* express the basic essence of the church as one, holy, catholic, and apostolic.[8] Yet disagreement arises concerning the meaning of each *notae* or mark. While Cyprian attempted to posit *unity* in relationship to communion with the bishop, those in the Reformed tradition saw unity as "spiritual, not organizational or institutional," uniting around gospel ministry.[9]

The church's *holiness* is rooted in God's holiness (Lev. 11:44–45; 19:2; 20:7; 1 Peter 1:14–16), separating it from the world to the service of God.[10] *Catholicity* describes the universality of the church, uniting local congregations across the

---

intentionally sent on a particular mission by the church. Acts 15:3, "Therefore, *being sent* on their way by the church" uses *propempo*, a term that indicates the mission team had received support from the church to make the journey, BDAG, 873. So the Antioch church officially sent out Paul and Barnabas, tangibly supporting them as they acted as official representatives of the church.

6   See John S. Hammett, "How Church and Parachurch Should Relate: Arguments for a Servant-Partnership Model," *Missiology: An International Review* XXVIII.2 (April 2000): 200–207, who demonstrates the priority of the church in Scripture, while calling for parachurch groups to serve as an arm of the church in partnership for mission and ministry. He further details the strain between parachurch groups and the Southern Baptists, and offers an appropriate servant-partnership paradigm in Hammett, "Selected Parachurch Groups and Southern Baptists: An Ecclesiological Debate," (PhD diss.; The Southern Baptist Theological Seminary, 1991). See a complementary position with a number of practical recommendations for bringing the parachurch into a servant-partnership with the church, in Larry J. McKinney, "The Church-Parachurch Conflict: A Proposed Solution," *Didaskalia* 6.1 (Fall 1994): 47–57.

7   J. D. Greear, "Great Commission Multiplication: Church Planting and Community Ministry," in *Great Commission Resurgence: Fulfilling God's Mandate in Our Time*, Chuck Lawless and Adam W. Greenway, eds. (Nashville: B&H Academic, 2010), 333–336, explains "signs" as a part of the apostolic message, with "the local church itself" as "the greatest kingdom sign of the gospel in Acts" (334).

8   Donald G. Bloesch, *The Church: Sacraments, Worship, Ministry, Mission* (Christian Foundations; Downers Grove, IL: IVP Academic, 2002), 39.

9   Hammett, *Biblical Foundations*, 52–55.

10  Mark E. Dever, "The Church," in Daniel L. Akin, ed., *A Theology for the Church* (Nashville: B&H Academic, 2007), 776–777.

globe. Yet no one church holds the domain of catholicity. The church locally and universally belongs to Christ alone (Rev. 5:9); consequently, he sets the agenda for his church, including its mission.[11]

Donald Bloesch asks whether *apostolicity* signifies an unbroken link between the ministers of a church and the early apostles signified through the laying on of hands, or "does it not refer to a continuity in the message of faith that was first articulated by the apostles?"[12] Churches in the Reformation tradition object to the former view, while agreeing on apostolicity pointing chiefly to the proclamation of God's Word in the tradition of the apostles.[13] John Calvin saw gospel proclamation as the clearest mark of a genuine church, accompanied by the sacraments: "Whenever we see the Word of God purely preached and heard, and the sacraments administered according to Christ's institution, there, it is not to be doubted, a church of God exists."[14] Martin Luther concurred: "The holy Christian people are recognized by their possession of the holy word of God."[15] The church distinguishes itself from parachurch agencies by its biblical foundation and possession of the four *notae*—especially in its apostolicity.

### The Local Church Leading in Mission and Ministry

The focus of the redemptive work of Jesus Christ centers on the church (Eph. 1:3–14; 2:11–22; 1 Peter 1:17–2:10; Rev. 5:1–10). Christ mandated and entrusted the church—which he redeemed and empowers by the Holy Spirit—with making disciples of all nations, baptizing, and teaching them to observe all that he commanded (Matt. 28:18–20; Luke 24:44–49; John 20:19–23; Acts 1:6–8). This post-resurrection command of Christ fueled a missionary mindset in the early church—particularly evident by the way the church in the book of Acts functioned to make disciples.[16]

The church continues what Yahweh promised Abraham (Gen. 12:1–3), unrealized through Israel and "fulfilled through Jesus in the mission of his followers," as Peter O'Brien and Andreas Köstenberger note, "which nevertheless remains

---

11   Dever, "The Church," 777.
12   Bloesch, *The Church*, 39–40.
13   See R. B. Kuiper, *The Glorious Body of Christ: A Scriptural Appreciation of the One Holy Scripture* (Edinburgh: The Banner of Truth Trust, 1967), 68, who explains apostolicity as "that the church is founded upon the *teaching* of the apostles" (italics original).
14   John Calvin, *Institutes of the Christian Religion*, LCC; John T. McNeill, ed; Ford L. Battles;, trans. (Philadelphia: Westminster, 1960), 21:1023 (4.4.9).
15   Timothy F. Lull, ed., *Martin Luther's Basic Theological Writings*, 2d ed. (Minneapolis: Fortress Press, 2005), 366.
16   Leon Morris, *The Gospel According to Matthew* (Grand Rapids: Eerdmans, 1992), 744.

his own mission."[17] Consequently, they explain, "mission is the church's primary task between Christ's first coming and his return."[18] Paul's statement to the Thessalonians illustrates how the church embraced this missionary practice: "For the word of the Lord has sounded forth from you, not only in Macedonia and Achaia, but also in every place your faith toward God has gone forth, so that we have no need to say anything" (1 Thess. 1:8). The early twentieth-century missionary Roland Allen observed of Paul, "His converts became missionaries."[19] Just as demonstrated with the Thessalonian church, Jesus calls the church to faithfully proclaim the gospel and to pray with "earnest, faith-filled prayers" as the gospel goes forth.[20] Therefore the church, so entrusted with and empowered for mission, stands above every Christian institution in God's eyes.

God's strategy for propagating the gospel of Jesus Christ to the world, as J. D. Greear asserts, "is the planting of healthy, local churches in strategic cities in the world."[21] Yet, the radical individualism promoted in the West seems to leave the church as merely an aid to discipleship rather than the community necessary in God's economy for spiritual formation.[22] Often the Western Christian paradigm focuses on the individual's personal relationship to Christ over his or her relationship to the body of Christ. But in the New Testament era, a person was saved to enjoy God *and* the redeemed community, "not saved for the sole purpose of enjoying a personal relationship to God."[23] Rather, "According to the New Testament," writes Joseph Hellerman, "a person is saved *to community*."[24]

Paul further demonstrated this truth by his use of corporate language to describe Christian behavior (Eph. 4:1–6:20). Christian lifestyle reflects the congregation's good name in the community, as well as the character of Jesus Christ who called the body into relationship with him and his family (Eph. 4:1–6).[25] Paul's focus on mutual relationships, rather than merely the individual, shows the

---

17  Andreas J. Köstenberger and Peter T. O'Brien, *Salvation to the Ends of the Earth: A Biblical Theology of Mission*, NSBT 11; D. A. Carson, ed. (Downers Grove, IL: IVP, 2001), 106.

18  Ibid., 108.

19  Roland Allen, *Missionary Methods: St. Paul's or Ours?* (Grand Rapids: Eerdmans, 1962), 93.

20  John Piper, *Let the Nations Be Glad! The Supremacy of God in Missions* (Grand Rapids: Baker, 1993), 66.

21  Greear, "Great Commission Multiplication," 325. Greear further explains that these vibrant, healthy churches are to bless their communities in the same fashion as the Acts 2:42–47 style churches.

22  Joseph H. Hellerman, *When the Church Was a Family: Recapturing Jesus's Vision for Authentic Christian Community* (Nashville: B&H Academic, 2009), 2–5.

23  Ibid., 124.

24  Ibid.; italics original.

25  F. F. Bruce, *The Epistles to the Colossians, to Philemon, and to the Ephesians*, NICNT (Grand Rapids: Eerdmans, 1984), 334.

strong sense of how his disciple making took place with a view to community.[26] This community, in turn, would be trained to do the work of ministry by those the Lord had gifted to equip and build up the church (Eph. 4:11–16). Every member has a part to contribute toward the growth (spiritually and numerically) and building up of the church body. The body functions according to the direction and determination of the Head (Eph. 4:15–16).[27] The *missio Dei* exercised by the Head will inevitably direct the body toward mission.[28]

Although not intentionally in every case, Christian organizations have unwittingly fostered an individualistic attitude.[29] Even those seeking to plant or revitalize churches may consider themselves fully equipped for their mission despite lack of a church community's influence. Yet Jesus identifies no other institution in which he claims to be its head or calls it his body or describes it through Paul as "the fullness of Him who fills all in all" (Eph. 1:22–23). The church alone is given "the keys of the kingdom" by which forgiveness of sins might be communicated by the church through the regular explanation and application of gospel promises (Matt. 16:19).[30]

Parachurch organizations, then, need to regularly evaluate their philosophy and practice in light of Christ's priority on the church. Similarly, individual Christians, especially those focusing on ministry, should consider whether or not they have slipped into a pattern in which a parachurch group holds more value to them in life and ministry than the local church. No doubt, most parachurch groups are easier to maneuver and get along with than a lot of churches. Yet Jesus sets his affections upon and entrusts the church with his mission in the world. So should we.

So, if those embarking on the mission of planting and serving churches would maintain a New Testament ministry, they must be honed and shaped by local churches that leave an imprint in their ministries. A church-shaped focus rather than an institutional or individual focus in ministry, ties future ministers to a foundation in the church that will be mirrored in the churches they serve.

With the Great Commission given to the church, with Christ as the church's Head, with the church uniquely marked by the *notae ecclesiae*, and with the New

---

26  Ibid.

27  D. Martyn Lloyd-Jones, *Christian Unity: An Exposition of Ephesians 4:1–16* (Grand Rapids: Baker, 1980), 273.

28  Timothy Keller, *Center Church: Doing Balanced, Gospel-Centered Ministry in Your City* (Grand Rapids: Zondervan, 2012), 259; see also his discussion of the various uses and applications of *missio Dei* and how it frames an understanding of the church as missional (255–261).

29  Bloesch, *The Church*, 24, warns against the ecclesiological dangers of individualism and institutionalism.

30  Calvin, *Institutes*, 21:635–36 (4.1.21–22).

Testament's corporate emphasis on the church, then the church stands apart from other Christian-oriented organizations. While we give thanks for the specialization of so many parachurch organizations to help the church in its mission and ministry, we acknowledge that these organizations cannot take the church's place in God's economy.

### The Local Church and Theological Education

Those preparing for ministry who desire to build strong, healthy churches need the experience of having lived in community with a local congregation to understand the dynamics of a New Testament church worked out in daily life (e.g., Acts 13:1–3). This it not to suggest that academic training in a theological seminary offers no benefit to future ministers. On the contrary, developing a strong foundation in biblical languages and exegesis, homiletics, theology, church history, and missions will assist the future minister in enriching his congregation through faithful preaching, teaching, and leadership. Yet to subtract the experience of application through faithful mentoring in the local church diminishes the value and effectiveness of a theological education.[31]

This need seems evident to Professor Robert Ferris, who refers to a 1984 proposal by theologian John Frame, in which Frame tersely wrote that we should "dump the academic model once and for all." He then called for a return to a Christian community where teachers, students, and families live out the Christian life and serve together in the trenches of local ministry. In other words, Frame does not want to abandon theological study but to see it best learned and practiced in the context of local church ministry.[32] Timothy George, dean at Beeson Divinity School, concurs, preferring a residential community for seminarians where professors and students live, work, play, and flesh "out the meaning of the gospel together."[33]

The focus in much theological education, with the influence of the Enlightenment, has been on amassing information, digging into minutiae, and devel-

---

31  While offering observations on theological schools, it should not be construed that conferences and networks are unaffected by the same issues. The *idealistic* atmosphere often portrayed in conference settings might fail to connect to the realities of congregational life, as well. This does not imply that attending conferences or participating in networks for church planting or missions lacks value. They do hold great value, just as do theological schools, but they must not be substituted for life in community offered by faithful participation in the church. For this reason, pastoral mentoring in the context of the local church, living out Christian community together, best prepares for ministry.

32  Robert Ferris, *Renewal in Theological Education: Strategies for Change*, BGC Monograph (Wheaton, IL: The Billy Graham Center, Wheaton College, 1990), 16.

33  "50 Years of Seminary Education: Celebrating the Past, Assessing the Present, Envisioning the Future," *Christianity Today* 50/10 (Oct 2006): [Special] S13.

oping narrow categories of scholarship while failing to apply biblical knowledge and wisdom to life in community.[34] Yet theological education without spiritual formation in community fails to prepare graduates for servant leadership in local congregations. This separation of academic preparation from the realities of community distorts the task in Christian ministry by isolating theological studies from local church ministry.[35] Instead, a more intentional partnership between seminaries and local churches requiring mentoring with pastoral leaders can close the gap on better preparation for ministry.[36]

The experience of relationships in the body living out the gospel, modeling forgiveness, service, and accountability will best be found in the church rather than through other institutions. Due to the church's importance to Christ, he has made it "the chief instrument for glorifying God in the world."[37] As such, the church not only proclaims the gospel audibly but also makes it known *visibly* through the way believers live together in community.[38] As this experience shapes those preparing for Christian ministry, they approach their ministries with a unique dynamic that cannot be found by relying upon short-term conferences or academic settings.[39] This will be evident when those preparing for ministry experience the model of a healthy church.

---

34  Robert W. Ferris, "The Role of Theology in Theological Education," in *With an Eye on the Future: Development and Mission in the 21ˢᵗ Century—Essays in Honor of Ted Ward*, Duane Elmer and Lois McKinney, eds. (Monrovia, CA: MARC, 1996), 102. See also Max L. Stackhouse, *Apologia: Contextualization, Globalization, and Mission in Theological Education* (Grand Rapids: Eerdmans, 1988), 30–31; and Dennis M. Campbell, "Theological Education and Moral Foundation: What's Going on in Seminaries Today?" in *Theological Education and Moral Formation*, Encounter Series 15; Richard John Neuhaus, gen. ed. (Grand Rapids: Eerdmans, 1992), 1–21. Campbell observes that American Seminaries may have unwittingly drifted toward "the principles and visions of the secular Enlightenment" in the heavily academic approach to theological education that has not adequately prepared graduates for returning to their communities as servant leaders (10–11).

35  Ibid., 103–105, 110.

36  For a helpful look at seminary and local church in partnership, see Matt Rogers, "Holistic Pastoral Training: Strategic Partnership between the Seminary and the Local Church in the United States," (PhD diss.; Southeastern Baptist Theological Seminary, 2015).

37  Dever, "The Church," 767.

38  Ibid.

39  Robert Banks, *Reenvisioning Theological Education: Exploring a Missional Alternative to Current Models* (Grand Rapids: Eerdmans, 1999), 11, investigates "the widening gap between the seminary and the church," citing the academy's sometime failure to develop spirituality and community that connects with the local church. He demonstrates that a sterile academic approach to ministry training lacks support from educational models in the biblical narratives and Jewish history (pp. 83–91). He further describes, with affirmation, a seminary cohort model with twenty-five to thirty students who work through the entire master of divinity degree together. They worship and serve together; minister in local churches; enter into mentoring relationships with both ministers and lay leaders; attend retreats with faculty and faculty families; maintain growth covenants for areas of spiritual formation; and receive feedback from faculty and fellow students on their progress and development in ministry (228).

## THE ECCLESIOLOGICAL RATIONALE:
## THE MODEL OF A HEALTHY CHURCH

Nineteenth-century Baptist theologian J. L. Dagg defines the local church as "an assembly of believers in Christ, organized into a body, according to the Holy Scriptures, for the worship and service of God."[40] "An assembly" or "a community" best captures the New Testament idea of *ekklesia* rather than merely an organization, although organization remains necessary for carrying out its mission.[41] While other religions have various acts of worship and service, that practiced by the Christian church has a theological foundation in the person and work of Jesus Christ. Worship takes place "in spirit and truth" (John 4:23–24) through the bloody, sacrificial death of Jesus Christ (Heb. 13:10–16), setting Christian worship apart from other religions. Instead of worshiping and serving as acts of achievement and merit, Christians worship and serve because they have already been declared righteous through the work of Jesus Christ (Gal. 2:16).

Serving God means that we are joined together as "God's fellow workers" (1 Cor.. 3:9), engaged in fulfilling both the Great Commission (Matt. 28:18–20) and the Great Commandment (Luke 10:25–37) through the power of the Holy Spirit (Luke 24:49; Acts 1:8). Certainly, individual Christians can worship and serve God on their own, yet in regularly doing so, they miss the pattern for worship and service evident throughout the New Testament by which believers worshiped, and served in and through a healthy church community (Acts 2:42–47; 4:23–35).

Ideas of church health vary from generation to generation. Nineteenth-century Baptist leader Francis Wayland thought of the church as a group that possessed a particular moral character. The better the moral character, the better the church's health.[42] In the early twentieth century, seminary president E. Y. Mullins, with a bent toward radical individualism, viewed a theology of soul competency "as the constitutive principle of Baptist church life."[43] Democracy, rather than community, gave the church its distinction, leading to pragmatism trumping biblical ecclesiology.[44] In contrast, Calvin centered the church's health on its declaration,

---

40  J. L. Dagg, *Manual of Church Order* (Harrisonburg, VA: Gano Books, 1990 from 1858 reprint), 74.
41  Ibid., 82. BDAG, 303, further identifies *ekklesia* as "people with shared belief, *community, congregation*," (italics original). The popular phrase, *community*, conveys well the Greek term.
42  Norman H. Maring, "The Individualism of Francis Wayland," in *Baptist Concepts of the Church: A Survey of the Historical and Theological Issues Which Have Produced Changes in Church Order*, W. S. Hudson, ed. (Chicago: Judson Press, 1959), 146.
43  Winthrop S. Hudson, "Shifting Patterns of Church Order in the Twentieth Century," in Hudson, ed., *Baptist Concepts*, 215.
44  Ibid., 215–218.

hearing, and reception of the gospel.[45] Despite weaknesses in other areas, as long as the gospel remained central, the church existed, according to Calvin, with the potential for growth and health.[46]

While acknowledging the right preaching of God's Word and proper administration of baptism and the Lord's Supper (with church discipline implied in the latter) as the Reformation marks of the church, Washington, DC. pastor Mark Dever sought to expand on the marks in order to "set off healthy churches from true but more sickly ones."[47] Churches can agree with and hold to the same marks identified in the Reformation but slip into nominal Christianity that follows pragmatism to achieve goals that fail to aim for the glory of God.[48] So, while maintaining ecclesiastical orthodoxy churches can still be sickly instead of healthy. In such settings, those training to plant, serve, and revitalize churches inevitably find greater inspiration and direction from other Christian institutions rather than from the local church. Skewing the place of a healthy local church as foundational to the shaping of Christian ministers leads to later confusion on what the church should look like. Healthy churches tend to reproduce healthy churches since anything less will be unsatisfactory to those sent out from them to serve.

Healthy churches, by contrast, "are self-consciously distinct from the culture," measuring success by "persevering biblical faithfulness," and uniting around the distinguishing elements of biblical Christianity.[49] While various lists might be noted to identify healthy churches (e.g., Luther's seven marks of the true church),[50] Dever recognizes nine distinguishing marks of a healthy church: expositional preaching, biblical theology, the gospel, biblical understanding of conversion, biblical understanding of evangelism, biblical understanding of church membership, biblical church discipline, concern for discipleship and growth, and biblical church leadership.[51] The adjective "biblical" reveals the intention of the marks of a healthy church: a return to the Scripture's sufficiency for all things related to the church (2 Tim. 3:16–17).

---

45  Paul D. L. Avis, *The Church in the Theology of the Reformers* (Eugene, OR: Wipf and Stock Publishers, 2002 from Marshall, Morgan, and Scott, 1981), 31.
46  Ibid., 40–42.
47  Mark E. Dever, *Nine Marks of a Healthy Church* (expd. ed.; Wheaton, IL: Crossway, 2004), 24.
48  Ibid., 25.
49  Ibid., 28.
50  Lull, *Martin Luther's Basic Theological Writings*, 366–375. Dever, *Nine Marks*, 249–266, in Appendix Two, shows the variety of church "marks" through forty Christian authors, making it evident that the discussion continues on what constitutes a healthy church.
51  Dever, *Nine Marks*, 29–32.

*Healthy churches* imply congregations where the gospel is central, member-ship is taken seriously, members care for one another, robust disciple making takes place (locally and internationally), and polity seeks to follow the teaching of Scripture. Healthy congregations continually reflect the Lordship of Christ in their relationships, ministries, and gospel outreach. Therefore, I am asserting that pastors, church planters, missionaries, and church revitalizers trained and mentored in the atmosphere of healthy churches have a better understanding of what a healthy congregation looks like, a comprehension of the leadership skills necessary for developing a healthy congregation, and a longing to reproduce similarly healthy congregations through their own patient, faithful labors. As my colleague Matt Sliger notes, "If the ultimate goal for a trainee is to become like the mentor, then one-on-one discipleship is sufficient. However, if the goal for a trainee is to become like Jesus, then he needs mentoring by Jesus's body."[52]

In conversations with young pastors who had been mentored in healthy con-gregations, inevitably they talked about the influence of their mentoring church upon their present ministries. For some, it gave a clear model at which to direct their ministry. For others, it gave encouragement that the churches they were leading *could* move toward a healthy model. Those planting churches start with a clear picture in mind of where they teach, pray, organize, and labor with their young congregations.

Training young ministers through academic institutions or conferences or networks might give excellent tools for going about the work of ministry, but *only the setting of healthy congregations provides the experiential model for them to emulate.*[53] With this healthy model, young ministers possess a clear goal at which to aim and a foundation from which to work in establishing healthy congrega-tions. Leaders in healthy congregations become a significant factor in shaping a generation of Christian workers—a matter to which we now turn.

## THE PRACTICAL RATIONALE:
## MENTORS IN THE LOCAL CHURCH LEADERSHIP STRUCTURE

The local church does not amorphously train Christian workers. It involves the pastoral leaders in the congregation exercising their gifts, sharing their experi-

---

52  Matt attributes this thought to ideas gleaned from Jeff Vanderstelt, *Saturate: Being Disciples of Jesus in the Everyday Stuff of Life* (Wheaton, IL: Crossway, 2015), 105.

53  James K. A. Smith, *You Are What You Love: The Spiritual Power of Habit* (Grand Rapids: Bra-zos Press, 2016), 21, in similar emphasis notes, "We learn to love, then, not primarily by ac-quiring information about *what* we should love but rather through practices that form habits of *how* we love."

ences, and coming alongside their less experienced protégés to mentor in minis-try. In this fashion, local church leadership models proclamation, pastoral care, disciplemaking, church discipline, vision for the nations, administration, god-liness, and leadership.[54] Trainees find the living examples to hone their under-standing in ways that textbooks and lecture halls cannot.

For instance, when young pastors face membership issues in the churches they eventually serve, having witnessed their local church mentors addressing mem-bership training and acceptance, membership care, and discipline of members, they have a clear reference point for doing the same. Otherwise, they might treat membership in the typically unhealthy manner so common among churches.[55] Or they might be idealistic or impatient or unrealistic when it comes to a congregation's understanding of Scripture rather than patiently teaching God's Word week by week from the pulpit, in small groups, and in one-on-one discipling relationships. Healthy models of proclamation and discipling enable Christian workers to approach their ministries with realism and patience (e.g. 2 Tim. 2:24–26).[56]

In the setting of plural, servant leaders, trainees find the best model of biblical leadership.[57] Plurality follows the biblical pattern for church leadership.[58] Pastors, elders, and deacons engaging the training cohort provide a helpful framework for modeling and training for ministry in new and existing churches.

---

54  See Thomas K. Ascol, ed., *Dear Timothy: Letters on Pastoral Ministry* (Cape Coral, FL Found-ers Press, 2004), that offers the insights of nineteen national and international pastors who identify a variety of areas in pastoral work, with practical letters addressing each. Derek Prime and Alistair Begg, *On Being a Pastor: Understanding Our Calling and Work* (Chicago: Moody, 2004), also address the multiple areas of pastoral work. See also Derek Tidball, *Ministry by the Book: New Testament Patterns for Pastoral Leadership* (Downers Grove, IL: IVP Academic, 2008), who works through the NT book by book, identifying the breadth of pastoral ministry exercised by Jesus Christ, the Apostles, and the early church elders.

55  Dever, *Nine Marks*, 147–149.

56  See Timothy Z. Witmer, *The Shepherd Leader: Achieving Effective Shepherding in Your Church* (Phillipsburg, NJ: P&R, 2010), 107–189, who identifies the pastor's responsibilities as know-ing, feeding, leading, and protecting the church. Pastoral trainees who observe these multi-dimensioned duties faithfully modeled are much better prepared to do the same when they begin service as pastors.

57  Hellerman, *When the Church*, 186; he also cites Matt. 23:8–12, e.g., "But the greatest among you shall be your servant."

58  Wayne Grudem, *Systematic Theology: An Introduction to Biblical Doctrine* (Grand Rapids: Zondervan, 1994), 913. See also Benjamin L. Merkle, *40 Questions about Elders and Deacons* (Grand Rapids: Kregel, 2008), 161–187; Phil A. Newton and Matt Schmucker, *Elders in the Life of the Church: A Guide to Ministry* (Grand Rapids: Kregel, 2014); Mark E. Dever, "The Church," in *A Theology for the Church* , Daniel L. Akin, ed. (Nashville: B&H Academic, 2007), 802–805, where the argument for plurality is made. In some settings there may be only one qualified elder, so in that case, the pastoral mentor will need to include those whom he may be cultivating toward eldership as part of training mentees.

Local pastors live under the charge given to Peter, "Tend My lambs . . . shepherd My sheep" (John 21:15–16; see also Acts 20:28; 1 Peter 5:1–4). Yet, as members of the larger body of Christ, pastors/elders face the challenge to train up pastoral leaders to serve in other churches and to start new congregations. Dagg argued that to think only of one local church without correspondingly laboring for other churches for the sake of God's kingdom "degrades his [pastoral] office."[59] He went so far as to call this "the antichristian spirit which substitutes external organization for spiritual religion."[60] While laboring to feed Christ's sheep in a local church, pastors and elders should also look beyond their own congregations to contribute toward establishing and revitalizing churches nationally and internationally.

A plurality of pastors and elders should take the lead for mentoring those whom the church would send out to serve Christ's kingdom.[61] Pastors/elders should possess the character and maturity necessary to train others for ministry (cf. 1 Tim. 3:1–7; Titus 1:5–9).[62] They are the ones engaged in the ongoing work of shepherding the flock, including teaching, preaching, membership care, counseling, leadership, discipline, administration, disciple-making (i.e., evangelism and missions), leadership development, and decision making—all gospel-centered actions the future ministers face. Seeing how faithful pastors and elders practice each arena of ministry, and walking with them through the process, shapes the thinking of those in training to emulate what they have observed.

Practically, since pastors/elders already engage in the breadth of local church ministry, they naturally possess the platform for training others in

---

59  Dagg, *Manual of Church Order*, 135; he cites John 21:15–17.

60  Ibid.

61  Due to the limitation of this chapter's scope, see the additional resources that address elder ministry and the equivalency of pastors and elders as constituting one office with multiple applications: Hammett, *Biblical Foundations*, 161–189; Mark Dever and Paul Alexander, *The Deliberate Church: Building Your Ministry on the Gospel* (Wheaton, IL: Crossway, 2005), 131–160; Benjamin L. Merkle, *The Elder and the Overseer: One Office in the Early Church*, SBL 57 (New York: Peter Lang, 2003). Merkle convincingly argues that the office of elder and overseer constitute one NT office.

62  Distinguishing both pastors and elders for the same biblical office, is done out of deference for churches that may not recognize non-staff elders comprising part of their pastoral leadership. While neglecting to set apart qualified non-staff elders diminishes the strength of a church's leadership, one would be presumptuous to think this is agreed upon across the spectrum of churches. In using *pastors*, I am particularly distinguishing those men called by the congregation as staff to serve as elders in the church's leadership, even if the title of elders is not utilized. See Newton and Schmucker, *Elders in the Life of the Church*, 45–57; Merkle, *40 Questions*, 169–172.

future ministry. As an example, elders meetings (or staff meetings) provide a wealth of insight on pastoral care, short-and-long-range planning, addressing critical problems, balancing ministry and budget, the dynamic of leadership relationships, missional challenges, and developing vision for ministry. Including a training cohort in the meetings allows for productive time to soak up the years of wisdom and experience bound up in any elder board or staff. Having opportunity for questions and debriefing after meetings gives more opportunity to clarify and shape the critical thinking skills of those engaged in future service.[63]

Reggie McNeal rightly notes that "Jesus created a learning community," demonstrated by his time with disciples in preparing to send them out, sending them on mission, and debriefing them upon return.[64] Similarly, by establishing a *training cohort* in a local church, pastors and elders lay groundwork for trainees to serve Christ's churches. Involvement in their lives—a sense of belonging and community[65]—leaves the training cohort with a consciousness of support and vision for accomplishing their ministry calling.[66] While ministering together in the larger context of the local church and community, the relationship between the training cohort and pastors/elders interacting together in small group settings, reinforces and hones the trainees just as Jesus did with the Twelve.[67]

So, while encouraging the use of parachurch organizations and theological seminaries for training those preparing to pastor or to do mission work or to plant churches, those organizations stop short in the preparation necessary for

---

63   The plural language of Acts 16:10 may suggest some precedent for trainees participating in elders' meetings, since Paul and Silas, as missionary team leaders, allowed their trainees—Luke, Timothy, and perhaps others involved in their missionary team—to participate in the discussion and seminal decision to take the gospel to Europe.

64   Reggie McNeal, *Practicing Greatness: 7 Disciplines of Extraordinary Spiritual Leaders* (San Francisco,: Josey-Bass, 2006), 68.

65   Hellerman, *When the Church*, 120–143, asserts that Christ's saving work in a person is "a community-creating event" (120). This counters the common "American Christian paradigm that understands salvation to have everything to do with how the individual relates to God and nothing to do with how we relate to one another" (123).

66   McNeal, *Practicing Greatness*, 124.

67   D. Michael Crow, "Multiplying Jesus Mentors: Designing a Reproducible Mentoring System—A Case Study," in *Missiology: An International Review*, 36:1 (January 2008), 92. See also the classic work by A. B. Bruce, *The Training of the Twelve* (Grand Rapids: Kregel, 1971; orig. published 1871), who patiently works through the process that Jesus used to train his disciples. He explains Jesus's training of the Twelve as, "Most formidable, for nothing is harder than to train the human will into loyal subjection to universal principles, to bring men to recognize the claims of the law of love in their mutual relations, to expel pride, ambition, vainglory, and jealousy, and envy from the hearts even of the good" (200). Contemporary pastoral mentors must keep this in mind, so that they do not grow weary in training others.

ministry. They are *specialists* that can offer plenty of help for young ministers. Yet those preparing to serve local churches need *generalists* to hone them toward their future work. A healthy church model, cultivation and mentoring in a community, and influence of faithful pastors and elders gives those preparing for ministry a unique edge in the work before them.

CHAPTER 9

# LEADERS SHAPING LEADERS

A few months into the start of our church, a young man moved to our community to begin theological studies. His home church sent us out to plant a church in Memphis, so we felt a natural bond. Kevin soon became a member of our fellowship. After a couple of years, he seemed to be a good candidate for our first pastoral intern. While my few years of pastoral experience failed to prepare me toward a structured internship, the love that the congregation and I had for Kevin more than compensated for poor plans.

Over the next few years, we did pastoral and evangelistic visits together, prayed together, and discussed Scripture, theology, and ministry. He accompanied me on our church's first and second mission trips. We shared a room on the first, leading to much praying and strategic conversations. Back home, he spent time with my family, so much so that my kids considered him as a big brother. We walked through joys and sorrows, advances and setbacks in our church. We shared life and ministry together. After a few years, my oldest son and I walked to the departure gate at our city's airport to pray for Kevin and send him away to serve as a missionary to Albania, a country that had only recently opened its borders to outsiders.

Twenty-five years later, Kevin remains vitally connected to our congregation and my family. He spent several years in Albania, married a wonderful young lady from Brazil whom I introduced to him on our second trip to that country, welcomed a daughter and a son, and experienced a country emerging from a generation of dictatorship. As Albania struggled, a coup developed, with anarchy on the streets around the clock. I prayed over the phone with him while hearing gunfire in the background. The United States Marines finally evacuated Kevin, his family, and a number of other missionaries.

With friendships that our church had developed in France, after the evacuation they found a respite with a wonderful congregation. A few months later, they returned to Memphis to seek the Lord and to let our congregation love them out of the shock of the warzone they had left in Albania. The Lord pointed them to Brazil and our leadership confirmed the decision, having watched Kevin's steadiness in Christian walk and ministry passion. He planted a church that continues today under national pastoral leadership with a brother that Kevin mentored. For a decade, Kevin and his wife have served with Fiel Ministries that focuses on training pastors and leaders in the Portuguese-speaking world. Kevin's work involves equipping, encouraging, and mentoring pastors.

The footprint of Kevin's relationship to our church, elders, and this pastor that first tried to mentor him, continues today. Through our experience with Kevin, we began to learn the importance of pastors, elders, and congregation partnering together to train those committed to serving Christ and his church. What does that partnership look like?

The Lord God grows his people through the church by those he gifts to preach and teach his Word (Eph. 4:11–16).[1] These gifts focus on teaching and training the entire congregation as learners—disciples—who grow in unity and maturity as one body in Christ.[2] Those preparing to serve Christ's churches need, therefore, to not only prepare to preach and teach but also to regularly receive the Word from those who lead the church. They must become learners if they would exercise teaching gifts for the church.

Tom Schreiner identifies the teaching gift with the "pastors and teachers" of Ephesians 4:11, adding that this gift "does not involve a spontaneous word [e.g., that of the prophet] but rather *an explication of a word already given.*" His point calls for mentors to test and hone the gifts of trainees in the area of teaching so that their trainees might best serve future congregations.[3]

In that setting of hearing, receiving, and interacting on God's Word, those involved in a training cohort begin to develop the foundation necessary toward

---

1 John Calvin, *Institutes of the Christian Religion,* John T. McNeill, ed.; Ford L. Battles, trans. (Philadelphia: Westminster, 1960), 4.1.5; in summary, notes that *the church is essential* as God's appointed means for the process of growth, particularly through being governed by those appointed to teach the Word. See also G. K. Beale, *A New Testament Biblical Theology: The Unfolding of the Old Testament in the New* (Grand Rapids: Baker Academic, 2011), 645–646, who explains that the church's growth and expansion in anticipation of the age to come, takes place "through the church's exercise of its gifts" ( 645).
2 Thomas R. Schreiner, *New Testament Theology: Magnifying God in Christ* (Grand Rapids: Baker Academic, 2008), 720.
3 Ibid., 721, italics added.

their ultimate goal of ministry in churches. As effective *learners* they will better prepare to be leaders, teachers, and preachers. Through this process of learning they must also *unlearn* theology, methodology, and ecclesiastical concepts that prove biblically deficient.[4] Pastors and elders can provide regular challenge to the training cohort's understanding and application of Scripture (see 1 Tim. 4:15–16; 2 Tim. 3:10–17, where Paul called for understanding and application of the Word).[5] Such a training process provides a safety net for the cohort members as they learn, unlearn, and relearn before embarking on their own ministries where mistakes in theology and methodology become more costly.

I've found occasional theological errors in pastoral trainees' sermon notes or even in their presentations. Typically, the errors arose out of bad theology that they heard in conversations. Calling attention to the errors, which have often been met with shocked looks, help to set them on a better theological footing. I've been thankful for those who have done that with me. The same is true, whether in structure or delivery, for sloppiness in sermons or unengaging teaching in Bible studies. They have formed poor habits that need to be unlearned by a firm, loving correction in order to aim them toward more theologically sound and effective communication.

Due to the contemporary tendency to gravitate toward the latest fads in church life, the training cohort needs to see biblical preaching and teaching modeled. Pastors Mark Dever and Paul Alexander correctly explain, "The most important and fundamental role of the pastor is to preach the Gospel clearly. The primacy of preaching will never change, no matter what stage of life the church is in."[6] So, whether planting a new church or revitalizing one that seems to be gasping to

---

4  Reggie McNeal, *Practicing Greatness: 7 Disciplines of Extraordinary Spiritual Leaders* (San Francisco: Jossey-Bass, 2006), 62–63, writes, "Lifelong learning actually means lifelong *unlearning*" (italics original). Huldrych Zwingli made learning and unlearning a regular part of his life. He welcomed correction, stating, "Whoever brings the truth to light, be it even through a calumny of myself, becomes thereby my friend; he enriches, rejoices my soul, and leads her to higher heights of accomplishment," in R. Christoffel, *Zwingli: or The Rise of the Reformation in Switzerland—a Life of the Reformer, with Some Notices of His Time and Contemporaries*, trans. John Cochran (Edinburgh: T & T Clark, 1858), 381.

5  This learning and honing process has effective examples in Zwingli's regular critiquing of his students' sermons in the *Prophezei* and in Calvin and the *Venerable Company's* use of the Saturday afternoon sermons by their protégés; see Timothy George, *Reading Scripture with the Reformers* (Downers Grove, IL: IVP Academic, 2011), 237–241, 248–249; Karin Maag, *Seminary or University? The Genevan Academy and Reformed Higher Education, 1560–1620* (Aldershot, Hants, England: Scolar Press, 1995), 130ff.; Randall C. Zachman, *John Calvin as Teacher, Pastor, and Theologian: The Shape of His Writings and Thought* (Grand Rapids: Baker Academic, 2006), 148ff.

6  Mark Dever and Paul Alexander, *The Deliberate Church: Building Your Ministry on the Gospel* (Wheaton, IL: Crossway, 2005), 89.

survive, faithfully and uncompromisingly preaching God's Word must anchor the pastor's ministry. Rather than effective ministry happening due to the uniqueness of the pastor's leadership skills, it's the Word that changes lives.[7] He may be excused for administrative mistakes or scheduling mixups but he must not let preaching slide or make corporate worship a second-tier part of his ministry (1 Cor. 1:18–25; 2 Cor. 4:1–6; 2 Tim. 4:1–5). Good models of preaching and leading corporate worship help to impress upon those involved in the training cohort to set priority on the ministry of the Word in their future work.[8]

In this chapter we'll consider how the local church develops future pastors and missionaries through investigating the shape of leadership development and then by understanding its dynamic in the life of the training cohort. We will also think about some specific ways that the trainees may be shaped, including the role of formal education.

## THE SHAPE OF LEADERSHIP DEVELOPMENT: WHAT IT LOOKS LIKE

One veteran missionary notes that mentoring others for ministry sometimes fails due to the attitude of those doing the mentoring. "We must be willing to ask ourselves, 'With what attitude do we approach those who are developing in the ministry?'"[9] Gene Daniels explains that "ministry is divine art," and as such "we should pay most careful attention to how we relate to those maturing into ministry." He offers clarification through the use of a helpful metaphor: "We need to see the person with a calling on his or her life as a painting still in the sketch, or a sculpture under construction, rather than raw material to be exploited." Barnabas did this with Saul. Rather than reacting to suppress one more gifted than him in ministry, he encouraged Saul. Paul did the same with Timothy, exposing generations to his nurturing heart in 1 and 2 Timothy. By

---

7  Derek Tidball, *Ministry by the Book: New Testament Patterns for Pastoral Leadership* (Downers Grove, IL: IVP Academic, 2008), 166–167, points out the neglect in recent books on leadership in recognizing the partnership of leadership and preaching in pastoral ministry. "[P]reaching as God's instrument of change and growth in people's lives" should give pastors new confidence in the place of preaching to bring about change in individuals and in the community (167).

8  Dever and Alexander, *Deliberate Church*, 89–91. This practice remains true for seasoned pastors as well. As a example, read or listen to excellent sermons, e.g., Martyn Lloyd-Jones, John Stott, Ligon Duncan, Kent Hughes, Mark Dever, etc. Read the older generation of expositors to see how they preached Christ from every text, e.g., Charles H. Spurgeon, Samuel Davies, Andrew Fuller, Thomas Watson, etc.

9  Gene Daniels, "Receive or Use," EMQonline.com (July 2006): n.p. [cited 8 February 2012], http://www.emisdirect.com/emq/issue-294/1966. "Gene Daniels" is a pseudonym.

contrast, Laban sought to exploit Jacob for his own profit rather than investing in him.[10]

As pastors and elders begin to mentor those in a training cohort, they build unique relationships. Günter Krallmann offers a helpful description of these relationships. "A mentor in the Biblical sense establishes a close relationship with a protégé and on that basis through fellowship, modeling, advice, encouragement, correction, practical assistance and prayer support influences his understudy to gain a deeper comprehension of divine truth, lead a godlier life and render more effective service to God."[11] Although some levels of mentoring may take place through long-distance communication or even through the writings of historical figures,[12] it best takes places through *life-on-life mentoring* (1 Thess. 2:7–8).

Consider how Paul impressed this idea of life-on-life mentoring with the Ephesian elders: "Therefore be on the alert, *remembering* that night and day *for a period of three years* I did not cease to admonish each one with tears. . . . I have coveted no one's silver or gold or clothes. *You yourselves know* that these hands ministered to my own needs and to the men who were with me. *In everything I showed you* that by working hard in this manner you must help the weak and remember the words of the Lord Jesus, that He Himself said, 'It is more blessed to give than to receive'" (Acts 20:31, 33–35; italics added). Paul had no hesitation in reminding the elders of the example that he modeled, and by which they learned the manner of serving the church at Ephesus. The up-close relationship has more lasting impact than mentoring from a distance.[13] While more time consuming and costlier than sending a trainee to a seminar, the life-on-life mentoring involves one more experienced and mature in ministry pouring his life into another who stands on the edge of future ministry. As the mentoring takes place within community, it deepens the lessons practiced and observed in real-life settings—so there's no mentoring in *theory* but in *tangible reality*.

As an example, Australian pastor Colin Marshall outlines a mentoring strategy that he and Philip Jensen developed in New South Wales. They call it "Ministry Training Strategy" and base it on 2 Timothy 2:2, "The things which you have heard

---

10  Ibid., n.p. He cites C.S. Lewis, *An Experiment in Criticism* (Cambridge: Cambridge University Press, 1992), n.p., as supplying the idea for his metaphor.

11  Günter Krallmann, *Mentoring for Mission: A Handbook on Leadership Principles Exemplified by Jesus Christ* (Waynesboro, GA: Gabriel Publishing, 2002), 122. Dave Kraft, *Leaders Who Last* (Wheaton, IL: Crossway, 2010), 41, explains mentoring through a statement he encountered that redirected his life: "Some people come into our lives and quietly go. Others stay awhile, and leave footprints on our hearts, and we are never the same."

12  McNeal, *Practicing Greatness*, 138, writes, some of these mentors "may have been dead for centuries."

13  Kraft, *Leaders*, 129. This practice appears evident in the mentoring models of Jesus and Paul.

from me in the presence of many witnesses, entrust these to faithful men who will be able to teach others also." It is an "apprenticeship in Word ministry" that prepares ministry candidates through a two-year apprenticeship prior to attending seminary or Bible college. Marshall does not advocate a one-size-fits-all approach to "apprenticeship," but rather the mentor and trainee work out a plan that fits the unique needs of the trainee.[14] Marshall wisely counsels, "By far the best and most important thing you can do as a trainer is to be involved in the life and ministry of your apprentice, giving them suggestions on how to do various tasks, teaching them from the Word, encouraging them from what you've been reading in Scripture and giving them feedback on how they are doing."[15] Trainees likely learn more lessons about life and ministry outside a classroom setting through the mentoring relationships.[16]

Trainees also need to receive assignments from their mentors (e.g., that modeled by Jesus and Paul in Luke 9:1–11; 10:1–20; Acts 17:14; 19:22; Titus 3:12). Pastors and elders can involve trainees in various aspects of pastoral ministry, giving them guidance in fulfilling their responsibilities, while offering feedback and critique on their response. They can assign reading related to ecclesiology and pastoral ministry, followed by discussion of the reading in order to clarify and layer a better understanding of life in the local church.

For instance, as I prepare for a new semester with our pastoral trainees, I've proposed that each man select a book from a list that I provided about a particular preacher and then work through a template that I developed for evaluating the preacher's life and ministry. With notable preachers such as John Owen, J. C. Ryle, and Martyn Lloyd-Jones under consideration, each trainee will provide the other trainees a written analysis of his selection. That analysis will serve as a framework for discussion when we gather for our meetings. I will add to it pointed questions that help to synthesize insights that might be applied to the trainees. In this approach, the trainee must analyze material, write in cogent fashion, and then be prepared to lead discussion for the rest of the group. Each skill prepares for future ministry, plus I will be able to press particular characteristics from those we're studying with the training cohort.

Pastoral mentors need to utilize questions with their trainees as Jesus did with his disciples (e.g. Matt. 13:51–52; 16:13–20). He saw questions as "a compelling

---

14  Colin Marshall, *Passing the Baton: A Handbook for Ministry Apprenticeship* (Kingsford, Australia: Matthias Media, 2007), 9–24. He advocates three areas of training: Christian conviction, Christian character, and "competence in doing the work of Christian ministry" (25).

15  Ibid., 55.

16  Mike Nichols, "Teaching Outside the Classroom: The Power of Relationship," EMQonline. com (January 2012): n.p. [cited 8 February 2012], http://www.emisdirect.com/emq/issue-318/2636.

teaching method," according to Craig Parro, forcing the disciples and others to "grapple with issues, moving them from passive listeners to active learners."[17] Although not easy to measure, pastoral mentors must seek to recognize where the grace of God has been at work in their trainees. Questions, involvement, and observation of their protégés provide opportunity to tailor training to best shape them for future ministry.[18] Their training must not be isolated from the congregation's life, since that's where growth in grace will be most evident.

While institutional and conference settings can enlarge trainees' knowledge of Scripture, theology, and methodology, only a *relational approach* to training can give trainees the accountability they need to best prepare for ministry.[19] Paul certainly modeled relationally with Timothy, so that he could write, "Now *you followed* my teaching, conduct, purpose, faith, patience, love, perseverance, persecutions, and sufferings" (2 Tim. 3:10–11; italics added).[20] A trainee may possess superb knowledge of all fields related to his future ministry, yet lack the necessary character and personality traits to lead a congregation. Mentors in a local church setting establish accountability with trainees so that character and personality issues, as well as ministry concepts, may be addressed and honed.[21]

In Acts 16:1–2, Luke indicates that the congregations and their leaders in Lystra and Iconium considered the accountability between them and Timothy to be at such a level that they gladly recommended him to serve with Paul in his missionary work. Here we find a great example of both congregational involvement with trainees and their observation of his life and ministry so that they might send him on mission work. Similarly, by their example, pastoral mentors modeling Christian character and faithful ministry in the local church provide correction and redirection to their pastoral trainees.[22]

---

17 Craig Parro, "Asking Tough Questions: What Really Happens When We Train Leaders," EMQonline.com (January 2012): n.p. [cited 8 February 2012], https://www.emqonline.com/node/2634.

18 Ibid.

19 Tom Julien, "Training Leaders by Planting Seed Truths," EMQonline.com (October 2008): n.p. [cited 8 February 2012], http://www.emisdirect.com/emq/issue-305/2193.

20 BDAG, 767, explains "Now you followed," as conforming one's "belief or practice by paying special attention, *follow faithfully, follow as a rule*" (italics original). So it implies an intensity of observation and attentiveness to learn from and mimic one's mentor.

21 Juha Jones, "Four Ways to Mentor Church Planters," EMQonline.com (October 2008): n.p. [cited 8 February 2012], http://www.emisdirect.com/emq/issue-305/2205. Accountability is found in the closeness of relationships between the pastoral mentor and the training cohort. They learn to live out the gospel together, to learn from each other's examples, to speak into one another's lives, and to engage together in service and ministry.

22 Julien, "Training Leaders," n.p., observes, "Truth that is not watered through personal example remains theoretical."

Praxis is critical before sending trainees to their pastoral work. As Tom Julien explains, "The learning process is not complete until truth is put into practice."[23] This gives mentors the opportunity to trust the work of the Holy Spirit in their protégés just as they have learned to trust the Spirit's enabling in their own ministries (2 Thess. 3:4).[24] We observe Jesus doing this with both the Twelve and the Seventy (Luke 9:1–6; 10:1–20). A. B. Bruce noted that Jesus "sent the twelve on this trial mission, even when they were comparatively unfitted for the work, and notwithstanding the risk of spiritual harm to which it exposed them."[25] He further explains, "But while thus encouraging the young evangelists, Jesus did not allow them to go away with the idea that all things would be pleasant in their experience," a reality that mentors should keep in mind with their protégés.[26] Mentors will profit from studying how Jesus gave his disciples opportunities for *praxis* and then debriefed them afterward, obviously shaping their minds for future mission (Luke 9:10).

While the local church training model offers life-on-life mentoring, closely supervised training assignments, accountability, and praxis, the role of formal education remains vital for those who serve Christ's churches. The rigor of theological education in an academic setting equips future ministers with basic skills in biblical languages, hermeneutics, biblical theology, and church history, all of which will be necessary for developing a healthy church and effective preaching/teaching ministry.[27]

For instance, if a church planter lacks an understanding of church history, he will be deficient in recognizing dangers that have affected the church for centuries. Likewise, if he has little knowledge of biblical theology then his preaching and teaching will be anemic, failing to preach "the whole purpose of God" (Acts 20:27). The expertise afforded ministers by academic rigor deepens their ability to minister long term with their congregations.

As Ben Sawatsky explains, "Paul did not plant churches during weekend evangelistic blitzes! He spent 18 months at Corinth and two to three years at Ephesus."[28] In order to continue that type of ministry, those involved will need a deep well from which to draw in weekly ministry. Substantial theological education helps to develop

---

23  Ibid.
24  Krallmann, *Mentoring for Mission*, 193.
25  A. B. Bruce, *The Training of the Twelve* (Grand Rapids: Kregel, 1971; reprint from 1894 edition), 109.
26  Ibid., 114.
27  Darren Carlson, "The Tension between Reaching and Teaching," EMQonline.com (January 2012): n.p. [cited 8 February 2012], http://www.emisdirect.com/emq/issue-318/2644.
28  Ben Sawatsky, "What it Takes to Be a Church Planter," EMQonline.com (October 1991): n.p. [cited 8 February 2012], http://www.emisdirect.com/emq/issue-139/602. Writing particularly with international missions in view, he insists, "Cross-cultural church planters must be trained to cope with the text of Scripture and the context of culture."

the thinking and research skills necessary toward this end. A combination of academic training with local church training cohorts seems best in preparing aspiring pastors for the depth and breadth of future ministry.[29] It also sharpens study skills and invigorates pastors to continue to read and think, broadly and deeply, having developed the intellectual and spiritual tools toward that continuation.

## THE DYNAMIC IN LEADERSHIP DEVELOPMENT: WHAT TAKES PLACE

The central theme of this book calls for leaders in the local church—pastors and elders—to train their protégés in the context of the local church. That call brings the contemporary concept of mentoring to a different level. Rather than just focusing on the one-on-one relationship that stands at the heart of mentoring—a necessary practice—the mentors and trainees take the journey of mentoring *within the sphere of the local church*. They conduct the mentoring relationship in the midst of the ups and downs, ins and outs of congregational life. They do not shield trainees from the church. In this respect, the entire congregation *adds* to what the mentors seek to accomplish with their pastoral trainees. One need only recall that Paul's description of ministry gifts to the church is given, as well, in the context of the church as a body, with all of the stress and strain of body life as the sphere of exercising ministry gifts (Rom. 12:3–13; 1 Cor. 12:1–31; Eph. 4:7–32).

Consequently, if the mentor/trainee neglects building relationships with others in the church due to being too focused on the mentoring relationship or substitutes the demands of mentoring for participation in corporate worship or neglects serving in the various ministries and outreach of the local church, then the mentorship lacks the necessary qualities to shape those who will serve churches. The mentor needs the church to keep him from seeing his mentorship as the end-all. The trainee needs the church to fill the broader gaps in his life and ministry. The church, according to Paul, is necessary for the mentors and trainees' sanctification, as well as for the rest of the body (Eph. 4:14–16). We "grow together among ourselves," Calvin notes, not apart from the body, so that we might be brought into the unity, love, and fullness for which Christ has redeemed his church.[30]

While citing Paul's description of the church in Ephesians 2:14–22, Joseph Hellerman correctly remarks that "salvation is a community-creating event."[31]

---

29  Julien, "Training Leaders," n.p. See also Matt Rogers, "Holistic Pastoral Training: Partnership Between the Seminary and the Local Church in the United States," (PhD diss.; Southeastern Baptist Theological Seminary.

30  Calvin, *Institutes*, IV.3.2 (p. 1055).

31  Hellerman, *When the Church*, 130–131.

Within this community, growth and maturity take place due to the corporate indwelling and work of the Holy Spirit.[32] Consequently, both mentor and trainee need intense involvement with the local church as the focal point of Jesus Christ's redemptive and restorative work.[33] Apart from such corporate engagement, growth on the part of either will be stunted.

No doubt, corporate involvement likely makes the mentoring process somewhat messy! Rather than a sterile laboratory of learning, the church setting congregates redeemed sinners still wrestling with the effects of indwelling sin. Some struggle with lingering habits, others with quick tempers, and still others with untamed tongues. Plus, no monolithic personality can be found among them. Pastoral mentors need not gloss over such blemishes in the congregation when working with trainees. They will soon face the people-challenges common to pastoral ministry. Instead, training protégés within the framework of the church, with all of its faults, struggles, and weaknesses, takes pastoral training to a new level. Trainees discover through their mentor's faithful pastoral model, how to lovingly conduct ministry as servant-leaders. In an academic setting, professors can relate stories of ministry to their students. But in the local church setting, trainees see these stories up close, often participating in them, while learning firsthand from their mentors' patience, grace under pressure, gentleness, boldness, and integrity in ministry.

In multiple discussions with our church's former pastoral interns, they have consistently expressed appreciation for experiencing the realities of church life during their mentorship. Seeing firsthand matters of conflict, church discipline, doctrinal questions, and other shepherding issues gave them an edge as they stepped into pastoral and missionary roles. Even organizational responsibilities delegated during mentorship better prepared these men with their present responsibilities in ministry.

While agreeing that the key ingredient to mentoring is the connection or relational process, as Daniel Egeler notes,[34] the circle must widen to the congregation. Granted, mentoring relationships need to be narrow in order to develop accountability and transparency. Yet, as Paul Stanley and Robert Clinton explain,

---

32  James G. Samra, *Being Conformed to Christ in Community: A Study of Maturity, Maturation and the Local Church in the Undisputed Pauline Epistles*, LNTS 320; Mark Goodacre, ed. (London: T & T Clark, 2006), 135. Samra notes 1 Corinthians 3:16–17; 5:4; 11:17–34; 12:7; 14:15; and 2 Corinthians 6:16 to validate this assertion.

33  Albert M. Wolters, *Creation Regained: Biblical Basics for a Reformational Worldview*, 2d ed. (Grand Rapids: Eerdmans, 2005), 69–86.

34  Daniel Egeler, *Mentoring Millennials: Shaping the Next Generation* (Colorado Springs: NavPress, 2003), 75.

no one mentor can adequately cover all the bases necessary for a trainee.[35] Although differing in the level of engagement as with mentors, trainees will find the broadening circle of relationships built in the local church to fill the inevitable gaps of any mentor. These wider, Christ-centered relationships in a local congregation, actively seeking to live out the gospel, further hones them as pastors and missionaries.

For example, Mike McKinley's work of revitalizing Guilford Baptist Church (Sterling, VA) and planting other churches was obviously impacted by his mentoring relationship with Mark Dever and the church's elders. However, McKinley notes the influence of the congregation at Capitol Hill Baptist Church (Washington, DC), not just his mentors, in helping to shape his understanding of what a healthy church looks like and how churches are revitalized.[36] Therefore, building relationships within the local church *before* launching a new church or answering a pastoral charge, changes the idealistic perspective that one might embrace by training limited to an academic or conference setting, into a realistic and relational perspective. In this sense, the local church shapes gospel ministers.

Dever explains, "God intends to work on us by His Spirit *through each other.*"[37] The training cohort functioning within the local church builds trust, accountability, and transparency as cohort members prepare for serving churches. Rather than competition with one another as might take place in an academic setting, the training cohort's ongoing relationship in the body of Christ, as well as their regular mentoring relationships, opens a level of discussion and sharpening that prepares for future church leadership.[38]

## CONCLUSION

The church's leadership structure—with pastors and elders—offers a natural framework for mentoring future ministers, particularly as they expose their pastoral trainees to the reality—sometime harsh reality—of church life. As we have noted, the experience of community while being mentored for future ministry, prepares trainees for the multifaceted relationships, with the variety of issues

---

35  Paul D. Stanley and J. Robert Clinton, *Connecting: The Mentoring Relationships You Need to Succeed in Life* (Colorado Springs: NavPress, 1992), 40–45. This statement argues for plural leadership.

36  Mike McKinley, *Church Planting Is for Wimps: How God Uses Messed-Up People to Plant Ordinary Churches That Do Extraordinary Things*, 9Marks Books (Wheaton, IL: Crossway, 2010), 14, 19.

37  Dever, *Nine Marks*, 245; italics added.

38  I was helped in this conclusion by observations from and discussion with Matt Sliger, my colleague in ministry and former pastoral intern.

they will likely face in their work of serving churches. With this church-oriented mentoring, those preparing for ministry will approach their responsibilities with an understanding of where they will lead the congregations that they will one day serve. As they do so, models from the practice of healthy community will inspire perseverance toward the same in the trainees. Additionally, expanding the training cohort's relationships with the broader church family—beyond the mentor—sharpens the edges of relational skills, anchors them in the priority of the local church, and challenges them to build healthy congregations in their own ministries.

# MODELS: ECCLESIOLOGY BOOT CAMP

W hy not just entrust training future pastors and missionaries to seminaries? Seminaries, as we know them today, are a recent phenomenon, coming on the scene in the eighteenth and nineteenth centuries. Prior to the advent of professional ministerial training in seminaries, most pastoral development took place in the local church or in an ecclesiastical setting, such as a monastery. As shown previously, Huldrych Zwingli, John Calvin, and Charles Haddon Spurgeon trained ministers in a collegial setting closely aligned with their churches. In such settings, Capitol Hill Baptist Church (CHBC), Washington, DC, senior pastor Mark Dever explains, the aspiring pastor would be known in the context of a community of believers who could affirm his conversion and testify to his giftedness for ministry. "Raising up [pastoral] leaders is part of the church's commission."[1] In the local church setting, the potential minister experiences a level of learning that comes only through "life-on-life" relationships in community. The local church develops "a 360-degree view of somebody's life," thus recognizing gifts, refining spiritual development, and providing opportunities for ministry with accountability to the congregation.[2]

The pastor, through faithful shepherding and discipling his congregation, is the key to the local church raising up aspiring pastors and missionaries. This training takes place in the context of regular ministry. "And if you don't start with faithful pastoring and discipling, neither internships nor seminaries amount to much,"

---

1 Mark Dever, "Raising Up Pastors Is the Church's Work," *9Marks eJournal*, n.p. [cited 21 September 2011], https://9marks.org/article/raising-pastors-churchs-work/; this is an interview transcript.
2 Ibid.

Dever notes.[3] He encourages pastors to take "the long view" regarding training and mentoring potential pastors in their congregations, noting that it will never be a quick process. The pastor must seek to pour as much of his life and passion into potential ministers as he can, depending on the Lord to eventually shape the men for ministry.[4] Dever has embraced this model.

## THE STRUCTURE FOR TRAINING PASTORS

With the approach to pastoral internships aimed at a "boot camp in ecclesiology," CHBC keeps the structure simple. The church describes its internship as follows: "We simply want to unveil regular, day-to-day ministerial life and provide men aspiring to be pastors with an ecclesiological and pastoral grid for doing the work of ministry."[5] The church does not try to build its ministry on the backs of pastoral interns. Instead, the five-month program hosts five to six men in an intensive time of reading five thousand pages from Puritan through twenty-first century authors. Interns write one hundred reflection papers that respond to the reading and various questions regarding local church ministry. Subjects include church health, the church's nature, the marks of the church, practices of Christian ministry, reformation of the church, the church's mission, polity, elder plurality, evangelism, church membership, church discipline, evangelicalism, mercy ministry, worship, baptism, and Christian doctrine.[6] This leads to discussion on how the church is organized, who leads it, biblical teaching on membership, and how polity affects the way the church functions. The leadership intentionally aims to engage the interns in conversations "with great pastors and theologians from the past," who demonstrate that the "church is the main sounding board of the gospel."[7] This past-to-present analysis of the church builds a strong ecclesiological foundation for the pastoral interns.

Dever and the entire pastoral staff spend three hours each Thursday morning leading a discussion through the issues raised in the interns' papers. Additionally, the pastoral interns are required to attend staff and elders meetings, church

---

3  Mark Dever, "How Do Pastors Raise Up Pastors?" *9Marks eJournal*, n.p. [cited 21 September 2011], http://www.9marks.org/ejournal/how-do-pastors-raise-pastors; this is an interview transcript.

4  Ibid.

5  "Capitol Hill Baptist Church: Internship Full Description," n.p. [cited 14 September 2011], http://www.capitolhillbaptist.org/internship-full-description.

6  "Fall 2011 Pastoral Intern," August 5–December 15, 2011, Washington, DC: CHBC, 2011. By my count, 28 books of varying length are required for the semester, along with more than twenty articles, essays, and ejournal posts.

7  "Capitol Hill Baptist Church: Internship Full Description," n.p.

services, prayer times, intern meetings, sermon reviews, weddings, funerals, and mentoring meetings. They also volunteer for administrative work in the children's ministry and church office. They learn about small groups by participating as members of the church. Interns also travel with Dever on various speaking engagements, adding another layer of interaction in the broader Christian community.[8] Matt Schmucker, former CHBC administrator and elder, compares this approach as "something akin to a teaching hospital for a medical student." They mentor by giving the interns a good picture of what it means to serve as a pastor, particularly in an urban setting.[9]

The initial five-month internship does not include times to teach or preach. That is reserved for those who serve as pastors. Interns are required to schedule lunch meetings with church leadership and with old and new members at CHBC to interact about the church's history and life.[10] Housing and a small stipend are provided to assist the interns to focus their entire attention to the five months of boot camp ecclesiology.[11]

## MENTORING FOR CHURCH MINISTRY

The pastoral internship sets the goal for trainees to live in two worlds: first, in the richness of former generations' understanding of ecclesiology; and second, in the present urban setting that seeks to work out biblical principles for the church.

Observation, discussion, and mentoring, according to associate pastor Jamie Dunlop, are the primary components of the internship. Through *observation* at elders meetings, funerals, weddings, staff meetings, luncheons with leaders and members, pastoral interns "get a more personal, one-on-one understanding and interpretation of what is going on in the church." Often, observation gives them a framework for future contexts of ministry. *Discussion* takes place in formal settings with Pastor Dever, but also in casual settings with elders, staff, and fellow interns.[12]

One of the strongest portions of the internship involves *mentoring* by a pastor or pastoral assistant. Inevitably, the pastoral interns bring with them the realization of past mistakes in ministry and the unsettling reality that they have adopted unbiblical models for ministry. Through accountability and involvement in the lives of the interns, the mentors seek to offer counsel and friendship that carries

---

8  Ibid.
9  Matt Schmucker, "Evaluation of Training Church Planters and Revitalizers," 29 August 2011.
10  Ibid.
11  Brad Wheeler, "Internships," n.p. [cited: 14 September 2011], http://www.capitalhillbaptist. org/we-provide/internships/.
12  Jamie Dunlop, "Evaluation of Training Church Planters and Revitalizers," 8 September 2011.

beyond the five-month internship. Those involved in mentoring have themselves been mentored over many years in ministry.[13]

In addition to the Thursday morning discussions, Dever meets regularly with the interns for Sunday night sermon/service reviews. Adding to this, "He has the interns 'live' in his study whenever possible," according to Schmucker. "He is intimately involved in evaluation and selection of each intern. Mark really takes a personal interest and has a working knowledge of each man which aids his evaluation of future placement."[14] The fruit of this involvement shows up in those sent out by CHBC for church planting, revitalization, and mission work.[15] The mentoring relationships allow the leadership to identify men that interact well with God's Word and with the leaders, indicating good potential for future service. At times they are able to recommend these men to other churches or to send them out to serve with the CHBC's support.[16]

## DETAILS OF TRAINING

Although interns have no opportunity to teach or preach, they spend time observing and interacting on biblical exposition. Under Dever's influence, former trainees responsible for pulpit ministry have given evidence of strong commitment to expository preaching.[17] They follow Dever's call for a threefold application grid in preaching: "preach to the ignorant, the doubtful, and sinners."[18] He demonstrates how the pastor can make application to three different strugglers from the same text. This calls for being just as excited over the indicative statements in Scripture as the imperatives. It also demands arguing for the truthfulness of Scripture while pressing the urgency of believing its message. His application challenge further points "people to a life of holiness that will reflect the holiness of God himself." Dever concludes, "The main message that we need to apply every time we preach is the gospel." The preacher applies the gospel to himself as he applies himself to the work of biblical preaching.[19] Dever's

---

13  Dunlop, "Evaluation of Training."

14  Schmucker, "Evaluation of Training."

15  As an example, see the story of Mike McKinley, *Church Planting Is for Wimps—How God Uses Messed-Up People to Plant Ordinary Churches That Do Extraordinary Things*, 9Marks Books (Wheaton, IL: Crossway, 2010), as he traces CHBC and Dever's involvement in the process of his ministry. See also Capitol Hill Baptist Church, "Where Are They Now?" n.p. [cited 14 September 2011], http://www.capitolhillbaptist.org/we-provide/internships/where-are-they-now/.

16  Schmucker, "Evaluation of Training."

17  McKinley, "Evaluation for Church Planters," 24 August 2011.

18  Mark Dever, "Preach to the Ignorant, the Doubtful, and Sinners," *9Marks eJournal*, n.p. [cited 21 September 2011], http://www.9marks.org/ejournal/preach-ignorant-doubtful-and-sinners.

19  Ibid.

philosophy agrees with the major Reformers that the first mark of the church is expositional preaching.[20]

Despite the pastoral internship's lack of extensive teaching on preaching, it does take place. First, it is modeled by Dever and others preaching from the CHBC pulpit. Second, trainees participate in the weekly Sunday night sermon review. Staff and interns interact on every detail of the day's services: preaching, music selections, prayers, baptismal testimonies, and even announcements. So while they are not preaching, they are hearing and participating in detailed critiques. Schmucker notes, "We want our people to learn to receive godly encouragement and criticism." The sermon review models and serves as an indirect teaching tool for preaching.[21]

As might be expected, over the years of training men for pastoral ministry, the curriculum regularly goes through refinement. The focus in Mike McKinley's training in 2004 was more refined than material utilized with Aaron Menikoff in the mid-1990s.[22] Consequently, McKinley points to little direct training in evangelism/disciplemaking while stating that it was divided rather equally between pastoral work, church planting, church revitalization, and polity.[23] On the other hand, Menikoff, now pastoring outside Atlanta, stated that little was done on church planting but much on evangelism and disciplemaking.[24] California pastor Jeremy Yong points out that despite lack of curricula on subjects of international mission, church planting, evangelism/disciplemaking, and church revitalization, the subjects were regularly discussed in elders meetings and in other settings. He indicated heavy exposure to each of these areas even without specific curricula designed for the trainees.[25]

Former intern Harshit Singh from Lucknow, India, found that the training had been carefully thought through and that the breadth of church life was learned, not just from reading and discussing the church, but also by sitting and observing life at CHBC.[26] When asked about the level of evangelism and disciplemaking-disciplemaking training in the current model, Singh observed that there is talk about evangelism and discipleship, but "the most important thing is the *culture*

---

20   Mark Dever, *Nine Marks of a Healthy Church,* new exp. ed. (Wheaton, IL: Crossway, 2004), 36–55. See the discussion of Paul D. L. Avis, *The Church in the Theology of the Reformers* (Eugene, OR: Wipf & Stock, 1981, 2002), 2–3, 6, 8–9, et al.

21   Matt Schmucker, interview with the author, Washington, DC, 4 October 2011.

22   Schmucker interview.

23   McKinley, "Evaluation for Church Planters."

24   Menikoff, "Evaluation for Church Planters," 8 September 2011.

25   Yong, "Evaluation for Church Planters," 16 September 2011.

26   Harshit Singh, interview with the author, Washington, DC, 4 October 2011.

*of discipleship* found in the congregation rather than [simply] in the staff." Instead of expecting the staff to do the evangelizing or even all the leadership in this area, he stated, "There is a pervasive influence of discipleship among the members." He indicated that a visitor off the street to a CHBC service would likely receive an invitation to meet for coffee or lunch where intentional disciplemaking takes place. He experienced this personally before the congregation knew he was present to participate in an internship. He commented on the remarkable consciousness in the congregation's DNA to engage others in the gospel.[27] That DNA rubs off on the trainees.

## PREPARATION FOR CHURCH PLANTING AND REVITALIZATION

Although the CHBC internship program is not solely designed for training men to plant and revitalize churches, much focus leans intentionally in that direction. McKinley, who is heavily involved in church planting, stated that training at CHBC, "gave us the vision for the local church as the Great Commission strategy. Therefore, more churches = more evangelism."[28] His fascinating book, *Church Planting Is for Wimps*, narrates the journey he took from his punk-rock persona to a member at CHBC under Mark Dever and Matt Schmucker's shepherding, to planting Guilford Baptist Church in Sterling, Virginia. Dever's revitalization work at CHBC sparked McKinley's love for the church.[29] When the Guilford Church called him, he followed Dever's counsel to "do everything you can to preach excellent sermons," contending that this priority will put everything else in its place.[30] As the dying church began to revitalize, they adopted CHBC's constitution, cleaned up the church rolls of the failed Guilford Fellowship, practiced church discipline, and maintained an atmosphere of disciplemaking.[31] McKinley's understanding of church membership and the way that he has shaped it in his own church planting involvement clearly bears the influence of his CHBC training.[32]

---

27   Ibid., italics added.
28   McKinley, "Evaluation for Church Planters."
29   McKinley, *Church Planting Is for Wimps*, 13–14. He explains that Guilford Fellowship Church in Sterling, Virginia had died down to twelve active members. Seven CHBC members went with him to restart as Guilford Baptist Church. His book combines an insightful look at both church planting and revitalization since his experience, technically, included both.
30   Ibid., 51.
31   Ibid., 55–71; also McKinley, "Evaluation for Church Planters."
32   Michael McKinley, "Implementing Membership in a Church Plant," *9Marks eJournal*, n.p. [cited 21 September 2011], https://9marks.org/article/journalimplementing-membership-church-plant/. He explains the benefits of church membership in a church planting set-

Aaron Menikoff continues the CHBC discipling culture by instilling it in his suburban Atlanta church revitalization. He participated in multiple evangelism training classes while at CHBC and watched Dever evangelize using *Christianity Explained* as a tool.[33] Menikoff embraces the same approach. He found "the heart for evangelism . . . so large" at CHBC, that he "sought to fold personal evangelism into [his] life."[34] That's why he can call evangelism his church's "central task." He follows Dever's lead in his preaching ministry, by preaching the gospel in every sermon.[35]

Trainees from the varying geographical regions represented in my research of CHBC's pastoral internship, found the principles taught and modeled there to be transferable in their unique settings. None expressed the idea of trying to clone CHBC but each bears something of the church's DNA in their philosophy and practice.

## PRÉCIS OF THE CAPITOL HILL BAPTIST CHURCH TRAINING MODEL

For other churches to utilize the same training process as CHBC, requires taking a look at the critical facets of their training model. Obviously, their unique urban setting, gifted pastor and staff, and demographics cannot be cloned. Yet, despite the differences in the Washington setting compared with Memphis or Atlanta or Denver, they offer a useful framework for modeling ministry and training pastors to plant and revitalize churches. The following observations identify areas that other churches may be able to practice in learning from the CHBC model.

First, *this model calls for strong pastoral leadership and commitment to invest in training others.* Dever models this by the significant time that he puts into mentoring the trainees.[36]

Second, *this model calls for strong church support.* The pastoral training process is not simply Dever's work. The entire church engages the trainees, having them in their homes for meals, folding them into their small groups, and praying for their future ministries. The church also provides a stipend and housing for the interns.

---

ting as, "membership calls attenders to ramp up their commitment . . . membership increases accountability . . . membership enables the church to fulfill its biblical responsibilities."

33  See the *Christianity Explained* website, n.p. [cited 16 February 2013], http://www.christianity-explained.com/.

34  Menikoff, "Evaluation for Church Planters."

35  Aaron Menikoff, "Preach to the Non-Christian, Christian, and Church Member," *9Marks eJournal*, n.p. [cited 21 September 2011], http://www.9marks.org/ejournal/preach-non-christian-christian-and-church-member.

36  Schmucker, "Evaluation of Training."

Third, *this model calls for a healthy congregation that seeks to apply the gospel in their lives and make the gospel known in their community*. Trainees reported that they observed the church taking the gospel seriously in every part of their lives. Singh explained that the "CHBC DNA" had impacted him.[37]

Fourth, *this model calls for concentration on ecclesiology*. While one might wish for other subjects to be addressed in the internship, ecclesiology intersects with most everything that the local church does: its worship, membership, leadership, outreach, mission, and service.

Fifth, *this model calls for observation and shadowing*. When interviewed, Schmucker used the term "shadowing," explaining that the trainees *shadow* Dever and other elders in their ministries, so that they learn by observing the practice of healthy church ministry.[38]

Sixth, *this model calls for personal mentoring of trainees by pastor, staff, and elders*. Everyone is involved, might be the best way to put it. Mentoring trainees must not be left only to the senior pastor. The rich diversity in ministry experience becomes fuller for trainees when the broad range of those involved in church leadership invest in their lives. In numerous conversations with former interns now serving in pastoral ministry around the country and outside of the US, they spoke of an elder or staff member at CHBC who greatly influenced their present ministries.

Seventh, *this model calls for maintaining an ongoing investment in those sent out by the church*. Not every trainee ends up being a missionary, church planter, or church revitalizer sent out by CHBC, but some do. The congregation continues to pray for these pastors and missionaries, as well as others who have gone through the internship and returned to their ministries. Schmucker noted that there has been an increase in internationals applying for the training, with the result that CHBC's model is being contextualized and replicated indigenously. The church continues to pray for and encourage this kind of work.[39]

## CONCLUSION

The focus on *boot camp ecclesiology*, while seemingly narrow, may actually be wider than it appears, particularly when it is fleshed out in the context of a healthy congregation. Seeing the gospel lived out in a congregation, and observing a passion to disciple others in the Christian faith, makes a study of ecclesiol-

---

37  Singh interview.
38  Schmucker interview.
39  Ibid.

ogy more than an academic exercise. In this kind of setting, pastoral trainees at
CHBC learn theology and practice, structure and method, while experiencing it
in the life of the church.

Were Dever to transfer his teaching material to a seminary setting without
the benefit of trainees observing the practice of ecclesiology in a healthy congregation, it would be useful but have far less impact, appearing only theoretical.
Instead, each trainee that I communicated with expressed the profound way that
the congregation modeled the lessons learned through reading, discussion, and
writing. In this kind of setting, aspiring pastors catch a glimpse of what a healthy
church looks like, what it values, and how it applies the gospel to the breadth of
life. It gives him a living picture of what to aim for in his pastoral work. While
he should allow the personality of his congregation to develop, he can inculcate
some aspects of the CHBC ministry culture into his own setting.

Those facing the daunting challenge of missions, church planting, or church
revitalization *need* not only careful biblical/theological study but also transferable
models, to guide them in plans and decisions in the years ahead. The Capitol Hill
Baptist Church pastoral internship offers such a model and opportunity for future
pastors to hone their understanding of local church life and practice. As Aaron
Menikoff remarked, "Even where I do things differently, CHBC is always a sense
of benchmark."[40] And as such, he, along with dozens of other young ministers,
find the "benchmark" as a providential means to stay on course in planting and
serving churches.

---

40   Menikoff, "Evaluation for Church Planters."

# CHAPTER 11

# MODELS:
# A SENDING CHURCH

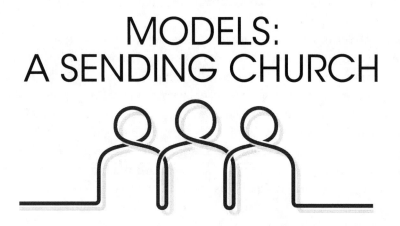

Most churches try to keep their members. The Summit Church in Raleigh-Durham, North Carolina intentionally tries to send members away. With the goal to plant one thousand churches in the next forty years, the church leadership understands the necessity of training and deploying large numbers of their membership throughout the world.[1] The church has launched an equipping arm, the Sam James Institute, to train and mobilize its members for mission.[2] On a regular basis, the church announces missions and church planting opportunities, inviting Summit members to "consider relocating their lives and jobs for at least two years to live and work in a strategic city that desperately needs the gospel."[3] And members are responding! In 2016–2017, Summit anticipates sending out 225 people to plant churches in strategic cities in North America and internationally.[4] Training and sending are woven into the Summit DNA.

More than a dozen years ago, that was not the case with Summit Church, which for forty years had been called Homestead Heights Baptist Church. Plateaued and even declining, in 2002 the church called J. D. Greear to serve as its senior pastor. Greear followed a pastor removed due to immorality, another that attempted to impose a Willow Creek church model,[5] and a third who was a theological moder-

1 J. D. Greear, "A Pastor Defends His Multi-Site Church," in *9Marks e-Journal*, n.p. [cited 12 February 2013], www.9marks.org/journal/pastor-defends-his-multi-site-church.
2 "The Sam James Institute," n.p. [cited 13 June 2016], sji.summitrdu.com.
3 Mike McDaniel, "Church Planting Interest Meeting" (31 January 2013), n.p. [cited 12 Feb. 2013], www.summitrdu.onthecity.org/plaza/events/8b4aad4c6a634aa48a336d27226e20304085ed8c.
4 "About: The Summit Church," n.p. [cited 6 June 2016], http://www.summitrdu.com/multiply/about.
5 See G. A. Pritchard, *Willow Creek Seeker Services: Evaluating a New Way of Doing Church*

ate. With revitalization as his first order of business, Greear focused on preaching the gospel rather than establishing a new program or model for the church. The gospel would be the central focus of the church's preaching, teaching, worship, and ministries. A new love for unbelievers led to change in church structures. Greear sought to develop a "sending culture," which affected the congregation's generosity and its desire to reach its own city.[6] By sending culture, he implies, "Sending means giving away some of your best leaders and letting go of resources. It means giving away opportunities in the kingdom, and watching others get credit for successes that you could easily have obtained for yourself."[7] With the church embracing a sending culture, Greear began to focus on training and deploying leaders.

## A SENDING CULTURE

"We're a sending church; it's part of our DNA," Curt Alan, missions pastor at The Summit Church, told me. He explained that the sending culture starts with the senior pastor and works it way down through the leadership to the congregation.[8] Examples of members embracing the sending culture abound.

Trevor Atwood, trained at The Summit Church, planted City Church in Murfreesboro, Tennessee in 2011, with twenty-four Summit members as the planting team. He had no intention of planting a church when he moved to the Raleigh-Durham area in 2006. His testimony reveals the way that the sending culture permeating the congregation impacted him. "God used The Summit Church to spark a desire to plant and to equip me to do it."[9] He heard testimonies by church planters and of how the Lord worked to transform those under their ministry. As the leadership team invested in training him, they also began to affirm his gifts of leadership and preaching.[10] He explained that Summit shaped his life and ministry by refocusing his attention on the centrality of the gospel. As the church's leadership had invested in him, he learned to do the same with others.[11]

---

(Grand Rapids: Baker, 1995), for details on the Willow Creek model. See Greg L. Hawkins and Sally Parkinson, *Reveal: Where Are You?* (South Barrington, IL: Willow Creek Association, 2007), for their inside critique of the spirituality in the Willow Creek model.

6 J. D. Greear, "Five Factors That Brought Life to a Dying Church," in *9Marks e-Journal*, n.p. [cited 12 February 2013], www.9marks.org/journal/five-factors-brought-life-dying-church. See also "Pastor J. D. Greear," The Summit Church, n.p. [cited 12 February 2013], www.summitrdu.com/about/pastor-j-d-greear.

7 J. D. Greear, *Gaining by Losing: Why the Future Belongs to Churches That Send* (Grand Rapids: Zondervan, 2015), 45.

8 Curt Alan, private conversation with author, 12 June 2012, at The Summit Church, Durham, NC.

9 "Meet a Church Planter: Trevor Atwood—City Church," *SendRDU* (17 May 2011), n.p. [cited 12 February 2013], www.sendrdu.com/blog/page/11.

10 Ibid.

11 Trevor Atwood, "Evaluation for Church Planters and Revitalizers," 12 October 2012.

In 2013, a Summit Church plant took root in Baltimore, Maryland, called Redeemer City Church. The church planter, Brad O'Brien, joined the Summit pastoral staff in 2003. He served as a college pastor, missions pastor, and campus pastor for one of the multi-site locations.[12] He had no intention of planting a church because he so much enjoyed his ministry at Summit. But his role shifted after nine years on staff when he was accepted in the church planter residency program at Summit in 2012.[13] After establishing his church in Baltimore, the congregation began using an older, established church's facility. Their relationship went so well that it led to the merger of the two congregations into one church in 2014, now called Jesus Our Redeemer Church.[14] Ironically, as a church planter resident, Brad was under supervision of Mike McDaniel, a staff member for whom he had been supervisor during his time as missions pastor. He expressed how positive the experience has been to learn from McDaniel's perspective.[15]

## EQUIPPING LEADERS TO PLANT
## AND REVITALIZE CHURCHES

To say that Summit is intentional in equipping leaders is an understatement. The church strategically trains its members at seemingly every level, whether they will plant churches or not. Greear affirms, "The Great Commission is not a calling for some; it is a mandate for all."[16] There are three arms to Summit's Sam James Institute: equipping believers, developing leaders, and engaging culture. Through the "equipping believers" arm, members can participate in discipleship classes and monthly forums. Forums address the broad spectrum of spiritual formation, gospel-centered living, evangelism, missions, leadership, family, etc. Discipleship classes offer hands-on training in these areas. The leaders consider these to be a serious time of discipling a large segment of the congregation and developing potential church planters and missionaries, as well as leaders on their multi-site campuses. Participants can be found at all stages of life, e.g., college students, seminarians, career people, etc.[17]

The "developing leaders" arm of Sam James equips members of the church to be leaders, "ministers" and pastors. This includes not only future missionaries and church planters but also lay "ministers." For those sensing a call to vocational

---

12   Brad O'Brien, "Evaluation for Church Planters and Revitalizers," 12 October 2012.
13   Ibid. See also SendRDU, "Our Next Church Plant" (16 April 2012), n.p. [cited 12 February 2013]: n.p. Online: www.sendrdu.com/blog/page/3/.
14   "Jesus Our Redeemer: Staff," n.p. [cited 6 June 2016], www.jesusourredeemer.com/#!staff/npgl7.
15   Ibid.
16   Greear, *Gaining by Losing*, 80.
17   Ibid.

ministry, Summit offers a one-year internship followed by a two-year apprenticeship. The initial study of ecclesiology, leadership, and other subjects related to church planting in these programs sets the stage for two major developments. First, it brings to the surface potential leaders that might serve in pastoral staff positions in one of the multi-site campuses or in the general leadership. Second, it allows the staff to discover potential church planters who might be moved toward planting a future congregation.[18] Future international church planters are directed toward an international church planting cohort, where they will be equipped by former and current missionaries to be part of a church planting team overseas. Domestic planters are invited to participate in one of the most intensive phases of leadership training at the The Summit Church: the church planting residency.

Mike McDaniel, who heads up the church planting residency, describes it as a one-part leadership finishing school, one-part church planting incubator, and one-part training in Gospel DNA.[19] Whereas everything prior to this point has been designed to develop lead pastors, residency focuses on training pastors to be planters. While they do accept people from the outside, Summit's primary goal is to raise up as many planters internally as possible. It's not uncommon for residents to spend several years on staff prior to residency. O'Brien spent nine years on staff before entering the residency program, Andrew Hopper spent four years, and Atwood three years before admission.[20] Each held strategic positions in leadership so that the church leaders might affirm their gifts and abilities to lead a new congregation.

The church planting residency accepts only as many potential church planters as Summit's leadership intends to start new churches. McDaniel identifies six reasons for the residency program. First, church planting is hard. Many church planters fail due to inadequate spiritual preparation, deficient training, and unrealistic expectations. While a number of church planting networks provide assessment tools to help sponsoring churches determine a planter's potential to persevere in the new work, the residency gives the Summit leadership the opportunity to observe the potential planter for nine months while "speaking into his life, his marriage, and his ministry." McDaniel adds, "*The best assessment tool we have for church planting is the local church.*"[21] In other words, rather than a some-

---

18  Ibid.

19  "Plant: We Equip Leaders to Plant Churches" [cited 13 June 2016], thesummitnetwork.com/#plant.

20  O'Brien, "Evaluation"; Andrew Hopper, "Evaluation for Church Planters and Revitalizers," 12 October 2012; Atwood, "Evaluation."

21  Mike McDaniel, "Why You Should Do a Church Planting Residency," SendRDU (6 February 2012), n.p. [cited 12 February 2013], www.sendrdu.com/blog/page/5. Italics original.

what sterile academic atmosphere for learning the gamut of church planting, the Summit residents engage in the full spectrum of church life.

Second, training takes place in gospel community rather than in isolation. "The best place to learn how to plant healthy churches," McDaniel notes, "is in a healthy church." He correctly remarks that some plant churches because they know what they do not want in a church while never having experienced a healthy church as a model to direct their leadership decisions.[22] Consequently, they may approach church planting somewhat blindly rather than intentionally. Third, those who have planted churches provide the coaching for the residents, speaking candidly of their successes and failures, so that the residents learn from the experiences of those who have preceded them. Church planters learn to value mentoring relationships that prepare them for the array of unknowns they will face in the planting process.

Fourth, due to the expense of church planting, residents receive training in fund raising, with allowances given while they travel to raise needed funding. The Summit Church also provides substantial resources to underwrite the church planting expenses. Fifth, McDaniel explains that residents are given "a hunting license on the church to recruit whoever they can get to go" with them in the church start.[23] Residents are allowed to assess and train their own teams to make sure that each volunteer shows signs of fitting well into the fabric of the team and adaptable to the context of the plant's location. This allays future problems with those who may lack the spiritual maturity, adaptability, and stamina to work through the planting process.[24] It also mobilizes more of the church to be involved in church planting. Summit sees its church planting teams as bands of missionary disciples grouped with a church planting pastor. Finally, the residency provides an ongoing relationship to The Summit Church and its leadership, as they seek to support the planter in the sometime lonely work of church planting.[25]

As part of the internship and apprenticeship programs, Summit has established a pulpit supply ministry for local churches. This ministry provides opportunities for those being trained to pastor and plant churches to gain more experience in preaching before being sent out by The Summit Church. Summit leadership invites pastors requesting pulpit supply to take the time to offer feedback on the sermon in lieu of an honorarium.[26] Each preacher sent out has demonstrated preaching

---

22  McDaniel, "Why You Should."
23  Ibid.
24  Mike McDaniel, private conversation, 12 June 2012; Summit Church, Durham, NC.
25  McDaniel, "Why You Should."
26  Mike McDaniel, "Preachers, Do You Need a Week Off?" (16 December 2012), n.p. [cited 12 February 2012], www.sendrdu.com/blog/page/2.

abilities through basic and advanced level preaching laboratories conducted by their mentors.[27]

What Summit does on the weekend provides guidance and plants seeds which lead to the intensive church planting residency. The specifics of the residency offer a good insight into the areas that Summit leadership values for training church planters.

## TRAINING THE RESIDENTS TO PLANT CHURCHES

While other training environments may be much bigger, the residency is typically limited to five to seven people. Those admitted to the residency have come out of various leadership roles at the church or other churches.[28] The basic curriculum for the residency is broken down into three phases: preparing the leader and the vision, gathering a team and resources, and developing strategies and systems. Residents read broadly from a variety of sources, including *Center Church* by Timothy Keller and the *Redeemer Church Planting Manual.*[29] The books specifically target church planting in an urban setting, written as a tool to aid those trained at Keller's Redeemer City to City, who seek to plant churches in metropolitan New York.[30] In the manual, Keller first tells his inspiring story of planting Redeemer Presbyterian Church.[31] It serves as a remarkable model for those intending to plant in an urban region. After setting forth a biblical rationale for church planting in the city, the book thoroughly examines the need for understanding the context of the church plant, followed by assessing the potential church planter's gifts to labor for Christ's kingdom in the city.[32] The balance of the book explores what it means to be a servant leader planting in an urban context, with numerous examples of how to develop a core group, leadership team, and reaching the community. Since a number of Summit's international and North American church plants are located in strategic urban centers, this church planting manual seems to be the most appropriate tool for preparation.

In addition to *Center Church* and the *Church Planting Manual*, residents read numerous authors dealing with multiple subjects for church planting and pastoral ministry, e.g., leadership, self-awareness, ecclesiology, church planting, urban ministry, mercy ministries, cultural contexts, preaching, and the gospel.

---

27  McDaniel, private conversation.
28  Ibid.
29  Timothy J. Keller, *Center Church: Doing Balanced, Gospel-Centered Ministry in Your City.* (Grand Rapids: Zondevan, 2012); Timothy J. Keller and J. Allen Thompson, *Redeemer Church Planting Manual* (New York: Redeemer Church Planting Center, 2002).
30  Keller and Thompson, *Church Planting Manual*, 24.
31  Ibid., 7–20.
32  Ibid., 27–71.

Discussion of the books with McDaniel and other leaders help to bring application to the residents' future church plants.[33]

Each former resident interviewed about his training pointed to McDaniel as the primary mentor during the residency. However, each had also been personally discipled by Greear while serving in a church staff position but had less direct mentoring contact with him during the residency. Greear shaped their understanding of gospel application to life, ministry, and preaching. Weekly meetings with McDaniel and other mentors honed their roles as church planters, coached them through everything they encounter preparing to plant, and kept them on pace to launch the new churches.[34] The team approach to mentoring by the Summit leadership appears evident in the residents.

The influence of the church permeates the training process. Rather than isolate the residents, the Summit leadership involves them in multiple church ministries. The leaders see this involvement as more important than the training times since the leaders receive feedback on the gifts, abilities, and character of the residents as they serve the congregation.[35] This practice highlights the value of the local church as the focal point of training church planters over training in an academic setting. In the actual experience of church life, the residents are tested and shaped for their future role as church planters. Training becomes more than theory. The residents see it as reality.

In the case with Summit's church planting residency, involvement in the varied church ministries by the residents allow them the opportunity to scout for potential team members. It also gives potential team members a realistic setting to evaluate the leadership skills and pastoral abilities of the church planter before joining the team. Such an arrangement bonds the team members and the resident church planter before they relocate to another city or country to plant a new congregation.

## PRÉCIS OF THE SUMMIT CHURCH'S
## LEADERSHIP TRAINING MODEL

First, *this model has strong support by the congregation, including financial support during the church planting residency and with the new church plant.* Residents are able to devote their full energies to preparation for planting a new church.

Second, *this model intentionally plans to launch a church plant with members from The Summit Church.* Residents are allowed to "go hunting" for prospective team members and are encouraged to train them prior to the church launch.

---

33  O'Brien, "Evaluation"; Atwood, "Evaluation"; Hopper, "Evaluation."
34  Ibid.
35  McDaniel, private conversation.

Third, *this model intensively studies church planting and pastoral ministry, with less attention to other areas of ministry.* Since the trainees must have a master of divinity degree before starting a residency, many of the broader subjects in Christian ministry have been covered in seminary classes.

Fourth, *this model puts the pastor of church planting as the primary mentor for the trainees, rather than the senior pastor.* He devotes full-time energies to the training and preparation for new churches. For smaller congregations, the senior pastor, partnered with other leaders, would assume this role.

Fifth, *this model gives trainees intentional assignments with various Summit ministries and assesses the trainees in order to mentor toward improvement in ministry.*

## CONCLUSION

Summit did not wait to become a megachurch before developing leadership training. By embracing a sending church mentality, training became a regular part of church life early on. The years of investing in their members so that they might send them into ministry has sharpened the church's ability to train leaders. The size of the church has allowed them to devote specific staff members to train leaders to plant churches. While the process used in the church planting residency is not designed to mass produce church planters, it does provide superb preparation for the planters and their teams as the church sends them to begin new congregations. Greear emphasizes the long-term multiplication of leaders and new churches rather than rapid addition for immediate gratification.[36]

The Summit church planting residency also serves as a replicable model for smaller churches who are willing to invest time and resources into training church planters, missionaries, or church revitalizers. Sometime that is best done by banding with other congregations to do training together. Summit's Denver church plant has done so with two other churches. In other settings, the pastor and staff members or church elders might share the mentoring of potential ministers, keeping in mind that their involvement in the church's ministry provides the best preparation for future pastoral work.

The sending church DNA necessitates leadership development. The Summit Church has risen to the challenge to equip their members for diversity of ministry by its Sam James Institute.[37]

---

36  Greear, *Gaining by Losing*, 31–35.
37  I am grateful for Mike McDaniel's assistance with the details in this chapter.

CHAPTER 12

# MODELS: FACE-TO-FACE

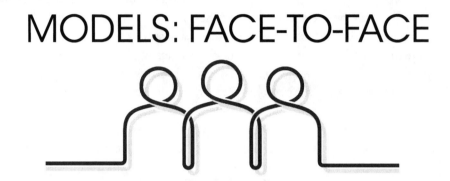

A small group gathered in 1992 to pray and discuss planting a new church in Nashville, a city known for its variety of churches. Out of this time of prayer, Bible study, and vision meetings, Grace Community Church (GCC) began in January 1993, with Nashville native Scott Patty serving as the first pastor. From the small beginnings, GCC has steadily grown in number, depth, and ministry, with three services each Sunday morning, multiple community and small groups meeting across Nashville throughout the week, and an array of evangelistic and mercy ministries in the community and beyond.[1] Patty continues to serve as senior pastor, seeking to teach the Scripture and instill "a biblical vision for all of life" through expositional preaching.[2]

Jamie Mosley served on the GCC pastoral staff as director of church ministries and administration (May 2005–December 2008) and director of church ministries (January 2009–July 2010). During the latter phase of his pastoral work at GCC, Mosley began the process for planting a new church about thirty minutes away from GCC in Hendersonville. After submitting a proposal to the elders at GCC for their affirmation and leadership support, the elders and congregation sent Mosley and two other leaders to serve as the initial leadership team. He recognized that the months leading up to his church launch would be critical, as he sought to hone his pastoral skills through Patty's and the elders' direction.[3] He learned about the details of pastoral ministry by "walking with Scott Patty for five years," followed by weekly meetings with Patty and another church planter in 2009–2010,

---

1 "History," n.p. [cited 12 February 2013], www.gccnashville.org/about-grace/history.
2 "Leadership," n.p. [cited 12 February 2013], www.gccnashville.org/about-grace/leadership.
3 Jamie Mosley, "Hendersonville Church Planting Proposal: Presented to the Elders of Grace Community Church" (non-published, 4 February 2010).

as Patty mentored both in preparation for beginning new churches.[4] He described the relationship with Patty as "intentional, humble and transparent," expressing his own desire to be like his pastor in those areas. He found this intentional mentoring relationship to be the best preparation for planting Redeemer Church in Hendersonville, Tennessee.[5]

Matt McCullough moved to Nashville to pursue a doctor of philosophy degree at Vanderbilt University, with a goal to eventually pastor and teach. He and his wife joined GCC shortly after arriving. Through a seven-year membership at GCC, McCullough actively engaged in ministry through the church, including teaching, community group leader, and mission work. He acknowledged that from the start, the training for ministry began in an informal way through relationship to Patty and the church's elders. He began a part-time pastoral internship in 2009 that turned into a full-time internship in early 2010, as he proposed planting a church in late 2010 in the university district of Nashville, near Vanderbilt and Belmont universities.[6] McCullough realized that not only did he need leadership training from Patty and the GCC elders, but also those who would form the leadership team for the new Trinity Church did as well.[7] The GCC elders came alongside to further mentor McCullough and his leadership team as they prepared to plant a new church.

## TRAINING YOUNG MEN FOR MINISTRY

From years of pastoral ministry, Scott Patty recognized the need to train young men for serving Christ's church. The first yearlong internship started in 2007 with a simple purpose: "To give the intern a broad exposure to church ministry so as to assist him in discerning his call to a specific ministry within the church." This would be accomplished by giving "special attention to the pastoral ministry."[8] Future internship syllabuses specifically identified the purpose as developing "pastors and/or church planters for service in a local congregation."[9] The internship process involved active ministry work at GCC, attending staff and elders' meet-

---

4  Jamie Mosley, "Evaluation for Church Planters and Revitalizers—Grace Community Church Nashville," 31 October 2012.

5  Ibid. See the church's website: http://www.redeemertn.org.

6  Matt McCullough, "Evaluation for Church Planters and Revitalizers—Grace Community Church Nashville," 31 October 2012, n.p. McCullough spent two summers interning at South Woods Baptist Church, Memphis, TN, during his college days.

7  "Matt McCullough, "A Church Planting Proposal: Presented to the Elders of Grace Community Church" (non-published, 5 November 2009), n.p. See the church's website: http://www.trinitynashville.org.

8  Scott Patty, "Grace Community Church Intern Program 2007–2008" (non-published; no date).

9  Scott Patty, Grace Community Church Pastoral Intern Program 2009–2010, (non-published).

ings, regularly meeting with Patty, rotating with other staff members, reading and listening assignments, and assisting the church staff in various projects. The intern was allowed the flexibility of designing some particular aspects of the internship to fit his ministry goals.[10] The reading list for the internship focused on five areas: the church, church leadership, preaching, counseling, and evangelism/missions.[11]

McCullough highlighted the access that Patty gave him throughout the internship as the most useful aspect of his experience. He had the opportunity to see Patty in the breadth of pastoral leadership, so that he learned by watching, interacting, and freely asking questions. Additionally, McCullough regularly sat in on staff and elders' meetings, profited from Patty's weekly preaching, and discussed ministry and church planting details in the standing weekly meeting with Patty.[12]

With the added duties of his staff position, Mosley found the face-to-face time with Patty to be invaluable in preparing him to plant Redeemer Church. He described the interaction as "pastoral, paternal (in a good way) and directed to investing [in] and shaping me."[13] He also found the regular interaction and mentoring by the GCC elders to be critical in developing him toward future ministry.

The internship program at GCC involves the pastor, elders, and the congregation. Patty pointed out that without congregational involvement, the internship would look much different and would be less effective.[14] Mosley's "paternal" comment reveals something of the way that Patty and the congregation view their ongoing relationship with Mosley, McCullough, and another former intern who planted a church in the Madison area of Nashville. They have demonstrated this appropriate paternal spirit by planning a joint leadership retreat with GCC and the church leaders serving with the three former pastoral interns. The former GCC interns continue to meet with Patty on a monthly basis for ongoing mentoring and coaching in their respective ministries.[15]

## THE MENTORING PROCESS

What is the GCC process for mentoring church planters? Patty believes that the Lord brings along the right men to mentor, adding that he has found it healthy to his ministry at GCC to be involved in mentoring.[16] The mentoring relationship starts with a written agreement between the elders and the pastoral intern. The

---

10  Ibid.
11  "GCC Pastoral Ministry Reading Schedule" (non-published; no date).
12  McCullough, "Evaluation."
13  Mosley, "Evaluation."
14  Telephone conversation with Scott Patty and the author, 16 August 2012.
15  Ibid.
16  Ibid.

interns have some flexibility with portions of the internship to adjust toward best preparing them for future ministry. McCullough stated that sixty percent of his training focused on pastoral work and church planting, with the balance spread on missions, evangelism/discipleship, proclamation, polity, and personal spiritual disciplines.[17] Half of the focus during the mentorship with Mosley focused on church planting and another twenty percent on proclamation.[18] This indicates that Patty tailored the internship to fit the particular needs of each intern rather than taking a one-size-fits-all approach.

### Face-to-Face Time

The regular meetings with Patty involve time to discuss readings, ministry plans, and personal walks with Christ. McCullough pointed out that the focus in these meetings on caring for his soul has proven invaluable. While the specific instruction on church planting and pastoral ministry has prepared him well for his present ministry, the attention to soul care and the cautions to guard against pride and the insecurities of the heart has buoyed him as a Christian and pastor.[19] Patty recognizes that mentoring is not simply about the x's and o's of pastoral work; more importantly, mentoring must focus on directing young men to give careful attention to walking humbly and faithfully in obedience to Christ and the gospel.

### Team Approach

The pastoral mentoring also includes regular, although less formal, interaction with the GCC elders. These men provide a different perspective than Pastor Patty, since they focus on the role of lay-elders in local church ministry. McCullough found extensive interaction with them to be useful in helping him to guide those serving as lay-elders in his congregation.[20] Pastoral mentoring can become unbalanced when non-staff leaders have little involvement in the trainees' lives and ministries. Patty has wisely designed the internship to include regular engagement with his elder-counterparts.

### Pointed Reading

Pastoral mentors prudently direct their trainees in substantial reading. Patty has selected a list of notable authors to read and discuss with his protégés, e.g. D. A.

---

17  McCullough, "Evaluation."
18  Mosley, "Evaluation."
19  McCullough, "Evaluation."
20  Ibid.

Carson, Graeme Goldsworthy, John Stott, Wayne Grudem, C. John Miller, David Powlison, Robert Coleman, J. I. Packer, Mark Dever, and Tim Keller. Both Mosley and McCullough found C. John Miller's *The Heart of a Servant Leader* and David Powlison's *Seeing with New Eyes*, as particularly formative in understanding soul struggles and gospel-centered counseling, respectively.[21] McCullough further noted the impact of John Stott and Graeme Goldsworthy on his understanding and practice in preaching Christ from all of Scripture while ministering in a secular city.[22]

### Training Male Leaders

Patty also models for his trainees the training of male leadership in the congregation. Both McCullough and Mosley commented on how they learned the value of training men from Patty and the GCC elders. The same practice continues in their ministries.[23] It appears to flow naturally out of one of the key expressions of faith found at GCC: "We *grow* in our relationship with Christ and with one another."[24] The leadership demonstrates their seriousness on building relationships through community groups widely distributed throughout the Nashville metropolitan area—a ministry practice adopted by their church planters.[25] Patty leads men in small group format to address issues specific to them and their leadership. Women are involved in small groups as well. Mosley's comment indicates something of the intensity given to training men and making disciples when he stated that GCC's ministry bears fruit in his ministry through the "emphasis on *being present in the lives of people* and using every life moment as an opportunity for discipleship."[26] Pastoral presence in the lives of the congregation, modeled consistently by Scott Patty, continues in the ministry of his trainees.

---

21  Ibid.; Mosley, "Evaluation." See C. John Miller, *The Heart of a Servant Leader: Letters from Jack Miller* (Phillipsburg, NJ: P&R, 2004) and David Powlison, *Seeing with New Eyes: Counseling and the Human Condition through the Lens of Scripture* (Phillipsburg, NJ: P&R, 2003).

22  McCullough, Ibid. See John Stott, *Between Two Worlds: The Challenge of Preaching Today* (Grand Rapids: Eerdmans, 1982) and *The Contemporary Christian: Applying God's Word to Today's World* (Downers Grove, IL: IVP, 1995); and Graeme Goldsworthy, *Preaching the Whole Bible as Christian Scripture: The Application of Biblical Theology to Expository Preaching* (Grand Rapids: Eerdmans, 2000).

23  Ibid.; Mosley, "Evaluation."

24  "Grace Community Church" [cited 12 February 2013], www.gccnashville.org. Italics original.

25  "Community Groups" [cited 12 February 2013], gccnashville.org/ministries/adult/small-groups/community-groups-2.

26  Mosley, "Evaluation." Italics added.

## *Keep Ministry Simple*

From the start of GCC, Patty sought to keep ministry simple. Rather than adding a long list of programs and activities that stray from the church's vision, he has led them to focus on expositional teaching of Scripture, building relationships through small groups and ministries together, reaching out and serving in the community, and connecting with ministry internationally. Their mission footprint continues to expand locally and in other places around the world.[27] Both McCullough and Mosley have adopted the same ministry philosophy learned from their mentor. McCullough explains, "I seek to prioritize the things God has promised to use to change lives: preaching/teaching the Bible, prayer, personal discipleship/gospel-centered counsel, and evangelism. I try to minimize time spent on anything else."[28] Mosley agrees. "We want to be simple and intentional." He further stressed that most of what they do as a church is relationally driven—much like what he observed for five years under Patty's leadership.[29]

## *Cultivate the Congregation*

In celebrating the twentieth anniversary of GCC, a number of members and former members wrote their stories about the church. The theme that resonated through each one focused on the strength of congregationally built relationships. One lady wrote of how the past few years at Grace "served as a shelter" for her. The reason, she commented, "is because of the people."[30] A couple spoke of friends and mentors at the church feeding the husband—physically and spiritually—during his membership as a single, and then further mentoring them as a married couple. They referred to GCC's intention to build small in order to serve as a launching pad for sending out church planters and missionaries. They rejoiced that they had been sent out as part of the team to plant Redeemer Church in Hendersonville with former staff member Jamie Mosley—mentored by Patty.[31] Another couple wrote, "We have experienced what the body of Christ really looks like expressed to us during times of great personal struggle and failure, without gossip or condemnation, by people walking with us through restoration." They continued by telling of the excellent preaching and teaching that

---

27  "History."
28  McCullough, "Evaluation."
29  Mosley, "Evaluation."
30  Emily Hudson, "Grace Has Served as a Shelter," in "Stories of Grace" [cited 12 February 2013], gccnashville.org/life-at-grace/20-year-anniversary/stories-of-grace.
31  Mike and Duffy Betterton, "Grace as a Launch Pad," in "Stories of Grace" [cited 12 February 2013], gccnashville.org/life-at-grace/20-year-anniversary/stories-of-grace.

they heard each week from unpretentious people who sought to faithfully serve the Lord.[32]

Under Scott Patty and the GCC elders, the church has not focused on buildings, programs, or personalities but rather on a community of Christ-followers living out the gospel and serving together in their city and beyond. In this setting, where the church understands the biblical sense of community, Patty mentors young ministers so that they might cultivate their congregations to reflect the life they experienced at GCC. The images finely imprinted on the protégés' minds of a body living together in unity, service, and love remain as a motivation to pursue the same in their own congregations.

### *Sound Doctrine, Biblical Polity, and Covenant Membership*

Patty's substantive discussions with his trainees left a strong mark in the way they have led their congregations in matters of doctrine, polity, and membership. Both McCullough and Mosley expressed a desire to model their church plants' doctrinal statement after what they followed at GCC. They observed how the church's doctrinal convictions directed their worship, evangelism, missions, and membership care. Patty and his church modeled the effectiveness of making doctrine foundational to mission and ministry, a practice his protégés fully embrace.[33]

Both McCullough and Mosley have adopted plural elder leadership within a congregational framework they saw modeled so effectively at GCC.[34] They intentionally started their congregations with plural elders that had been examined and affirmed by the elders at GCC. Just like at Grace, they also established a membership process that requires attendance at a new members' class, interview by the elders, commitment to the church covenant, and affirmation by the congregation. Placing high priority on church membership distinguishes these new churches from many of the churches in their area that maintain large "inactive members" rolls and who require no membership covenant. Patty's influence on what membership looks like for a healthy church continues to bear fruit in his protégés.[35]

McCullough and Mosley both expressed desire for additional help with their preaching. McCullough pointed out that the intern program was not intended to provide a preaching laboratory for participants. Nothing was mentioned in the

---

32  Julie and Bill Bryan, "Same Team, Same Hope," in "Stories of Grace" [cited 12 February 2013], gccnashville.org/life-at-grace/20-year-anniversary/stories-of-grace.

33  McCullough, "Church Planting Proposal"; Mosley, "Hendersonville Church Planting Proposal."

34  For an explanation of plural eldership within a congregational form of polity, see Phil A. Newton and Matt Schmucker, *Elders in the Life of the Church: Rediscovering the Biblical Model for the Church* (Grand Rapids: Kregel Ministry, 2014).

35  McCullough, "Church Planting Proposal"; Mosley, "Hendersonville Church Planting Proposal."

intern syllabus about preaching opportunities, only sermon preparation and delivery, reading, and discussion. However, he stated that he could have used more preaching opportunities, along with critiques to further hone his skills.[36] Mosley offered virtually the same comment, desiring more opportunities to preach and receive feedback from Patty and the elders.[37]

Since biblical proclamation is central to church life, emphasis on better preparing pastoral trainees for preaching can strengthen the training process. To do so requires sacrificing pulpit time for the regular ministers or developing a separate time of preaching similar to Huldrych Zwingli's *prophezi* and John Calvin's Saturday afternoon sermons (see chapter 5). The added level of preparation ensures readiness to preach each week by the church planters and work out rough edges in preaching skills while the protégés remain in the "safety net" of the training program.

## PRÉCIS TO THE GRACE COMMUNITY
## CHURCH TRAINING MODEL

First, *this model focuses intentional training on one or two trainees at a time, thus ensuring significant attention to pastoral development under the guidance of the senior pastor.* Although trainees miss the camaraderie of a training cohort, they make up for it with broader congregational involvement.

Second, *this model has strong involvement by the church's elders.* Patty recognizes the wisdom and life experience of lay elders to be of inestimable value in training future ministers.

Third, *this model places major emphasis on spiritual formation and pastoral ministry.* Former trainees attest to the lasting impression that this emphasis has had on their spiritual lives and ministries.

Fourth, *this model expects trainees to be fully involved in the breadth of Grace's ministries and community life.* They are active church members first, who happen to also be pastoral trainees.

Fifth, *this model devotes intentional training to church planting, with the senior pastor as an experienced church planter directing the process.* The model would work equally well with ministers preparing for revitalization or mission work.

Sixth, *this model has strong congregational support during and after completing the internship and on into planting a new church.* The congregation continues to encourage and pray for the former trainees even after their departures.

---

36  McCullough, "Evaluation."
37  Mosley, "Evaluation."

Seventh, *this model tailors the specific areas of study and discussion appropriate to each intern.* In doing so, Patty recognizes the particular gifts, strengths, and weaknesses in each pastoral intern, providing necessary structure to better prepare them for ministry.

## CONCLUSION

Several observations can be made about the GCC pastoral internship program. First, Scott Patty does not come across as a larger-than-life figure, but rather, as a warm, gracious, and caring pastor. His personal involvement through mentoring men during their internship—and even years later, as they continue in their pastoral work—commends him as an example of pastoral mentoring.

Second, GCC's pastoral internship is not large and unwieldy. Intensely mentoring one or two men for ministry appears to be the approach that Patty carries well with his other pastoral duties. His ongoing monthly meeting with his former mentees demonstrates the seriousness with which he has entered into the mentoring role. Third, the backdrop for every step of the mentoring process is the congregation at Grace. As the protégés regularly participate in the full range of church life, congregational life at Grace shapes what their mentor teaches them.

Finally, training at GCC implants a missional approach to ministry in Patty's trainees. McCullough's Trinity Church membership in urban Nashville regularly engages international refugee families in their community. Mosley's Redeemer Church utilizes their community groups to serve in mercy ministries. Both churches, like their model at Grace Community Church, participate in financial, ongoing prayer, and personnel support with international missions. Scott Patty and the elders at GCC have trained their protégés well.

# CHAPTER 13

# MODELS: CHURCH AND ACADEMY IN PARTNERSHIP

Theological seminaries—as typically structured to focus on academics, according to Robert Banks—cannot adequately prepare students for serving in Christian ministry. He does not deny the role or necessity of academic training, but Banks sees concentration solely on academics lacking in developing spiritual formation in both students and faculty. He explains, "An ecclesial group creates the best opportunity for this."[1] He contrasts the nature of an exclusive academic setting where one's educational achievements merit inclusion compared to the inclusive nature of the church that welcomes a diversity of believers to live out community and share at the Lord's Table. Banks calls for more community interaction between faculty, administration, students, spouses, and children, so that a more holistic approach to common life can be achieved.[2] What he proposes appears to be a combination of church and theological institution living as community in Christ.

What Banks rightly calls for to transform the entire process of theological education, bringing it back to the church, is precisely what pastoral interns participating in the internship/seminary program at Lakeview Baptist Church (LBC) in Auburn, Alabama experience everyday. Since 1996, LBC and the Southern Baptist Theological Seminary (SBTS) in Louisville, Kentucky have joined to train a ministry cohort to prepare them for service as pastors, church planters, mis-

---

1  Robert Banks, *Reenvisioning Theological Education: Exploring a Missional Alternative to Current Models* (Grand Rapids: Eerdmans, 1999; Kindle ed.), loc. 2080.
2  Ibid.

sionaries, and Christian workers.[3] Combining work toward a master of divinity degree through the Billy Graham School of Missions, Evangelism and Ministry, and the practical mentoring of the LBC pastor, staff, and deacons, a cohort of six to ten interns work, serve, grow, and participate together in the multidimensioned experience of seminary and church, wedded to train them for ministry.[4]

As LBC pastor Al Jackson sees it, their training cohort model resembles Jesus's training of the Twelve.[5] He contends that current practices in theological education fail to adequately prepare pastors for local church ministry. To counter this deficit, he recommends, "a return to church-based theological training for those called to pastoral ministry."[6] Just as Jesus did with the disciples, this approach gives ministry students on-the-job-training.

## A COMMITMENT TO MENTORING FOR MINISTRY

Long before Jackson and SBTS joined to train ministers, he had been training those called to ministry who attended Auburn University, near the LBC campus. For sixteen years, he met with students each Thursday morning for a "Preaching Class," where he addressed sermon preparation, evangelism, leadership, missions, and an array of pastoral subjects. Most of the first cohort members had participated in the preaching class, where Jackson had already engaged in mentoring them for ministry.[7] The move from Thursday class to the full-range of academic work toward a master of divinity degree, while simultaneously serving as a pastoral intern at LBC, emerged in Jackson's desire to equip young men to serve effectively in pastoral ministry.[8] His vision for this seminary/church partnership arose, not because of weak seminaries but because he realized that seminary training proved incomplete when graduates entered their first pastorate.[9] Without the experience of local church mentoring, graduates would be ill-prepared to serve Christ's church with effectiveness.

This pastoral scholar recognized the need for rigorous academic training under the tutelage of seasoned theological professors with simultaneous mentoring by experienced pastors in the full range of pastoral work. In cooperation

---

3   Al Jackson, "Evaluation of Church-Based Model of Seminary Training," (Lakeview Baptist Church/Southern Baptist Theological Seminary, 1999), 1.
4   Ibid.
5   Al Jackson, "Look, It's the Church's Job," *9Marks e-Journal*, n.p. [cited 12 February 2013], https://9marks.org/article/look-its-churchs-job/.
6   Ibid.
7   Jackson, "Evaluation of Church-Based Model," 1.
8   Ibid.
9   Jackson, "Look."

with SBTS, students would take twelve hours of seminary credit each semester, along with working at least twenty-five hours each week in ministry at LBC. They would also participate in on-campus classes at SBTS during January terms, and over two years, they would serve for six to ten weeks each summer in a North American and international mission setting—learning church planting and missiology on the field. The students would also take more Supervised Ministry Experience classes under the mentorship of LBC staff members than the traditional on-campus students. The three-year plan required diligence on the part of the cohort to maintain the rigor of academics and pastoral work.[10] Jackson would continue to serve as mentor for the students, along with assistance from staff and later, church deacons.

Jackson maintains a simple rationale for the program. "The model is church-based not classroom-based. We take things happening in the life of the church and interpret them historically, biblically, and theologically, which cannot be done in an academic setting."[11] The integration of real-life church experience, with the core courses found in most seminaries, broadens the ministry scope of the pastoral intern cohort. How do they quantify the success of this integration of seminary and church? Jackson identifies nineteen attributes that he and the seminary administration have agreed need to result in the three-year internship:

> spiritually alive and growing, balanced and disciplined lifestyle, biblically knowledgeable, theologically grounded, historically informed, competent to lead worship, homiletically prepared, evangelistically active, missions minded, competent to lead, people oriented, administratively competent, able to equip others for ministry, Christian education, congregational care, stewardship motivator, lifelong student, denominationally knowledgeable, culturally aware.[12]

At the end of the three-year process of academic training and local church mentoring, Jackson personally interviews each graduate, questioning the degree that the program had covered the nineteen attributes, and the level of competence for each graduate. This measurement has allowed Jackson and his fellow mentors

---

10  Robert Don Hughes, "Southern Seminary at Lakeview Project—July 9, 1996–May 20, 1999" (The Southern Baptist Theological Seminary, 1996), 1–3.
11  Telephone conversation with the author, 21 August 2012.
12  Al Jackson, "Churches Raising Up Pastors—Lakeview Baptist Church," *9Marks e-Journal*, n.p. [cited 12 February 2013], www.9marks.org/journal/churches-raising-pastors-lakeview-baptist-church.

to adjust the time and intensity of training for future cohorts, to ensure that they adequately address each attribute, as well as helping to mentor cohort members toward competency.[13]

## CHURCH-FOCUSED MENTORING

Jackson does not stand alone in the work of bringing on new students during each three-year cohort. Students must apply to both seminary and the Lakeview church and be accepted by both before admission to the pastoral internship. Applicants must complete a thorough questionnaire that evaluates their spiritual walk, call to ministry, and doctrinal fidelity. The deacon fellowship reviews the questionnaire before recommending the applicant to the church body, which holds the prerogative to vote to call the applicant into a three-year pastoral intern role.[14] Due to the church's vote, the congregation considers the pastoral interns as staff, although they do not receive compensation for their duties. Students have responsibility for raising their own support to participate on a full-time basis. The church provides books and covers any ministry expense while they conduct their congregational duties.[15]

The church-based model provides opportunities to see firsthand the range of typical congregational life. Pastoral interns attend funerals and debrief afterward to better understand the components of the funeral. They partner with pastors in visiting the sick and homebound, learning how to apply the gospel in their visits. They observe pastors and deacons as they engage in the practice of church discipline. They preach at Lakeview and other churches, receiving feedback on their sermons.[16]

Former intern Kameron Pugh, whose father is a long-time Southern Baptist pastor, reports that he spent three hours each month with pastors and deacons meeting together, as well as weekly meetings with an older man in the congregation to build accountability, offer and receive encouragement, and glean from his wisdom.[17] He acknowledged that in addition to several hours of class time and meetings with Al Jackson and other members of the congregation, Jackson also welcomed questions about life and ministry, generously giving of his time.[18]

LBC's staff tenure averages more than twenty-five years per staff member! Jackson has completed his thirty-seventh year as LBC pastor in 2016. This stability

---

13  Jackson, "Evaluation of Church Based," 2.
14  Jackson, "Churches Raising Up Pastors."
15  Chris Burns, form letter addressed to "prospective intern," no date.
16  Jackson, "Evaluation of Church-Based Model," 2.
17  Kameron Pugh, "Evaluation for Church Planters and Revitalizers," 14 November 2012.
18  Ibid.

and longevity with the staff adds another dimension to the training that pastoral interns receive. They learn about perseverance, forgiveness, cooperation, getting along together, and diversity in leadership by observing the staffs' relationships with one another, as well as their relationship to the congregation. At one point, the curriculum called for a leadership course, which Jackson taught. But after years of seeing leadership modeled by the church staff, Jackson and the seminary decided that the course could add nothing to what the students experienced firsthand in this church-based model.[19] The course was dropped to make room for another elective.

Since the LBC/SBTS partnership has already graduated forty-two students (and six more on the way to graduation), their former pastoral interns now serve across the United States and in other countries.[20] Nathan Tubbs, a graduate from LBC, planted a church in Brooklyn, New York that currently meets in a hotel.[21] In the summer of 2012, the LBC pastoral interns and their wives spent six weeks working and living in Brooklyn where they assisted Tubbs and the young congregation. They learned church planting by firsthand experience.[22] Pastoral interns spent six to ten weeks serving with International Mission Board (SBC) missionaries in Africa during one summer break, where students worked and learned missions by practice.[23] This complements the previous co-horts who have served in church planting settings in Pennsylvania, Maryland, and Nevada, and in international mission settings in Costa Rica, Ghana, and Sub-Saharan Africa.[24] The mission focus of LBC appears to root deeply in the pastoral interns during their time with the church, particularly by the way that graduates continue mission involvement.

The healthy church context at Lakeview instills a vision in the pastoral interns for leading their future congregations toward the same health. Jackson talks candidly about the difficult times and experiences as LBC's pastor. He relates details of how unhealthy the church was when he arrived. He also talks freely about his failures as well as successes over the thirty-seven years of his ministry at LBC. Out of this live-church discussion, the interns learn lessons that they may revisit when their time comes to serve as pastors, church planters, or missionaries.[25] As a

---

19  Jackson, telephone interview, 31 August 2013.
20  Jackson, "Churches Raising Up Pastors."
21  Cornerstone Church at Bay Ridge, where Nathan Tubbs serves as pastor. See the church's website: http://www.cornerstonebayridge.org/blog1.
22  Pugh, "Evaluation," n.p.
23  Ibid.
24  Jackson, "Look," n.p.
25  Pugh, "Evaluation," n.p.

seasoned pastor, he understands the need to persevere in the spiritual disciplines, so he teaches the incoming cohort a class on the spiritual disciplines.[26] Jackson models a spiritually healthy pastor leading a healthy church.

## A MODEL TO CONSIDER

After several years of observing the fruitfulness of the LBC/SBTS model for pastoral mentoring, Lakeview has set the pace for other congregations to follow in cooperation with theological seminaries. The Church at Brook Hills in Birmingham, Alabama began its Institute for Disciple-Making that couples theological education with their church's ministry, partnering with Southeastern Baptist Theological Seminary (SEBTS).[27] The Equip Center at SEBTS seeks to bring a limited number of seminary courses into local church settings, with pastors mentoring students toward future ministry.[28] Already, dozens of churches have partnered with SEBTS for training young ministers. This trend that Lakeview pioneered, could prove to be one of the best gifts to the contemporary church.

Granted, as Jackson admits, adding teaching and mentoring to his demanding pastoral duties at LBC sometimes leave him fatigued. Yet, he finds increasing satisfaction in "seeing God-called men go out to serve Christ and his church," making the fatigue and strain well worth the effort.[29] He finds it gratifying that his ministry multiplies by training the next generation of pastors and missionaries.

What are the strengths of the Lakeview model? From former SBTS administrator Hughes' perspective, the tight-knit community provides a good atmosphere for training. Additionally, Jackson's long-term mentoring of ministry students, as well as his pastoral longevity makes him an ideal leader for the program.[30]

Jackson evaluated the strengths of the first three years of training and identified a number of positive elements that can be found in the church-based training model. First, due to the connection with SBTS faculty and retired faculty from other seminaries, students were taught by an array of outstanding evangelical scholars, e.g., Tim Beougher, Danny Akin, Tom Nettles, George Martin, Adam Greenway, Bruce Ware, Rob Plummer, and Thom Rainer. Second, the small classroom setting allowed for exceptional student and professor interaction. Third, the

---

26  Conversation with Al Jackson and the author, 12 July 2016.
27  See the Church at Brook Hills, n.p. [cited 13 February 2013], http://www.brookhills.org/idm, for additional information.
28  See the SEBTS Equip website, n.p. [cited 13 February 2013], http://www.sebts.edu/Equip/default.aspx.
29  Jackson, "Look," n.p.
30  Hughes, "Lakeview," 2.

church-based model gave students the opportunity to be trainees to Jackson and other staff members. This led to observation and participation in the ongoing challenges faced by those in pastoral ministry, with mentors available to guide the students through the experience of church life.[31]

Fourth, the cohort-based model developed at Lakeview challenged the students to practice Christian community. Since the same group stayed together for three years, they had opportunity to experience the normal strains of relationships found in any congregation. Jackson thought that the first cohort did not gel as quickly in developing a sense of brotherhood, as he believed might happen, but in the end, the nine interns grew to love and care for one another.[32] Along with relationships to one another, the students also faced the normal demands found in congregational life. They had to learn to love and serve members of the church, too—a lesson well suited to future ministry. Fifth, the cohort had the chance to meet a number of Southern Baptist leaders and visit a number of agencies as part of their training. That gave them a broader exposure to SBC life. Finally, the cohort participated together during summer sessions in church planting and mission work, shaping their perspective on missions as they left to serve other churches.[33]

Both Hughes and Jackson identify a few weaknesses in the church-based model. First, aside from January terms, students were unable to avail themselves of the superb theological library at SBTS. While they had access to a general library at Auburn University and Jackson's extensive theological library, the source material, theological volumes, church history resources, and exegetical helps found at the seminary's library would have enriched the experience. Second, the cohort's distance from SBTS put them at a disadvantage for not hearing the guest speakers for chapel and lectures.[34] Third, Hughes points out that the necessity of living a Spartan lifestyle, while depending upon outside support for three years of living expenses, put a heavier burden on students with families than might be found in the traditional campus setting. Due to the Lakeview model requiring students to work more than twenty-five hours at the church each week and to refrain from any other occupation, they must raise substantial support for normal living expenses since they receive no stipend from the church. Fourth, the closeness of the cohort quickly exposes weaker students, putting additional pressure on them to keep up with the workload. This could also strain cohort morale if left

---

31 Jackson, "Evaluation," 2–3.
32 Ibid., 3.
33 Ibid., 3–4.
34 Ibid., 4.

unchecked. Fifth, the "lock-step nature of the program," as Hughes calls it, does not allow for variation in curriculum.[35]

## PRÉCIS FOR LAKEVIEW BAPTIST CHURCH'S PASTORAL TRAINING MODEL

First, *this model has a unique combination of academic and local church pastoral training.* The relationship with The Southern Baptist Theological Seminary and the Lakeview church enable trainees to complete their master of divinity degrees while serving as pastoral interns.

Second, *this model has the strength of the church staff's longevity, bringing depth to the layered mentoring relationships led by the church staff.* The twenty-five-year average of staff members means that the trainees will rarely raise a ministry situation that one of the staff members has not experienced.

Third, *this model's interaction with seminary professors and immediate access to pastoral staff provides an increased level of training.* They are able to immediately take theoretical and historical issues, bringing them into the Lakeview church context.

Fourth, *this model insists on accountability to not only pastoral staff but also to church laymen.* This practice broadens the spiritual formation and matures the relational development of the trainees.

Fifth, *this model's length—three years—exposes pastoral trainees to most congregational and pastoral issues during their tenure.*

Sixth, *this model provides the opportunity for developing community with the training cohort and congregation, thus deepening trainees' understanding of gospel application to all of life.*

Seventh, *this model places strong emphasis on preaching, hence giving trainees solid preparation for their future preaching ministries.*

## CONCLUSION

Hughes offered a good perspective on the students in the church-based model for ministry training found at Lakeview. "They are doubly prepared for real ministry."[36] By this statement he implied that the strong theological education they received coupled with the praxis found in the church-based mentoring relationships, amply prepared the cohort for entering into future ministry. As one graduate from the Lakeview program listened as a director of missions told of feeling

---

35  Hughes, "Lakeview," 4–5.
36  Ibid., 5.

clueless when he began his first church experience, the graduate mused, "After sitting through countless hours of staff, deacon, Sunday School and supervised ministry meetings, I have a good idea about what I should do when I first get to a church."[37] If his experience repeats with the rest of the cohort members, then it gives strong evidence to the need for increasing church-based ministry training across North America.

What will it take to see this model replicated? The commitment of the lead pastor, willing to invest six to ten additional hours each week to teaching and mentoring as modeled by Jackson, will be the first requirement. Second, the staff, leadership, and congregation must agree to invest the personnel, time, and resources for this training model to succeed. Third, an innovative seminary must recognize the usefulness of the church-based model, committing personnel, time, and resources to make it happen from the academic side. They will also have to recognize a level of flexibility from their traditional on-campus ministry model. Finally, students must covenant to live in community, submit to the pastoral mentors, maintain high academic standards, fully engage in the local church, and pursue spiritual formation with zeal throughout the process.

---

37  Jackson, "Evaluation," 5.

# CHAPTER 14

# A TEMPLATE FOR TRAINING LEADERS

W hen Mike McKinley visited Capitol Hill Baptist Church in Washington, DC as a college student, he appeared with green hair, combat boots, a kilt, and several face piercings—not the typical fashion for that congregation! Yet, no one seemed fazed by his appearance. Instead, the seventy-year-olds in the congregation welcomed him and even invited him to lunch. Several years later, the hair had returned to its normal color, God's call to ministry had led him to graduate from seminary, and a proposal by CHBC pastor Mark Dever stared him in the face. Dever brought McKinley on staff for one to two years so that he might be prepared and sent out to plant a church in the DC area. As the process developed, rather than starting from scratch, McKinley would seek to revitalize (and in some fashion, replant) a church in Guilford, Virginia that by every estimation appeared on the edge of death. With his punk-rock background, it seemed only natural to his peers that he would plant a church that focused on twenty-somethings from the same background. To the contrary, the diverse and healthy congregation at CHBC had impacted him. Although he read extensively in the area of ecclesiology under Dever's mentorship, the diversity in the CHBC congregation spoke even more volumes to him. He would not "target" one group, which would likely exclude another. Instead, the church would target the diversity of his community just as he had experienced at Capitol Hill Baptist Church.[1]

Seeing a diverse, healthy church up close affected McKinley more than second-hand reading about other churches. McKinley does not stand alone. Throughout

---

1   Mike McKinley, *Church Planting Is for Wimps—How God Uses Messed-up People to Plant Ordinary Churches That Do Extraordinary Things,* 9Marks Books (Wheaton, IL: Crossway, 2010), 11–22.

the biblical, historical, and contemporary portions of this book, we have considered that the influence of a healthy congregation while training for ministry leaves its mark on the trainees' future work. Timothy's understanding of the local church through the congregations at Lystra and Iconium prepared him well to serve for many years with Paul, who often sent him to strengthen young congregations (Compare Acts 16:1–2; 16:23–40; 17:10–15; 1 Thess. 3:2; 1 Tim. 4:14; 2 Tim. 1:5–6; 3:10–15). Martin Bucer's Strassburg church influenced John Calvin's future work in Geneva, which in turn shaped the ecclesial understanding of hundreds sent out from Geneva.[2] Pastoral mentors not only seek to develop and prepare their protégés through the depth of their experience, but also to train them in the framework of vibrant local churches. The effects of healthy congregations on pastoral trainees are foundational to pastoral mentoring.

The pastor who best trains protégés devotes himself to building a healthy congregation. That sets the stage for mentoring in a congregational context. In this case, the style, approach, and practice of mentorship may vary from one pastor to another—and that is certainly appropriate—but the praxis within the congregation shapes the pastoral trainee as much as the wise words of his mentor. The church setting for mentorship allows for majoring on praxis in real-life situations. This setting strengthens what a trainee may have gotten from time in the academy by putting the theoretical elements together in the congregational context in ways that the academy cannot replicate. Consequently, the pastoral trainee finds greater meaning from his time in the academic setting by his experience of practice in the congregation.

This kind of understanding led John Calvin, Charles Spurgeon, and Dietrich Bonhoeffer to combine academic and congregational elements in their approach to training young ministers. Al Jackson has been able to do the same at his church in Auburn, Alabama. The issues discussed in the seminary classroom play out in real-life scenarios in the congregation. Local church based training—with all of its service and mission at the disposal of the trainees—in combination with solid theological study in an academic setting, best prepare trainees for ministry.

Pastors desiring to train young ministers to plant or revitalize or serve a local church may consider pursuing relationship with a seminary and their churches, so that by a combination of academic and praxis through the church, they might conduct the ideal pastoral training. However, most cannot work from the ideal, and so must focus on training in ways available to them. Therefore, the goal of pastors burdened to train young ministers must be to do what they can to prepare the next generation for ministry rather than stopping short because they

---

2   W. Robert Godfrey, *John Calvin: Pilgrim and Pastor* (Wheaton, IL: Crossway, 2009), 43–45.

cannot achieve the idealistic model. With this in mind, this last chapter will set forth a workable local church training model. We will seek to show that the best pastoral training model will be one that draws from the biblical, historical, and contemporary training models, while adjusting to one's pastoral gifts, the church's leadership dynamics, and the congregational context.

## ESSENTIAL MENTORING ELEMENTS IN THE BIBLICAL, HISTORICAL, AND CONTEMPORARY MODELS

The goal in the previous chapters has been to identify various elements and practices utilized in training ministers for pastoral ministry. Every setting considered—biblical, historical, and contemporary—varies in terms of the capabilities of mentors, the strength of the congregation, the accessibility to theological education, the educational level and pastoral experience of those being trained, the local field of ministry, and the cultural issues that further shape preparation for ministry. Since each situation differs from the others, none of the models considered would likely fit *in toto* with contemporary pastors seeking to begin a pastoral training ministry. However, in analyzing the various models, five elements seem to run through virtually each one, which suggests their inclusion in any pastoral training ministry.

### *Mentoring within a Congregational Framework*

Whether one looks at the nascent church in the small community gathered around Jesus and his followers, or at the emerging house churches throughout the Roman Empire, the influence of the church upon those preparing to be sent into pastoral work seems prominent (see Acts 16:1–3; 20:4; Gal. 2:1).[3] Bonhoeffer's approach in training his students centered in the warp and woof of community life.[4] Charles Spurgeon considered the lively, zealous, and working atmosphere of the Metropolitan Tabernacle, despite its faults, to be the best center for train-

---

3  James George Samra, *Being Conformed to Christ in Community: A Study of Maturity, Maturation and the Local Church in the Undisputed Pauline Epistles*, Library of Biblical Studies 320; Mark Goodacre, ed. (London: T & T Clark, 2006), 31, notes, "[F]or Paul no individual exists apart from and unaffected by the group(s) to which he or she belongs." One does not go "solo" when it comes to ministry. The community of believers helps to shape the person for ministry. Samra further explains, "that for Paul the church was to some extent a 'laboratory' where truth could be learned by putting principles into practice" (163).

4  Eric Metaxas, *Bonhoeffer: Pastor, Martyr, Prophet, Spy—A Righteous Gentile vs. the Third Reich* (Nashville: Thomas Nelson, 2010; Kindle edition), loc. 5218. See also Dietrich Bonhoeffer, *Life Together/Prayerbook of the Bible*, DBW 5; Gerhard L. Müller, Albrecht Schönherr, Geoffrey B. Kelly, eds.; Daniel W. Bloesch and James H. Burtness, trans. (Minneapolis: Fortress Press, 2005), 30–47, for his discussion of community which he applied to his protégés.

ing his young preachers, since they would learn from the congregation about the healthy application of the gospel to all of life.[5] Each trainee interviewed in the contemporary models indicated a desire to take some of the training church's DNA into their own newly planted or revitalized congregations.

### Mentors Speak into Their Trainees' Lives

Jesus and Paul regularly spoke into the lives of their protégés, addressing issues of doctrine, character, relationships, and the exercise of their gifts (see Luke 9:10; 10:17–20; 1 Tim. 4:11–16; 2 Tim. 1:6–14; 4:1–5; Titus 2:1, 15).[6] Spurgeon took his pastoral trainees on preaching trips so that he might have additional time to speak directly into their lives.[7] The contemporary models illustrate the same practice, as protégés of Al Jackson, Scott Patty, and Mark Dever spoke of how accessible the pastors had been to them, and how directly they spoke into their lives. Effective mentoring does not take place from behind a lectern as much as in life-on-life relationships.

### Mentoring Focuses on Relationships

A person training for ministry might escape the messy and sometime difficult challenges of relationships in an academic setting, but not in a local church mentoring setting. Philip Spener recognized this when he established his *ecclesiola in ecclesia*, in which believers were brought into close proximity where they could learn to live out the gospel with one another. Bonhoeffer did the same in his Finkenwalde training model. He wrote, "One can joyfully and authentically proclaim the Word of God's love and mercy with one's mouth only where one's hands are not considered too good for deeds of love and mercy in everyday helpfulness."[8] He modeled focus on relationships to his protégés by serving one another in that close-knit setting. Each contemporary model intentionally puts their trainees into congregational situations where they learn to love and serve the body of Christ with all of its diversities. Effective mentoring makes much of relationships in the church.

---

5   Charles Haddon Spurgeon, *C. H. Spurgeon Autobiography*, 2 vols.; rev. ed. by Susannah Spurgeon and Joseph Harrald (Carlisle, PA: Banner of Truth, 1973), 1:98.

6   The simplicity of this approach to training others for ministry is set forth by Robert Coleman, *The Master Plan of Evangelism* (Old Tappan, NJ: Revell, 1964), 17–19. Coleman's concern is to follow the strategy of Jesus in training his disciples to make disciples. He contends that the gospel writers not only heard truth but they saw the way that Jesus lived and taught, recording the particular things that most influenced them to leave all and follow Christ. These things bear repetition in mentoring others.

7   Spurgeon, *Autobiography*, 2:110–111.

8   Bonhoeffer, *Life Together*, 100.

*Effective Mentoring Utilizes a Team Approach to Training*

Team approach refers to making good use of other leaders in the congregation to help shape and hone trainees for ministry. John Calvin incorporated Geneva's *venerable company of pastors*, as they were known, to assist in all aspects of training those that the Geneva Academy and St. Pierre Church would send out into ministry. Scott Patty at Grace Community Church and Mark Dever at Capitol Hill Baptist Church make good use of their elders joining in the training regimen of their mentees. Al Jackson at Lakeview Baptist Church utilizes his church staff and deacon body to mentor and build accountability with the mentees. An important lesson can be learned for those developing a training ministry: Do not try to do it alone. Recognize those whom the Lord has raised up in the congregation—elders, deacons, older members, members who have endured suffering with grace—and get them involved in training pastors for ministry.

*Mentors Trust Their Protégés*

Jesus placed a level of trust in his disciples by sending them out as beginners.[9] He demonstrated that mentors must willingly trust their protégés with responsibilities in order to train them. Paul certainly did the same by assignments he gave to Timothy and Titus. Spurgeon sent his trainees out to preach, often in difficult settings, trusting them with faithfully proclaiming the gospel. Al Jackson regularly gives his trainees various ministry responsibilities, trusting them to discharge their duties with integrity and dependability. Does this mean that the trainees are always on the mark with their assignments? Probably not, but it does mean that the mentor shows grace to them especially when they fail. The debriefing that follows likely proves to be an exceptional teaching opportunity, that brings trainees into greater usefulness in God's kingdom.

The five elements gleaned from the previous chapters do not constitute every possibility for incorporation into a developing training model, but do provide what I have found to be essential for effective local church mentoring. So, how does a pastor or church leadership establish an effective training model? We now turn our attention to an adaptable structure for mentoring young ministers to engage in local church ministry.

## AN ADAPTABLE STRUCTURE FOR
## LOCAL CHURCH MINISTRY TRAINING

Since I have argued that no single approach to mentoring can claim to be the *only* way to training pastors or missionaries, the structure proposed for men-

---

9  A. B. Bruce, *The Training of the Twelve* (Grand Rapids: Kregel, 1971), 102–103.

toring through the local church recommends a basic training model. To this model, three additional layers or angles of training will be described, with the basic model serving as foundational to each one. First, some preliminary considerations will be discussed, followed by a look at the basic mentoring model, and then by three additional layers of mentoring: a seminary/church partnership; a full-time pastoral internship; and a full-time church planter residency.

## *Preliminary Considerations*

### A Willing Pastor

The training process begins with a willing pastor, settled in his church ministry, committed to invest the time and resources necessary to train pastors, missionaries, and church planters.[10] He need not pastor a large church; he simply needs the commitment to do what will be necessary to mentor less experienced ministers toward the goal of future ministry. His conviction on the inerrancy of Scripture, practice of biblical exposition, passion to disciple others, and cooperation with those appointed/elected to serve in his congregation as leaders gives him the platform for training through the local church.[11] Certainly, a pastor can mentor someone outside of his congregational setting and can accomplish much.[12] But the best training takes place, as I have attempted to show, with the pastoral mentor shaping and honing his protégés in the lively experience of community.

The experience of giving oneself in mentoring others can take a toll on a pastor, so he must not presume upon his spiritual life anymore than he would expect his protégés to presume on theirs. How might a pastor maintain his spiritual edge? Joel Beeke and Terry Slachter take a page from Puritan writers by recommending that pastors make prayer a priority, enjoy friendship with God, meditate on the Scriptures, and journal to crystalize the present for the future experiences of life.[13] He must find time for reading and studying, fellowship with other believers, and

---

10  Scott Thomas and Tom Wood, *Gospel Coach: Shepherding Leaders to Glorify God* (Grand Rapids: Zondervan, 2012), 28, write, "Faithful leaders will make disciples, but great leaders focus on making other leaders."

11  Keep in mind the historical examples discussed in chapters 5–7, particularly the way that Zwingli and Calvin brought together their churches' leadership to assist with pastoral training.

12  Many of the books addressing mentoring and coaching take this approach rather than centering the training in the local church, e.g., Paul D. Stanley and J. Robert Clinton, *Connecting: The Mentoring Relationships You Need to Succeed in Life* (Colorado Springs: NavPress, 1992); Regi Campbell, *Mentor Like Jesus* (Nashville: B&H, 2009). While they offer valuable help on mentoring they do miss this critical aspect of the experience of local church community in mentoring.

13  Joel R. Beeke and Terry D. Slachter, *Encouragement for Today's Pastors: Helps from the Puritans* (Grand Rapids: Reformation Heritage Books, 2013), 25–37.

maintain accountability with his fellow elders (or staff or deacons) for his spiritual formation. Furthermore, he must give careful attention to his marriage and family life, recognizing that the example he sets in this vital area will be mirrored in his protégés.[14]

### An Involved Church

Paul Gupta and Sherwood Lingenfelter correctly point out, "The local church and pastor are the front line of leadership training."[15] Starting with a healthy congregation[16] that gives strong attention to the ministry of the Word and values ministry training, the pastor should lead the congregation toward ownership of the ministry training process. Just as Spurgeon did with his church,[17] the pastor must show them how essential a faithful, gospel-centered congregation will be to training future ministers. This calls for the church to get involved in praying for the training, supporting it financially, and encouraging the trainees at every opportunity. It means showing up to listen to them preach even when the trainees might struggle in the early attempts at preaching. It requires a willingness to accept the pastoral interns with their inexperience, slowly stepping into leadership roles under the mentorship of the senior pastor, staff, and elders. The congregation must realize that they hold a strong measure of responsibility, along with the pastor and elders, for assessing pastoral trainees' gifts for ministry or missions, while helping to prepare them for their future work.[18] If the trainees fail to minister with a healthy congregation then they do not need to launch into ministry until significant changes transpire. On the other hand, if their gifts show consistent development, the congregation must be willing to affirm and encourage them.

### A Committed Leadership Team

Elders (or deacons, if they are the *de facto* pastoral leaders) need to be involved in the planning and development of the pastoral training. They possess wonder-

---

14  Pastors will find Thomas K. Ascol, ed., *Dear Timothy: Letters on Pastoral Ministry* (Cape Coral, FL: Founders Press, 2004), to be an excellent resource for help in personal life and ministry.

15  Paul R. Gupta and Sherwood G. Lingenfelter, *Breaking Tradition to Accomplish Vision: Training Leaders for a Church-Planting Movement* (Winona Lake, IN: BMH Books, 2006), 209.

16  See Mark E. Dever, *Nine Marks of a Healthy Church*, new expanded ed. (Wheaton, IL: Crossway, 2004) and Mark E. Dever and Paul Alexander, *The Deliberate Church: Building Your Ministry on the Gospel* (Wheaton, IL: Crossway, 2005), for a description of a healthy church and an expanded description of healthy church practices.

17  Spurgeon, *Autobiography*, 1:98.

18  Rodney Harrison, Tom Cheyney, and Don Overstreet, *Spin-Off Churches: How One Church Successfully Plants Another* (Nashville: B&H Academic, 2008), 70.

ful insights on how to connect to a congregation, how to start a new work, how to nurture a small group, how to engage in local ministry and mission, and how to counsel and train church members. They should also be involved in aspects of mentoring the pastoral trainees by housing them, inviting them for meals, meeting with them on a regular basis, bringing them into an accountability group, etc. As they build relationships with pastoral trainees, the trainees will more readily receive their critiques and find joy in their affirmations.[19] The elders, along with church staff, are in the best position to shoulder the congregational work of pastoral care so that the senior pastor might devote additional time to training and mentoring his protégés. Otherwise, without this investment on the part of the church leadership, the senior pastor might soon burn out from the extra demands on his time.[20]

### A Process for Selecting Pastoral Trainees

Once the pastor, leadership, and congregation agree on investing time, personnel, and resources in training ministers, the pastor and elders will need to decide on a process for selecting pastoral trainees. If the candidates have been church members long enough to observe their Christian character, call to ministry, teachability, cooperative spirit, and zeal for pastoral work, the decision will be easy. Otherwise, develop an application process to include the following: *one page each*—Christian testimony, what is the gospel, basic description of a New Testament church, basic description of New Testament polity, testimony of call to ministry; *short answer*—agreement with the church's doctrinal statement, particular plans to pastor or plant or revitalize or do mission work, description of personal spiritual walk, description of family relationships, and the names of three or four references that have had opportunity to observe the candidate for at least one to three years; *one to two pages*—an essay explaining why the candidate desires pastoral training. Realizing that a candidate for the training ministry might lack a strong testimony or have critical fault lines in his understanding of the church would be reason to decline his participation in it. It is not that the pastor or leadership should expect a candidate to have arrived in his understanding and practice in each area, but there needs to be evidence that he will respond to the intensity of preparing for pastoral ministry.

---

19 See Sam Crabtree, *Practicing Affirmation: God-Centered Praise for Those Who Are Not God* (Wheaton, IL: Crossway, 2011).
20 Dever and Alexander, *Deliberate Church*, 133–136.

## Make Plans

Planning the pastoral training would be similar to planning for one to three courses on a master of divinity level. Students appreciate professors taking the time to think through on the details of class requirements and participation. In the same way, pastoral trainees should expect to know some details ahead of time so that they might invest in preparation. The following list offers some recommendations for what might be involved in planning for a six-to-twelve-month pastoral training ministry:

- **Develop a syllabus that shows reading and general requirements.**
- **Plan weekly schedules for face-to-face mentoring and small group classes.**
- **Acquire the necessary resources for the pastoral interns; decide if they are to bear some of the expense.**
- **Plan the level of duties in which the pastoral interns will be involved.**
- **Plan accountability relationships between interns and church leadership.**
- **Plan involvement with the congregation and the pastoral interns.**
- **Decide if the pastoral interns will be full-time and the amount of stipend, if any, for support; or part-time and the necessary stipend, if any; develop schedules accordingly.**
- **Identify specific and narrow areas of focus according to the interns' needs.**
- **Delegate responsibilities for training to pastors, elders, staff, and deacons.**
- **Consider partnering with a seminary:**
  - » **Will this be for academic credit?**
  - » **Do you have an established relationship with a seminary for leading in some courses?**
  - » **Do you have the academic credentials to lead a class or will you need a professor of record?**
  - » **Can you send the pastoral interns to a seminary for classes that you lack credentials to lead?**
  - » **Is there the possibility of hosting seminary classes at your church with seminary faculty teaching them?**
  - » **Do you have adequate library resources for the basics of pastoral ministry?**
  - » **Do you want to go the seminary route at all? Would you be better off letting the seminary do its work and try to come alongside as a local church making pastoral application?**

### Communicate with Pastoral Interns

Taking time to listen to the pastoral interns, to understand their struggles and questions will advance the direction of the pastoral training. Ask what the trainees expect with pastoral mentoring and training. Discover their fears related to various aspects of ministry. Spell out expectations during the training in both public and private lives. Establish a method of communication with them (email, texting, phone calls) and maintain it regularly. Develop a rubric or guideline that will allow you to evaluate progress made with the internship and mentoring. Be open and straightforward with the protégés concerning their progress in ministry.

## *The Structure for Pastoral Training*

Since one size does not fit all, the following offers a basic approach to pastoral training, with additional layers added as opportunity warrants. I recommend starting with the basic structure before working toward goals for ministry training that match the gifts and resources of the pastor, elders, and congregation. In doing so, pastors and churches will work out some of the issues that may be problematic with training before getting involved in a more complicated and expensive training model. If pastors and churches desire to be involved in missions, church planting, and church revitalization, they will need to invest in mentoring young leaders whom they can send into the work.[21] The cost in terms of time, energy, finances, and change cannot be measured when one considers the outcome of preparing a new generation to impact the world by establishing gospel-centered churches.[22]

### A Basic Mentoring Model

"Basic" does not minimize the effectiveness of this approach to mentoring and training; rather, it refers to uncomplicating the process. To begin with, the pastor will attempt to mentor only one or two young ministers at a time. They might be members of the church that the pastor and elders recognize demonstrate gifts for ministry. In such cases, the pastor should initiate pastoral training. If considering a trainee from outside the church, then the process for acceptance discussed earlier in this chapter would be useful. Spend time discussing the gospel, the church, and Christian ministry with the trainee in order to gauge where to begin

---

21 Bob Roberts Jr., *The Multiplying Church: The New Math for Starting New Churches* (Grand Rapids: Zondervan, 2008), 90.

22 Timothy Keller, *Center Church: Doing Balanced, Gospel-Centered Minisry in Your City* (Grand Rapids: Zondervan, 2012), 46–51.

with reading, discussion, and assignments. Take plenty of time to listen to the trainee. Bob Roberts correctly states, "Good mentoring doesn't start by hugging, but by listening, observing, and then challenging."[23] Tailor the mentorship according to the specific needs of the trainee.

Develop a plan for reading, discussion, ministry projects, sermon building, writing assignments, and opportunities to test gifts for preaching and teaching, and a way to evaluate the progress.[24] Decide on how often formal meetings will take place. Incorporate praxis as part of the training. The protégé will need the chance to preach before an audience and receive affirmation and critique—make plans for such occasions.[25] He will need opportunities to join the pastor, staff, or elders in various types of visits, attending funerals, attending weddings—including rehearsals, and, if possible, even taking part in counseling sessions. He will need to do actual administrative tasks that will affect church ministry. He needs to see the inside of daily church ministry and to try his hand at serving in these settings. Regular debriefing will be critical to training.

If the trainee is being prepared for church planting and revitalization, the pastor will need to direct reading and research in those fields.[26] The same will be true for those aiming to pastor or do mission work. Begin the reading and discussions by building a strong theology of the church. The pastor will need to help the trainee to sift through pages of material to discern biblically appropriate church methodology that have a good foundation in healthy ecclesiology. Regular discussion of these subjects, visits with newly planted and newly revitalized churches (or those in the process) will strengthen the discussions. Trainees accompanying pastors and elders on mission trips will give insight for those preparing for international missions. The mentor might give the protégé some case studies in his area of ministry interest to see how he works through the details.[27] This type of mentoring and training will go a long way in giving the future planter or

---

23  Roberts Jr., *Multiplying Church*, 92.
24  See Appendix for a suggested reading list.
25  In a yearlong mentorship, I suggest having the pastoral intern preach at least six to ten times, as well as providing small group teaching opportunities. The pastor will need to review sermon notes before the intern preaches in order to provide sufficient guidance, followed by post-sermon critique. Follow a book on preaching, e.g., Bryan Chapell, *Christ-Centered Preaching: Redeeming the Expository Sermon,* 2d ed. (Grand Rapids: Baker Academic, 2005), as a guide to the preparation process. Scheduling preaching times might be a challenge in the church's regular schedule, so utilizing an alternative, such as those followed by Zwingli, Calvin, and Spurgeon discussed earlier, might serve the process well.
26  See Ed Stetzer's extended bibliography on church planting, Ed Stetzer, "Church Planting Bibliography," n.p. [cited 25 January 2012], http://www.christianitytoday.com/edstetzer/2009/april/church-planting-bibliography.html. See Appendix for recommended books on revitalization.
27  Roberts Jr., *Multiplying Church*, 92, writes, "Give them bite-size things and watch them."

revitalizer the critical tools he will need. It also gives him time to sharpen his gifts and abilities before facing the pressure of ministry.[28]

After six to nine months into the mentoring process, the mentor should have an idea of whether his protégé appears ready to be sent out, needs another year or two of training, or needs to consider serving Christ's church in a different way. As the mentor labors to build a strong relationship with his trainee, he will have the capacity to speak into his life—even when it may be painful for both, as glaring weaknesses might be exposed.[29] Above all, the mentor needs to be a model to his protégé, even as Jesus was to his disciples, leading by example.[30] When the time comes for the official mentorship to end, the pastor needs to understand that it really does not end. He will likely remain a mentor for years ahead, although contact might be more infrequent, as the protégé moves on to his own ministry.

Each of the following training models will incorporate this basic structure as foundational to their development. These models add another dimension to the basic model.

### A Partnership for Training between Seminary and the Local Church

The pastor and church leadership will need to align with a particular seminary for the theological education of their pastoral interns. The seminary training might be full-time, e.g., as practiced by Lakeview Baptist Church in Auburn and The Southern Baptist Theological Seminary, as noted in chapter thirteen. Or it could be a part-time arrangement, e.g., as with the Southeastern Baptist Theological Seminary Great Commission Equipping Network. While the seminary provides much of the academic training, the local church develops plans to make the ecclesial application. They serve as partners, recognizing the strengths of each body to equip the pastoral intern toward future ministry.

If a student has completed at least the first or second year of his seminary work, he might be better adjusted to juggling seminary and local church work. As much as possible, it seems best if the academic work can intersect with the emphases in the church, e.g., courses in missions, ecclesiology, church planting, pastoral ministry, counseling, hermeneutics and homiletics, and leadership. If the church leadership has academic qualifications to teach, then arrangements should be sought out with the seminary to lead, if possible, some of the classes in the local church. This will give the pastor a stronger connection with the seminary and

---

28  Ben Ingebretson, *Multiplication Moves: A Field Guide for Churches Parenting Churches* (Grand Rapids: Faith Alive Resources, 2012), 116–117.

29  See Thomas and Wood, *Gospel Coach*, 23–108, for helpful discussion on this subject.

30  Ted W. Engstrom, *The Making of a Christian Leader* (Grand Rapids: Pyranee Books, 1976), 37.

vice versa. The normal method of course evaluation will be helpful to the pastoral mentor in building on the trainee's strengths and honing areas of weakness. The mentor and trainee will need to determine the length of the training.

During one season while training a pastoral intern who sensed a calling to global missions, the Southeastern Baptist Theological Seminary—where he was enrolled as a student—gave me the opportunity to tailor a class on international church planting that focused on a particular unreached people group. Later, this young man and his wife served among that people group. The investment in dealing with that narrowed focus proved helpful in preparing him for mission work, as well as informing me with more details as I led our congregation in praying for and supporting them.

## A Full-Time Pastoral Training Model

A full-time pastoral training model might resemble the residencies discussed in chapters 10–12 for Capitol Hill Baptist Church, The Summit Church, and Grace Church. Leadership will need to decide if the intern will need to have a master of divinity degree before participating or if the model better suits one preparing to attend seminary. The pastoral intern serves full-time with the church in capacities planned by the pastor and leadership. One would expect some measure of compensation to be provided in this model, so the church will need to determine compensation level and housing arrangements, if needed, ahead of time, as well as the time investment on the part of the pastor and staff. A long-term syllabus and weekly schedule of responsibilities and assignments will need to be developed. The syllabus might be best determined after spending some time getting to know the pastoral intern, so that assignments might be tailored to build his strengths and strengthen his weaknesses.

The possibility for praxis in a full-time pastoral internship seems limitless. The pastoral intern will need to experience the full range of local church ministry. If it goes on in a local church, he needs to get his feet wet in it!

Along with praxis, the pastoral intern will need substantial reading that coordinates with the areas of church life: preaching, teaching, theology, ecclesiology, polity, leadership, counseling, missions, disciple making, et al. Of course, the assignments will need to keep in mind a good balance between time for reading and time for praxis. The reading and discussion that follows with the mentor will help to probe, inform, and promote critical thinking skills regarding ministry. The mentor will also need to major on the intern's church involvement, relationship building, refining rough edges in personality and relational skills, fulfilling assignments in timely fashion, and developing work ethic.

Establish clear-cut goals or aims at the start of the internship, so that there will be a tool to measure progress. The length of the internship will also need to be established so that adequate time is allowed for cultivating the gifts and abilities of the intern for readiness in pastoral work.

### A Full-Time Church Planter Resident Model

This church planter residency model follows the practice of The Summit Church described in chapter 11. The intention is to train the church planting (CP) resident and then to send him out with members of the congregation to plant a church. This is the most strategic type of CP training since its entire focus centers on church planting. One could also do the same with the focus on church revitalization or missions or pastoral work.[31] In this case, all seminary work would need to be completed before entering the residency. While keeping in mind the basic pastoral training content, this training model also gives attention to church planting strategies, evangelism/disciple making, missions, cultural issues, mercy ministries, and relationship building. Reading, assignments, discussion, mentorship, and praxis will need to incorporate these areas of ministry. The goal for this model will be a hands-on approach to ministry that is complemented with intensive reading, discussion, and assignments. The mentor will need to keenly observe the protégé's consistency, humility, attitude, ability to work with others, submissiveness, diligence, work ethic, leadership skills, and spiritual disciplines throughout the praxis and mentoring sessions. He will need to affirm and correct, understanding that this trainee will soon be leading members from his own congregation to plant a new work.

Ben Ingebretson notes, "The selection of the lead planter is the most important decision in a new church start."[32] Consequently, the residency model provides the most thorough opportunity to assess the trainee's aptitude and gifts for church planting, since he will exercise them in a real-life, local church setting. As Mike McDaniel wisely points out, the local church is the best church planter assessment tool.[33] The timeline for the residency should aim toward releasing him to be sent out by the church with the members in whom he has invested time preparing to serve as part of the leadership team with the new church plant. In this structure, it seems best that not only will the resident receive a salary during

---

31  See also McKinley, *Church Planting*, 27, who described a similar process that he went through at Capitol Hill Baptist Church before they sent him out to revitalize a church in Virginia.

32  Ingebretson, *Multiplication Moves*, 114.

33  Mike McDaniel, "Why You Should Do a Church Planting Residency," in SendRDU (6 February 2012), n.p. [cited 12 February 2013], www.sendrdu.com/blog/page/5.

his time of residency, but the church will also invest financially in the startup of the new church.

## CONCLUSION

Before starting a pastoral training ministry, a church's pastor and leadership will need to evaluate their goals for getting involved in training young ministers. The work will add to the already heavy load of local ministry, so they need to enter into it with a passion for continuing the task. They will need to understand the unique aspects of their local church setting, leadership structure, and community that might enhance the training model. They will also need to consider how various members of the congregation might contribute toward training young ministers, e.g., those whose life experiences have taught them how to apply the gospel in times of need. Will they train with a goal to prepare a church planter or revitalizer? Or will they train to prepare for regular pastoral or mission work?

Whichever direction the training model takes, it serves to prepare the rising generation for the challenges of pastoral ministry. In doing so, the mentoring church serves Christ's kingdom by preparing those who follow the divine call to plant, revitalize, pastor, or do mission work toward leading gospel-centered churches—just like the churches that trained them.

My goal has been to demonstrate that the best mentoring for pastoral ministry takes place within the framework of a healthy congregation. Whichever training model one might select, aside from the pastoral mentor's strong walk with Christ, the most important element in the training will be a church that lives out and displays the gospel in its relationships, ministries, and mission. In such a setting, the future pastor begins to grasp the importance and weightiness of the work ahead. He also has a clear model etched in his mind that will take shape as he heads to a mission setting or takes on a revitalization work or plans a new church. The mentorship and training has helped him to understand how to lead a congregation toward becoming a healthy, gospel-centered church for the glory of God. A mentoring church—by the partnership of pastors and congregation—multiplies kingdom work through faithfully training and sending new pastors and missionaries into Christ's mission.

# NOW IT'S YOUR TURN

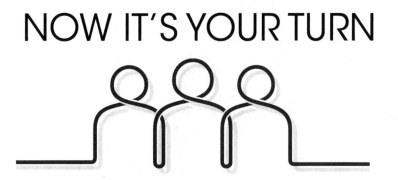

As one that needed an *organized mentorship* to prepare me for years of pastoral ministry, that just did not happen. But *it did happen* in countless other ways as members of churches served as God's instruments for honing and shaping me for pastoral work. The Lord brought just the right pastor or older Christian or hungry-hearted new believer into my life along the way to spur me forward. Biographies of those journeying before me gave me insight on ministry, challenged me at points of weakness, and inspired me toward faithfulness in God's calling to gospel ministry.

Yet, along the way, I made enough mistakes to fill a hefty book, not due to those who helped me through the years, but due to my misconceptions, idealism, stubbornness, ignorance, and inexperience about pastoral work. I think that's one reason that I'm so passionate about mentoring—I feel it every day in the weight of gospel ministry.

In all likelihood, some reading this conclusion feel the same weight of mentoring those preparing to step into pastorates, embark on mission work, launch into planting a new church, or serve a congregation as an elder or leader. No doubt, the task of mentoring can be compared to carving a figure out of a block of granite or forming a useful cup out of a lump of clay. The only way that the figure can emerge or the cup shaped will be by putting your hands to the work. It will not happen by staring at them.

That's the reason for the book you've just completed. By looking at the biblical models for mentoring in community, you've seen how mentoring works. The candidates shaped by Jesus, Peter, and Paul, were no different than the potential pastor or missionary in your congregation. They love Christ, desire to serve him, but they might falter without your guidance and willingness to speak into their lives about spiritual disciplines, interpreting the Scripture, preaching Christ, and shepherding the church.

My selection of Zwingli, Calvin, Spener, Gano, Spurgeon, and Bonhoeffer as historical mentoring models only touch the hem of the garment. Notice, as you read church history and biographies of pastors and missionaries, the influences on their lives that prepared them for ministry. You will likely find some patterns similar to what you've read concerning those chosen in this book. But you will also discover angles for mentoring that I've not mentioned. Continue learning from those who've gone before us.

The contemporary models, just like the historical ones, represent only a few out of hundreds of mentoring models. I make a practice of asking pastors how they train future gospel workers. I've learned so much just by asking, listening, and probing. I encourage you to do the same. We're not in competition but in partnership with one another, in training up the next generation who will faithfully serve Christ's church.

Now it's your turn. Who in your congregation shows interest in pastoral or mission work? Who is a potential elder candidate or church leader? Who do you see already doing the work of ministry that needs pastoral honing? *There are your trainees.* Pursue them. Using ideas that you've read in this book, develop a model that fits you, your trainees, and your pastoral context. Your model might not look like Spurgeon's or Al Jackson's or Mark Dever's or mine—all the better because it's your model, your mentorship that will serve your congregation and prepare new leaders for kingdom work. Trust the Lord of the Church for grace to engage in training the next generation.

# SUGGESTED BOOKS FOR PASTORAL TRAINING

## SPIRITUAL FORMATION

Beeke, Joel and Terry D. Slachter. *Encouragement for Today's Pastors: Help from the Puritans*. Grand Rapids: Reformation Heritage Books, 2013.

Bernard of Clairvaux. *Sermons on Conversion: On Conversions, a Sermon to Clerics and Lenten Sermons on the Psalm "He Who Dwells."* Cistercian Fathers Series 25. Translated by Marie-Bernard Saïd. Kalamazoo, MI: Cistercian Publications, 1981.

Brooks, Thomas. *Precious Remedies against Satan's Devices*. Puritan Paperbacks. Carlisle, PA: Banner of Truth, 2008 from 1652 edition.

Burroughs, Jeremiah. *The Rare Jewel of Christian Contentment*. Puritan Paperbacks. Carlisle, PA: Banner of Truth, 1964 from the 1648 edition.

Ferguson, Sinclair. *In Christ Alone: Living the Gospel-Centered Life*. Lake Mary, FL: Reformation Trust, 2007.

Hugh of Saint-Victor. *Selected Spiritual Writings*. Translated by a Religious of Community of St. Mary the Virgin. Eugene, OR: Wipt and Stock, 2009.

Köstenberger, Andreas J. *Excellence: The Character of God and the Pursuit of Scholarly Virtue*. Wheaton, IL: Crossway, 2011.

Owen, John. *Overcoming Sin & Temptation*. Edited by Kelly M. Kapic and Justin Taylor. Wheaton, IL: Crossway, 2006; from 1656, 1658, and 1667 editions.

Spener, Philip Jacob. *Pia Desideria*. Translated and edited by Theodore G. Tappert. Minneapolis: Fortress, 1964. Kindle edition.

Whitney, Donald. *Spiritual Disciplines for the Christian Life*. Colorado Springs: NavPress, 1991.

## ECCLESIOLOGY

Allison, Gregg R. *Sojourners and Strangers: The Doctrine of the Church*. Foundations of Evangelical Theology. John S. Feinberg, general editor. Wheaton, IL: Crossway, 2012.

Augustine. *City of God*. Translated by Marcus Dods. Nicene and Post-Nicene Fathers, edited by Philip Schaff. Peabody, MA: Hendrickson, 1994; from 1887 edition.

Dever, Mark E. *Nine Marks of a Healthy Church*. New expanded edition. Wheaton, IL: Crossway, 2004.

Hammett, John S. *Biblical Foundations for Baptist Churches: A Contemporary Ecclesiology*. Grand Rapids: Kregel, 2005.

Haykin, Michael A. G. *Rediscovering the Church Fathers: Who They Were and How They Shaped the Church*. Wheaton, IL: Crossway, 2011.

Hellerman, Joseph H. *When the Church Was a Family: Recapturing Jesus's Vision for Authentic Christian Community*. Nashville: B&H Academic, 2009.

Keller, Timothy. *Center Church: Doing Balanced, Gospel-Centered Ministry in Your City*. Grand Rapids: Zondervan, 2012.

*The Didache: The Lord's Teaching Through the Twelve Apostles to the Nations*. Kindle edition, n.d.

## HERMENEUTICS

Goldsworthy, Graeme. *Gospel-Centered Hermeneutics: Foundations and Principles of Evangelical Biblical Interpretation*. Downers Grove, IL: IVP, 2006.

Greidanus, Sidney. *The Modern Preacher and the Ancient Text: Interpreting and Preaching Biblical Literature*. Grand Rapids: Eerdmans, 1988.

Köstenberger, Andreas J. and Richard Patterson. *For the Love of God's Word: An Introduction to Biblical Interpretation*. Grand Rapids: Kregel Academic, 2015.

McCartney, Dan and Charles Clayton. *Let the Reader Understand: A Guide to Interpreting and Applying the Bible*. 2d ed. Phillipsburg, NJ: P&R, 2002.

## PREACHING

Ash, Christopher. *The Priority of Preaching*. Proclamation Trust Media. David Jackman and Robin Sydserff, eds. Fearn, Ross-shire, Scotland: Christian Focus Publications, 2009.

Chapell, Bryan. *Christ-Centered Preaching: Redeeming the Expository Sermon*. 2d edition. Grand Rapids: Baker Academic, 2005.

Clowney, Edmund P. *Preaching Christ in All of Scripture*. Wheaton, IL: Crossway, 2003.

Hall, Christopher A. *Reading Scripture with the Church Fathers*. Downers Grove, IL: IVP, 1998.

Jensen, Phillip D. and Paul Grimmond. *The Archer and the Arrow: Preaching the Very Words of God*. Kingsford, Australia: Matthias Media, 2010.

Johnson, Dennis E. *Him We Proclaim: Preaching Christ from All of Scripture*. Phillipsburg, NJ: P & R, 2007.

Lloyd-Jones, D. Martyn. *Preaching and Preachers*. 40th anniversary edition. Grand Rapids: Zondervan, 2011.

## PASTORAL MINISTRY

Armstrong, John H., editor. *Reforming Pastoral Ministry: Challenges for Ministry in Postmodern Times*. Wheaton, IL: Crossway, 2001.

Ascol, Thomas K., editor. *Dear Timothy: Letters on Pastoral Ministry*. Cape Coral, FL: Founders Press, 2004.

Bridges, Charles. *The Christian Ministry with An Inquiry into the Causes of its Inefficiency*. Carlisle, PA: Banner of Truth, 1967; from 1830 edition.

Croft, Brian. *Visit the Sick: Ministering God's Grace in Times of Illness*. Revised and updated. Practical Shepherding Series. Grand Rapids: Zondervan, 2014.

Croft, Brian and Phil A. Newton. *Conduct Gospel-Centered Funerals: Applying the Gospel at the Unique Challenges of Death*. Revised and updated. Practical Shepherding Series. Grand Rapids: Zondervan, 2014.

Dever, Mark and Paul Alexander. *Deliberate Church: Building Your Ministry on the Gospel*. Wheaton, IL: Crossway, 2005.

Gregory the Great. *The Book of Pastoral Rule*. Translated by James Barmby. Nicene and Post-Nicene Fathers, Vol. 12. Edited by Philip Schaff and Henry Wace. Peabody, MA: Hendrickson, 1994; from the 1895 edition.

Marshall, Colin and Tony Payne. *The Trellis and the Vine: The Ministry Mind-Shift That Changes Everything*. Kingsford, Australia: Matthias Media, 2009.

_____. *The Vine Project: Shaping Your Ministry Culture Around Disciple-Making*. Kingsford, Australia: Matthias Media, 2016.

MacArthur, John Jr., editor. *Rediscovering Pastoral Ministry: Shaping Contemporary Ministry with Biblical Mandates*. Dallas: Word, 1995.

Nettles, Tom. *Living by Revealed Truth: The Life and Pastoral Theology of Charles Haddon Spurgeon*. Fearn, Ross-shire, Scotland, UK: Mentor, 2013.

Piper, John and D. A. Carson. *The Pastor as Scholar & The Scholar as Pastor: Reflections on Life and Ministry*. Edited by Owen Strachan and David Mathis. Wheaton, IL: Crossway, 2011.

Purves, Andrew. *Pastoral Theology in the Classical Tradition*. Louisville: Westminster John Knox, 2001.

Saint Benedict. *The Rule of St. Benedict*. Translated by Boniface Verheyen. Atchison, KS: PlanetMonk Books, 2011. Kindle edition.

Sibbes, Richard. *The Bruised Reed*. Puritan Paperbacks. Carlisle, PA: Banner of Truth, 1998; from the 1630 edition.

Spurgeon, Charles Haddon. *Lectures to My Students*. Pasadena, TX: Pilgrim Publications, 1990 reprint; from 1881 edition.

Tidball, Derek. *Ministry by the Book: New Testament Patterns for Pastoral Leadership*. Downers Grove, IL: IVP Academic, 2008.

Witmer, Timothy Z. *The Shepherd Leader: Achieving Effective Shepherding in Your Church*. Phillipsburg, NJ: P&R, 2010.

## POLITY

Brand, Chad Owen and R. Stanton Norman, eds. *Perspectives on Church Government: Five Views of Church Polity*. Nashville, B&H, 2004.

Dever, Mark, ed. *Polity: Biblical Arguments on How to Conduct Church Life*. Washington, DC: Center for Church Reform, 2001.

Hammett, John S. and Benjamin L. Merkle, eds. *Those Who Must Give an Account: A Study on Church Membership and Church Discipline*. Nashville: B&H Academic, 2012.

Leeman, Jonathan. *Political Church: The Local Assembly as Embassy of Christ's Rule*. Studies in Christian Doctrine and Scripture. Downers Grove, IL: IVP Academic, 2016.

_____. *The Church and the Surprising Offense of God's Love: Reintroducing the Doctrines of Church Membership and Discipline*. Wheaton, IL: Crossway, 2010.

Newton, Phil A. and Matt Schmucker. *Elders in the Life of the Church: A Guide to Ministry*. Grand Rapids: Kregel, 2014.

## COUNSELING

Emlet, Michael R. *Cross Talk: Where Life and Scripture Meet*. Greensboro, NC:New Growth Press, 2009.

Köstenberger, Andreas J. and David Jones. *God, Marriage, and Family: Rebuilding the Biblical Foundation*. 2d ed. Wheaton, IL: Crossway, 2010.

Pierre, Jeremy and Deepak Reju. *The Pastor and Counseling: The Basics of Shepherding Members in Need*. 9Marks. Wheaton, IL: Crossway, 2015.

Powlison, David. *Seeing with New Eyes: Counseling and the Human Condition through the Lens of Scripture*. Phillipsburg, NJ: P&R, 2003.

_____. *Speaking the Truth in Love: Counsel in Community*. Greensboro, NC: New Growth Press, 2005. Church Planting

Murray, Stuart. *Church Planting: Laying Foundations*. Scottsdale, PA: Herald Press, 2001.

Keller, Timothy J. and J. Allen Thompson. *Redeemer Church Planting Manual*. New York: Redeemer Church Planting Center, 2002.

Ott, Craig and Gene Wilson. *Global Church Planting: Biblical Principles and Best Practices for Multiplication*. Grand Rapids: Baker Academic, 2011.

Payne, J. D. *Discovering Church Planting: An Introduction to the Whats, Whys, and Hows of Global Church Planting*. Colorado Springs: Paternoster, 2009.

Stetzer, Ed and Daniel Im. *Planting Missional Churches: Your Guide to Starting Churches that Multiply*. 2nd ed. Nashville: B&H Academic, 2016.

## CHURCH REVITALIZATION

Croft, Brian. *Biblical Church Revitalization: Solutions for Dying and Divided Churches*. Practical Shepherding Series. Fearn, Ross-shire, Scotland, UK: Christian Focus, 2016.

Liederbach, Mark and Alvin L. Reid. *The Convergent Church: Missional Worshipers in an Emerging Culture*. Grand Rapids: Kregel Academic, 2009.

McKinley, Michael. *Church Planting Is for Wimps: How God Uses Messed-up People to Plant Ordinary Churches That Do Extraordinary Things*. Wheaton, IL: Crossway, 2010.

Reid, Alvin L. *Revitalize Your Church through Gospel Recovery*. Amazon Digital Services, 2013.

"Revitalize: Why We Must Reclaim Dying Churches—and How," *9Marks Journal*. November-December 2011, www.9marks.org/journal/revitalize-why-we-must-reclaim-dying-churches-and-how.

Stetzer, Ed and John Michael Dodson. *Comeback Churches: How 300 Churches Turned Around and Yours Can, Too*. Nashville: B&H, 2007.

## RELATIONSHIPS

Crabtree, Sam. *Practicing Affirmation: God-Centered Praise for Those Who Are Not God*. Wheaton, IL: Crossway, 2011.

Lane, Timothy S. and Paul David Tripp. *Relationships: A Mess Worth Making*. Greensboro, NC: New Growth Press, 2008.

## LEADERSHIP

Bruce, A. B. *The Training of the Twelve*. Grand Rapids: Kregel, 1971; reprint of 1894 edition.

Mohler, R. Albert Jr. *The Conviction to Lead: 25 Principles for Leadership That Matters*. Minneapolis: Bethany House, 2012.

Sanders, J. Oswald. *Spiritual Leadership*. Chicago: Moody, 1967.

## DISCIPLE MAKING AND MISSION

Allen, Roland. *Missionary Methods: St. Paul's or Ours?* Grand Rapids: Eerdmans, 1962.

Ashford, Bruce Riley, editor. *Theology and Practice of Mission: God, the Church, and the Nations*. Nashville: B&H Academic, 2011.

Bonar, Horatius. *Words to Winners of Souls*. Phillipsburg, NJ: P&R, 1995; reprint of 1860 edition.

Coleman, Robert E. *The Master Plan of Discipleship*. Old Tappan, NJ: Revell, 1987.

_____. *The Master Plan of Evangelism*. Second edition, abridged. Grand Rapids: Revell, 1993.

Dever, Mark. *The Gospel and Personal Evangelism*. Wheaton, IL: Crossway, 2007.

Greear, J.D. *Gospel: Recovering the Power That Made Christianity*. Nashville: B&H, 2011.

Green, Michael. *Evangelism in the Early Church*. Revised edition. Grand Rapids: Eerdmans, 2003.

Helm, David. *One-to-One Bible Reading: A Simple Guide for Every Christian*. Kingsford, Australia: Matthias Media, 2011.

Metzger, Will. *Tell the Truth: The Whole Gospel to the Whole Person by Whole People*. 2d ed. Downers Grove, IL: IVP, 1984.

Packer, J. I. *Evangelism & the Sovereignty of God*. Downers Grove, IL: IVP, 1961.

Piper, John. *Let the Nations Be Glad! The Supremacy of God in Missions*. Grand Rapids: Baker, 1993.

Sills, M. David. *Reaching and Teaching: A Call to Great Commission Obedience*. Chicago: Moody, 2010.

Stiles, J. Mack. *Marks of the Messenger: Knowing, Living and Speaking the Gospel*. Downers Grove, IL: IVP, 2010.

Stott, John. *Christian Mission in the Modern World*. Downers Grove, IL: IVP, 2008.

# SELECTED BIBLIOGRAPHY

Akin, Daniel L., ed. *A Theology for the Church*. Nashville: B&H Academic, 2007.

Allen, Roland. *Missionary Methods: St. Paul's or Ours?* Grand Rapids: Eerdmans, 1962.

Alexander, J. W. *Thoughts on Preaching: Being Contributions to Homiletics*. Edinburgh: Banner of Truth, 1988.

Allison, Gregg R. *Sojourners and Strangers: The Doctrine of the Church*. Foundations of Evangelical Theology. John S. Feinberg, gen. ed. Wheaton, IL: Crossway, 2012.

Ascol, Thomas K. *Dear Timothy: Letters on Pastoral Ministry*. Cape Coral, FL: Founders Press, 2004.

Ash, Christopher. *The Priority of Preaching*. Proclamation Trust Media. David Jackman And Robin Sydserff, eds. Fearn, Ross-shire, Scotland: Christian Focus Publications, 2009.

Ashford, Bruce Riley, editor. *Theology and Practice of Mission: God, the Church, and the Nations*. Nashville: B&H Academic, 2011.

Avis, Paul D. L. *The Church in the Theology of the Reformers*. Eugene OR: Wipf and Stock Publishers, 2002; from Marshall, Morgan, and Scott, 1981.

Backus, Isaac. *A History of New England with Particular Reference to the Denomination of Christians Called Baptist*, 2nd ed. Vol. 2. Newton, MA: The Backus Historical Society, 1871.

_____. *Church History of New England from 1620 to 1804*. Philadelphia: American Baptist Publication and S. S. Society, 1844.

Bacon, Ernest W. *Spurgeon: Heir of the Puritans*. Arlington Heights, IL: Christian Liberty Press, 1996.

Banks, Robert J. *Paul's Idea of Community: The Early House Churches in Their Cultural Setting*. Rev. ed. Grand Rapids: Baker, 1994.

_____. *Reenvisioning Theological Education: Exploring a Missional Alternative to Current Models*. Grand Rapids: Eerdmans, 1999.

Barnett, Mike, ed. *Discovering the Mission of God: Best Missional Practices for the 21st Century.* Downers Grove, IL: IVP Academic, 2012.

Bauckham, Richard. *Jesus and the Eyewitnesses: The Gospels as Eyewitness Testimony.* Grand Rapids: Eerdmans, 2006.

Bauer, Walter, Frederick William Danker, W. F. Arndt, F. W. Gingrich. *A Greek-English Lexicon of the New Testament and Other Early Christian Literature.* 3d ed. Revised and edited by F. W. Danker. Chicago: University of Chicago Press, 2000.

Beale, G. K. *A New Testament Biblical Theology: The Unfolding of the Old Testament in the New.* Grand Rapids: Baker Academic, 2011.

Beeke, Joel R. and Terry D. Slachter. *Encouragement for Today's Pastors: Helps from the Puritans.* Grand Rapids: Reformation Heritage Books, 2013.

Benedict, David. *A General History of the Baptist Denomination in America and Other Parts of the World.* 2 vols. Boston: Lincoln & Edmands, 1813.

Berthoud, Jean-Marc. "La Formation des Pasteurs et la Prédication de Calvin." *La Revue Réformée* 201 (November 1998), cited 17 January 2013, http://larevuereFormee.net/articlerr/n201/la-formatino-des-pastuers-et-la-prediction-de-calvin.

Bethge, Eehard. *Dietrich Bonhoeffer: Man of Vision, Man of Courage.* Translated by Eric Mosbacher, Peter and Betty Ross, Frank Clarke, William Glen-Doepel. Edited by Edwin Robertson. New York: Harper & Row, 1977; from 1967 German edition.

Bird, Warren. "Churches Taking Back the Task of Theological Education." *Leadership Network* (no date): n.p., cited 12 January 2013, http://leadnet.org/churches_taking_back_the_task_of_theological_education/.

Blomberg, Craig L. *Jesus and the Gospels: An Introduction and Survey.* 2d ed. Nashville: B&H Academic, 2009.

Bloesch, Donald G. *The Church: Sacraments, Worship, Ministry, Mission.* Christian Foundations. Downers Grove, IL: IVP Academic, 2002.

Bock, Darrell L. *Luke.* 2 vols. Exegetical Commentary on the New Testament. Grand Rapids: Baker, 1994.

Bonhoeffer, Dietrich. *Discipleship.* Dietrich Bonhoeffer Works 4. Philadelphia: Fortress Press, Kindle Edition, 2003.

_____. *Letters & Papers from Prison.* Edited by Eberhard Bethge. New York: McMillan, 1972.

_____. *Dietrich Bonhoeffer—Life Together: Prayerbook of the Bible.* Vol. 5 of Dietrich Bonhoeffer Works. Translated and edited by Gerhard Ludwig Müller and Albrecht Schönherr. English edition edited by Geoffrey B. Kelly. Translated by Daniel W. Bloesch and James H. Burtness. Minneapolis: Fortress Press, 2005.

_____. *Dietrich Bonhoeffer—Theological Education Underground: 1937–1940.* Vol. 15 of Dietrich Bonhoeffer Works. Translated and edited by Dirk Schulz. English edition edited by Victoria J. Barnett. Translated by Victoria J. Barnett, Claudia D. Bergmann, Peter Frick, and Scott A. Moore. Supplementary material translated by Douglas W. Stott. Minneapolis: Fortress Press, 2012.

Bonnet, Jules, trans. and ed. *Letters of John Calvin: Complied from the Original Manuscripts and Edited with Historical Notes.* Vol. 2. Philadelphia: Presbyterian Board of Publication, 1858; no city: Repressed Publishing LLC, 2012 reprint.

Bornkham, Günther. *Paul (Paulus).* Translated by D. M. G. Stalker. New York: Harper & Row, 1971.

Bosch, David J. *Transforming Mission: Paradigm Shifts in Theology of Mission.* American Society of Missiology Series 16. Maryknoll, NY: Orbis Books, 2008.

Bridges, Charles. *The Christian Ministry: With an Inquiry into the Causes of its Inefficiency.* Carlisle, PA: Banner of Truth Trust, 1967; from 1830 edition.

Bromiley, Geoffrey, gen. ed. *International Standard Bible Encyclopedia.* 4 vols. Grand Rapids: Eerdmans, 1986.

Bromiley, Geoffrey, ed. *Zwingli and Bullinger.* Library of Christian Classics. Ichthus Edition. Philadelphia: Westminster Press, 1953.

Broome, John David. *Life, Ministry, and Journals of Hezekiah Smith, 1737–1805: Pastor of the First Baptist Church of Haverhill, Massachusetts and Chaplain in the Revolution.* Reprint of *The Journals of Hezekiah Smith, 1762–1805.* Springfield, MO: Particular Baptist Press, 2004.

Bruce, A. B. *The Training of the Twelve.* Grand Rapids: Kregel, 1971; reprint of 1894 edition.

Bruce, F. F. *New Testament History.* New York: Galilee/Doubleday, 1969.

_____. *The Spreading Flame: The Rise and Progress of Christianity from Its First Beginnings to the Conversion of the English.* Vol. 1 of *The Advance of Christianity Through the Centuries.* Edited by F. F. Bruce. Grand Rapids: Eerdmans, 1958.

Burrage, Henry S. *A History of the Baptists in New England.* Philadelphia: American Baptist Publication Society, 1894.

Calvin, John. *Calvin's Commentaries.* Translated by William Pringle. Grand Rapids: Baker, 2003.

_____. *Institutes of the Christian Religion.* Edited by John T. McNeill. Trans. by Ford L. Battles. Library of Christian Classics 20–21. Philadelphia: Westminster, 1960.

Campbell, Dennis M. "Theological Education and Moral Foundation: What's Going on in Seminaries Today?" Pages 1–21 in *Theological Education and Moral Foundation.* Encounter Series 15. Edited by Richard John Neuhaus. Grand Rapids: Eerdmans, 1992.

Campbell, Regi. *Mentor Like Jesus*. Nashville: B&H, 2009.

Carson, D. A. *Matthew*. 2 vols. The Expositor's Bible Commentary. Edited by Frank Gaebelein. Grand Rapids: Zondervan, 1995.

Carson, D. A., ed. *Entrusted with the Gospel: Pastoral Expositions of 2 Timothy*. Wheaton, IL: Crossway, 2010.

Christoffel, R. *Zwingli: or The Rise of the Reformation—a Life of the Reformer, with Some Notices of His Time and Contemporaries*. Translated by John Cochran. Edinburgh: T & T Clark, 1858.

Clarke, Andrew._A Pauline Theology of Church Leadership*. Library of New Testament Studies 362. Edited by Mark Goodacre. London: T & T Clark, 2008.

Clark, James L. *". . . To Set Them in Order": Some Influences of the Philadelphia Baptist Association upon Baptists in America to 1814*. The Philadelphia Association Series. Asheville, NC: Revival Literature, 2001.

Clowney, Edmund P. *Preaching Christ in All of Scripture*. Wheaton, IL: Crossway, 2003.

Coleman, Robert E. *The Master Plan of Discipleship*. Old Tappan, NJ: Revell, 1987.

_____. *The Master Plan of Evangelism*. Second edition, abridged. Grand Rapids: Revell, 1993.

Crow, D. Michael. "Multiplying Jesus Mentors: Designing a Reproducible Mentoring System—A Case Study." *Missiology: An International Review* 36:1 (January 2008): 87–109.

Dallimore, Arnold. *Spurgeon: A New Biography*. Carlisle, PA: Banner of Truth, 1985.

Dagg, J. L. *Manual of Church Order*. Harrisonburg, VA: Gano Books, 1990; reprint from 1858 edition.

D'Aubingé, Jean Henri Merle. *For God and His People: Ulrich Zwingli and the Swiss Reformation*. Translated by Henry White. Edited by Mark Sidwell. Greenville, SC: BJU Press, 2000.

De Greef, Wulfert. *The Writings of John Calvin: An Introductory Guide*. Translated by Lyle D. Bierma. Grand Rapids: Baker, 1993.

_____. *The Writings of John Calvin: An Introductory Guide*. Expanded edition. Translated by Lyle D. Bierma. Louisville: Westminster John Knox Press, 2008.

Dever, Mark. *A Display of God's Glory: Basics of Church Structure—Deacons, Elders, Congregationalism & Membership*. Washington, DC: Center for Church Reform, 2001.

_____. *By Whose Authority? Elders in Baptist Life*. Washington, DC: 9Marks, 2006.

_____. "How Do Pastors Raise Up Pastors?" *9Marks eJournal*, cited 21 September 2011, http://www.9marks.org/ejournal/how-do-pastors-raise-pastors.

_____. *Nine Marks of a Healthy Church*. New Expanded Edition. Wheaton, IL: Crossway, 2004.

_____. "Raising Up Pastors Is the Church's Work." *9Marks eJournal*, cited 21 September 2011, http://www.9marks.org/ejournal/raising-pastors-churches-work.

_____. *The Gospel and Personal Evangelism*. Wheaton, IL: Crossway, 2007.

Dever, Mark, ed. *Polity: Biblical Arguments on How to Conduct Church Life*. Washington, DC: Center for Church Reform, 2001.

Dever, Mark and Paul Alexander. *The Deliberate Church: Building Your Ministry on the Gospel*. Wheaton, IL: Crossway, 2005.

Dodd, Brian J. *Empowered Church Leadership: Ministry in the Spirit According to Paul*. Downers Grove, IL: IVP, 2003.

Earls, Rodney Douglas. "The Evangelistic Strategy of Charles Haddon Spurgeon for the Multiplication of Churches and Implications for Modern Church Extension Theory." PhD diss. Southwestern Baptist Theological Seminary, 1989.

Egeler, Daniel. *Mentoring Millennials: Shaping the Next Generation*. Colorado Springs: NavPress, 2003.

Engstrom, Ted W. *The Making of a Christian Leader*. Grand Rapids: Pyranee Books, 1976.

Eusebius. *Ecclesiastical History*. Translated by Christian F. Cruse. Popular Edition. Grand Rapids: Baker, 1995.

Ferris, Robert. *Renewal in Theological Education: Strategies for Change*. Billy Graham Center Monograph. Wheaton, IL: The Billy Graham Center, Wheaton College, 1990.

_____. "The Role of Theology in Theological Education." Pages 101–111 in *With an Eye on the Future: Development and Mission in the 21st Century—Essays in Honor of Ted Ward*. Edited by Duane Elmer and Lois McKinney. Monrovia, CA: MARC, 1996.

"50 Years of Seminary Education: Celebrating the Past, Assessing the Present." *Christianity Today* 50/10 (October 2006): Pages Special 4–Special 18.

Fitzmyer, Joseph A. *The Gospel According to Luke I–IX: A New Translation with Introduction and Commentary*. Anchor Bible 28. New Haven, CT: Yale University Press, 1970.

Furcha, E. J. and H. Wayne Pipkin, eds. *Prophet, Pastor, Protestant: The Work of Huldrych Zwingli After Five Hundred Years*. Eugene, OR: Pickwick Publications, 1984.

Gäbler, Ulrich. *Huldrych Zwingli: His Life and Work*. Translated by Ruth C. L. Gritsch. Philadelphia: Fortress Press, 1986.

Gano, John. *Biographical Memoirs of the Late Rev.. John Gano of Frankfort, Kentucky Formerly of the City of New York*. New York: Southwick and Hardcastle, 1806.

Gardner-Smith, Percival. "Factors in the Development and Expansion of the Early Church." *Modern Churchman* 41.3 (Spring 1951): 187–194.

Gaustad, Edwin S., ed. *Baptist Piety: The Last Will and Testament of Obadiah Holmes* Valley Forge, PA: Judson Press, 1994.

Genade, Aldred A. *Persuading the Cretans: A Text-Generated Persuasion Analysis of the Letter to Titus.* Eugene, OR: Wipf & Stock, 2011.

Timothy George. *Galatians.* New American Commentary 30. E. Ray Clendenen, gen. ed. Nashville: B&H, 1994.

_____. *Reading Scripture with the Reformers.* Downers Grove, IL: IVP Academic, 2011.

_____. *Theology of the Reformers.* Nashville: Broadman Press, 1988.

George, Timothy, editor. *John Calvin & the Church: A Prism of Reform.* Louisville: Westminster John Knox Press, 1990.

George, Timothy and David Dockery, editors. *Baptist Theologians.* Nashville: Broadman Press, 1990.

Gillette, A. D., editor. *Minutes of the Philadelphia Baptist Association 1707 to 1807: Being the First One Hundred Years of Its Existence.* Philadelphia: American Baptist Publications Society, 1851.

Godfrey, Michael. "The Role of Mentoring in the Developmental Experiences of Baptist Pastors in Texas: A Case Study." PhD diss., Baylor University, 2006.

Godfrey, W. Robert. *John Calvin: Pilgrim and Pastor.* Wheaton, IL: Crossway, 2009.

Goldsworthy, Graeme. *Gospel-Centered Hermeneutics: Foundations and Principles of Evangelical Biblical Interpretation.* Downers Grove, IL: IVP, 2006.

_____. *Preaching the Whole Bible as Christian Scripture: The Application of Biblical Theology to Expository Preaching.* Grand Rapids: Eerdmans, 2000.

González, Justo L. *A History of Christian Thought: From Augustine to the Eve of the Reformation.* Vol. 2. Rev.. ed. Nashville: Abingdon, 1987.

_____. *The Story of Christianity: The Early Church to the Present Day.* 2 vols. Peabody, MA: Prince Press, 2001.

Goodfriend, Joyce D. "The Baptist Church in Prerevolutionary New York City." *American Baptist Quarterly.* 16.3 (September 1997): 219–240.

J. D. Greear. "Five Factors that Brought Life to a Dying Church." *9Marks e-Journal,* cited 12 February 2013, www.9marks.org/journal/five-factors-brought-life-dying-church.

_____. *Gaining by Losing: Why the Future Belongs to Churches That Send.* Grand Rapids: Zondervan, 2015.

Green, Joel B. *The Gospel of Luke.* New International Greek Testament Commentary. Grand Rapids: Eerdmans, 1997.

Green, Michael. *Evangelism in the Early Church*. Grand Rapids: Eerdmans, 1970.

Gregory the Great. *The Book of Pastoral Rule*. Translated by James Barmby. Nicene and Post-Nicene Fathers, Vol. 12. Edited by Philip Schaff and Henry Wace. Peabody, MA: Hendrickson, 1994; from the 1895 edition.

Greidanus, Sidney. *The Modern Preacher and the Ancient Text: Interpreting and Preaching Biblical Literature*. Grand Rapids: Eerdmans, 1988.

Griffiths, Thomas S. *A History of Baptists in New Jersey*. Hightown, NJ: Barr Press Publishing Co., 1904.

Grudem, Wayne. *Systematic Theology: An Introduction to Biblical Doctrine*. Grand Rapids: Zondervan, 1994.

Gupta, Paul R. and Sherwood G. Lingenfelter. *Breaking Tradition to Accomplish Vision: Training Leaders for a Church-Planting Movement*. Winona Lake, IN: BMH Books, 2006.

Hall, Christopher A. *Reading Scripture with the Church Fathers*. Downers Grove, IL: IVP, 1998.

Hammett, John S. *Biblical Foundations for Baptist Churches: A Contemporary Ecclesiology*. Grand Rapids: Kregel, 2005.

_____. "How Church and Parachurch Should Relate: Arguments for a Servant-Partnership Model." *Missiology: An International Review* XXVIII.2 (April 2000): 200–207.

_____. "Selected Parachurch Groups and Southern Baptists An Ecclesiological Debate." PhD diss., The Southern Baptist Theological Seminary, 1991.

Hammett, John S. and Benjamin L. Merkle, eds. *Those Who Must Give an Account: A Study on Church Membership and Church Discipline*. Nashville: B&H Academic, 2012.

Harrison, Everett F. *A Short Life of Christ*. Grand Rapids: Zondervan, 1968.

_____. *Interpreting Acts: The Expanding Church*. Grand Rapids: Academie Books, 1986.

Harrison, Rodney, Tom Cheyney, and Don Overstreet. *Spin-Off Churches: How One Church Successfully Plants Another*. Nashville: B&H, 2008.

Haykin, Michael A. G. *Rediscovering the Church Fathers: Who They Were and How They Shaped the Church*. Wheaton, IL: Crossway, 2011.

Haykin, Michael, editor. *The British Particular Baptists 1638–1910*. Vol. 1. Springfield, MO: Particular Baptist Press, 2000.

Hellerman, Joseph H. *When the Church Was a Family: Recapturing Jesus's Vision for Authentic Christian Community*. Nashville: B&H Academic, 2009.

Helm, David. *One-to-One Bible Reading: A Simple Guide for Every Christian*. Kingsford, Australia: Matthias Media, 2011.

Hengel, Martin. _Acts and the History of Earliest Christianity_. Translated by John Bowden. Philadelphia: Fortress, 1979.

_____. _The Charismatic Leader and His Followers_. Eugene, OR: Wipf and Stock, 1968.

Hengel, Martin and Anna Maria Schwemer. _Paul between Damascus and Antioch: The Unknown Years_. Translated by John Bowden. Louisville: Westminster John Knox, 1997.

Hudson, Winthrop S., ed. _Baptist Concepts of the Church: A Survey of the Historical and Theological Issues Which Have Produced Change in Church Order_. Chicago: Judson Press, 1959.

Hughes, Philip E. _The Register of the Company of Pastors of Geneva in the Time of Calvin_. Grand Rapids: Eerdmans, 1966.

Hunt, Josh. "Finding Church Planters: Discovering and Discerning Those God Has Called to Start the Next Generation of Churches." Pages 1–17. _Leadership Network_, 2006.

Hunter, James Davison. _To Change the World: The Irony, Tragedy, & Possibility of Christianity in the Late Modern World_. Oxford: Oxford University Press, 2010.

Ingebretson, Ben. _Multiplication Moves: A Field Guide for Churches Parenting Churches_. Grand Rapids: Faith Alive Resources, 2012.

Ivimey, Joseph. _A History of the English Baptists_. Vol. 4. London: Isaac Taylor Hinton and Holdsworth & Ball, 1830.

Jackson, Al. "Churches Raising Up Pastors—Lakeview Baptist Church," in _9Marks e-Journal_, cited 12 February 2013, https://9marks.org/article/churches-raising-pastors-lakeview-baptist-church/.

_____. "Look, It's the Church's Job." _9Marks e-Journal_, cited 12 February 2013, https://9marks.org/article/look-its-churchs-job/.

_____. "The Strategy of Jesus," _The Union Pulpit: Sermons from Union University_ 7, 14–24. Jackson, TN: Union University Press, 2005.

Janz, Denis R. _A Reformation Reader: Primary Texts with Introductions_. Minneapolis: Fortress Press, 1999.

Jensen, Phillip D. and Paul Grimmond. _The Archer and the Arrow: Preaching the Very Words of God_. Kingsford, Australia: Matthias Media, 2010.

Johnson, Dennis E. _Him We Proclaim: Preaching Christ from All of Scripture_. Phillipsburg, NJ: P & R, 2007.

Johnson, Lee Sayers. "An Examination of the Role of John Gano in the Development of Baptist Life in North America, 1750–1804." PhD diss., Southwesternbaptist Theological Seminary, 1986.

Johnson, Luke Timothy. *The First and Second Letters to Timothy: A New Translation with Introduction and Commentary*. Anchor Bible 35A. General editors W. F. Albright and David N. Freedman. New Haven, CT: Yale University Press, 2001.

Jones, Juha. "Four Ways to Mentor Church Planters," EMQonline.com (October 2008), cited 8 February 2012, http://www.emisdirect.com/emq/issue-305/2205.

Julien, Tom. "Training Leaders by Planting Seed Truths." EMQonline.com (October 2008), cited 8 February 2012, http://www.emisdirect.com/emq/issue-305/2193.

Kaufman, Bob. *Worship Matters: Leading Others to Encounter the Greatness of God*. Wheaton, IL: Crossway, 2008.

Keller, Timothy J. *Center Church: Doing Balanced, Gospel-Centered Ministry in Your City*. Grand Rapids: Zonderan, 2012.

Keller, Timothy J. and J. Allen Thompson. *Redeemer Church Planting Manual*. New York: Redeemer Presbyterian Church, 2002.

Kelly, J. N. D. *Early Christian Doctrines*. New York: Harper One, 1978.

Kistemaker, Simon J. *Acts*. New Testament Commentary. Grand Rapids: Baker, 1990.

Kittel, Gerhard and Gerhard Friedrich, editors. *Theological Dictionary of the New Testament*. Translated by Geoffrey W. Bromiley. 10 vols. Grand Rapids: Eerdmans, 1964–1976.

Knight, George W. III. *The Pastoral Epistles*. New International Greek Testament Commentary. Edited by I. Howard Marshall and W. Ward Gasque. Grand Rapids: Eerdmans, 1992.

Köstenberger, Andreas J. *Excellence: The Character of God and the Pursuit of Scholarly Virtues*. Wheaton, IL: Crossway, 2011.

Köstenberger, Andreas J. and Terry L. Wilder, editors. *Entrusted with the Gospel: Paul's Theology in the Pastoral Epistles*. Nashville: B&H Academic, 2010.

Köstenberger, Andreas J. and David Jones. *God, Marriage, and Family: Rebuilding the Biblical Foundation*. 2d ed. Wheaton, IL: Crossway, 2010.

Köstenberger, Andreas J. and Peter T. O'Brien. *Salvation to the Ends of the Earth: A Biblical Theology of Mission*. New Studies in Biblical Theology. Edited by D. A. Carson. Downers Grove, IL: IVP, 2001.

Kraft, Dave. *Leaders Who Last*. Wheaton, IL: Crossway, 2010.

Krallmann, Günter. *Mentoring for Mission: A Handbook on Leadership Principles Exemplified by Jesus Christ*. Waynesboro, GA: Gabriel Publishing, 2002.

Kwon, Lillian. "Is the Church Dying in America's Bible Belt?" *Christianity Today* (April 28, 2010), cited 24 January 2012, http://www.christiantoday.com/article/is.the.church.dying.in.americas.bible%09.belt/25802.htm.

Lane, Timothy S. and Paul David Tripp. *Relationships: A Mess Worth Making*. Greensboro, NC: New Growth Press, 2008.

Larkin, William J. Jr. and Joel F. Williams, eds. *Mission in the New Testament: An Evangelical Approach*. American Society of Missiology Series 27. Maryknoll, NY: Orbis Books, 1999.

Lawless, Chuck and Adam. W. Greenway, eds. *The Great Commission Resurgence: Fulfilling God's Mandate in Our Time*. Nashville: B&H Academic, 2010.

Lea, Thomas D. and Hayne P. Griffin Jr. *1, 2 Timothy Titus*. New American Commentary 34. Edited by David Dockery. Nashville: Broadman Press, 1992.

Leeman, Jonathan. *The Church and the Surprising Offense of God's Love: Reintroducing the Doctrines of Church Membership and Discipline*. Wheaton, IL: Crossway, 2010.

Liederbach, Mark and Alvin L. Reid. *The Convergent Church: Missional Worshipers in an Emerging Culture*. Grand Rapids: Kregel Academic, 2009.

Lloyd-Jones, D. Martin. *Christian Unity: An Exposition of Ephesians 4:1–16*. Grand Rapids: Baker, 1980.

_____. *Preaching and Preachers*. 40th anniversary ed. Grand Rapids: Zondervan, 2012.

_____. *The Puritans—Their Origins and Successors: Addresses Delivered at the Puritan and Westminster Conferences 1959–1978*. Carlisle, PA: Banner of Truth, 1987.

Locher, Gottfried. *Zwingli's Thought: New Perspectives*. Leiden, The Netherlands: E. J. Brill, 1981.

Louw, Johannes P. and Eugene Nida. *Greek-English Lexicon of the New Testament Based on Semantic Domains*. Logos Bible Software 4.

Lull, Timothy F., ed. *Martin Luther's Basic Theological Writings*. 2d ed. Minneapolis: Fortress Press, 2005.

Luther, Martin. *The Table Talk of Martin Luther*. Edited by Andrew Dickson White, Alexander Chalmers, and William Hazlitt. Mineola, NY: Dover Publications/ Nabu Press, 2010.

Maag, Karin. *Seminary or University? The Genevan Academy and Reformed Higher Education 1560–1620*. St. Andrews Studies in Reformation History. Edited by Andrew Pettegree, Bruce Gordon, and John Guy. Aldershot, Hants, UK: Scolar Press, 1995.

Malherbe, Abraham J. *Paul and the Popular Philosophers*. Minneapolis: Fortress, 1989.

Manetsch, Scott M. *Calvin's Company of Pastors: Pastoral Care and the Emerging Reformed Chruch, 1536–1609*. Oxford Studies in Historical Theology. Edited by David Steinmetz. New York: Oxford University Press, 2013.

Manly, Basil, Jr. *History of the Elkhorn Association,* from *Sketches from the History of the Elkhorn Baptist Association,* 1–9; cited 9 February 2011, http://baptisthistoryhomepage.com/elkhorn.assoc.his1.manly.html.

Manson, T. W. *The Teaching of Jesus: Studies of Its Form and Context.* Cambridge: Cambridge University Press, 1967.

Marshall, Colin and Tony Payne. *The Trellis and the Vine: The Ministry Mind-Shift That Changes Everything.* Kingsford, Australia: Matthias Media, 2009.

Marshall, Colin. *Passing the Baton: A Handbook for Ministry Apprenticeship.* Kingsford, Australia: Matthias Media, 2007.

Marshall, I. Howard. *The Gospel of Luke.* New International Greek Testament Commentary. Grand Rapids: Eerdmans, 1978.

_____. *The Pastoral Epistles.* International Critical Commentary. Edited by J. A. Emerton, C. E. B. Cranfield, and G. N. Stanton. London: T & T Clark, 1999.

Mattson, Daniel L. "Church Planting through Leadership Formation." *Missio Apostolica* 3.2 (November 1995): 79–84.

McKinley, Mike. *Am I Really a Christian?* Wheaton, IL: Crossway, 2011.

_____. *Church Planting Is for Wimps—How God Uses Messed-up People to Plant Ordinary Churches That Do Extraordinary Things.* Wheaton, IL: Crossway, 2010.

McKinney, Larry J. "The Church-Parachurch Conflict: A Proposed Solution. Didaskalia 6.1 (Fall 1994): 47–57.

McLoughlin, William G. "The First Calvinistic Baptist Association in New England, 1754?–1767. *Church History* 36.4 (December 1967): 410–418.

McNeal, Reggie. *Practicing Greatness: 7 Disciplines of Extraordinary Spiritual Leaders.* San Francisco: Jossey-Bass, 2006.

Merkle, Benjamin. *40 Questions about Elders and Deacons.* Grand Rapids: Kregel, 2007.

_____. *The Elder and the Overseer: One Office in the Early Church.* Society of Biblical Literature 57. New York: Peter Lang, 2003.

Metzger, Bruce M. *A Textual Commentary on the Greek New Testament.* New York: United Bible Societies, 1971.

Metzger, Will. *Tell the Truth: The Whole Gospel to the Whole Person by Whole People.* 2d ed. Downers Grove, IL: IVP, 1984.

Metaxas, Eric. *Bonhoeffer: Pastor, Martyr, Prophet, Spy—A Righteous Gentile vs. the Third Reich.* Nashville: Thomas Nelson, 2010. Kindle edition.

Miller, C. John. *The Heart of a Servant Leader: Letters from Jack Miller.* Phillipsburg, NJ: P&R, 2004.

Minea, Paul S. *Images of the Church in the New Testament.* Philadelphia: Westminster, 1960.

Mohler, R. Albert Jr. *The Conviction to Lead: 25 Principles for Leadership That Matters*. Minneapolis: Bethany House, 2012.

Moreau, A. Scott, Harold Netland, and Charles Van Engen, eds. *Evangelical Dictionary of World Missions*. Grand Rapids: Baker, 2000.

Mounce, William D. *Pastoral Epistles*. Word Biblical Commentary 46. Edited by Bruce Metzger. Nashville: Thomas Nelson, 2000.

Murphy, Thomas. *Pastoral Theology: The Pastor in the Various Duties of His Office*. Willow Street, Pa.: Old Paths Publications, 1996; reprint from 1877 edition.

Murray, Iain. *Spurgeon v. Hyper-Calvinism: The Battle for Gospel Preaching*. Carlisle, PA: Banner of Truth, 1995.

_____. *The Forgotten Spurgeon*. Carlisle, PA: Banner of Truth, 1972.

Murray, Iain, ed. *D. Martyn Lloyd-Jones 1919–1981*. Edinburgh: Banner of Truth, 1994.

Murray, John. *Principles of Conduct: Aspects of Biblical Ethics*. Grand Rapids: Eerdmans, 1957.

Murray, Stuart. *Church Planting: Laying Foundations*. Scottsdale, PA: Herald Press, 2001.

Nettles, Tom. *Living by Revealed Truth: The Life and Pastoral Theology of Charles Haddon Spurgeon*. Fearn, Ross-shire, Scotland: Mentor, 2013.

_____. *The Baptists: Key People Involved in Forming a Baptist Identity*. Beginnings in Britain, Vol. 1–2. Fearn, Ross-shire, Scotland: Mentor, 2005.

Newton, Phil A. *Elders in Congregational Life: Rediscovering the Biblical Model for Church Leadership*. Grand Rapids: Kregel, 2005.

Newton, Phil A. and Matt Schmucker. *Elders in the Life of the Church: A Guide to Ministry*. Grand Rapids: Kregel, 2014.

Nichols, Mike. "Teaching Outside the Classroom: The Power of Relationship." EMQonline.com (January 2012), cited 8 February 2012, http://www.emisdirect.com/emq/issue-318/2634.

Nickel, Tim. "Luke 10 Strategy for Village Church Planting." *Missio Apostolica* 13.1 (May 2005): 43–48.

Nissen, Johannes. *New Testament and Mission: Historical and Hermeneutical Perspectives*. 3d ed. Frankfurt: Peter Lang, 2004.

Oliver, Robert W. *History of the English Calvinistic Baptists 1771–1892: From John Gill to C. H. Spurgeon*. Carlisle, PA: Banner of Truth, 2006.

Ott, Craig. "Matching the Church Planter's Role with the Church Planting Model." EMQonline.com (July 2001), cited 8 May 2012, http://www.emisdirect.com/emq/issue-251/1480.

Ott, Craig and Gene Wilson. *Global Church Planting: Biblical Principles and Best Practices for Multiplication*. Grand Rapids: Baker Academic, 2011.

Packer, J. I. *Evangelism & the Sovereignty of God.* Downers Grove, IL: IVP, 1961.

Parro, Craig. "Asking Tough Questions: What Really Happens When We Train Leaders." EMQonline.com (January 2012), cited 8 February 2012, http://www.emisdirect.com/emq/issue-318/2634.

Payne, J. D. *Discovering Church Planting: An Introduction to the Whats, Whys, and Hows of Global Church Planting.* Colorado Springs: Paternoster, 2009.

Peerbolte, J. Lietaert. *Paul the Missionary.* Biblical Exegesis and Theology 34. Leuven: Peeters, 2003.

Pesch, Rudolph. *Die Apostelgeschichte.* 2 vols. Evangelisch-Catholischer Kommentar zum Neuen Testament 5. Edited by Josef Blank, Rudolf Schnackenburg, Eduard Schweizer, and Ulrich Wilckens. Zürich: Benziger Verlag, 1986.

Peterson, David G. *The Acts of the Apostles.* Pillar New Testament Commentary. Edited by D. A. Carson. Grand Rapids: Eerdmans, 2009.

Pettegree, Andrew, Alastair Duke, and Gillian Lewis, eds. *Calvinism in Europe 1540–1620.* Cambridge: Cambridge University Press, 1994.

Phillips, Richard D., Philip G. Ryken, and Mark E. Dever. *The Church: One, Holy, Catholic, and Apostolic.* Phillipsburg, NJ: P&R, 2004.

Pike, G. Holden. *The Life & Work of Charles Haddon Spurgeon.* 5 vols. Carlisle, PA: Banner of Truth, 1991; originally published London: Cassell & Co., 1894.

Piper, John. *The Supremacy of God in Preaching.* Grand Rapids: Baker, 1990.

_____. *What Jesus Demands from the World.* Wheaton, IL: Crossway, 2006.

Piper, John and D. A. Carson. *The Pastor as Scholar & The Scholar as Pastor: Reflections on Life and Ministry.* Edited by Owen Strachan and David Mathis. Wheaton, IL: Crossway, 2011.

Pocock, Michael. "The Role of Encouragement in Leadership." Pages 301–307 in *Integrity of Heart, Skillfulness of Hands: Biblical and Leadership Studies in Honor of Donald K. Campbell.* Edited by Charles H. Dyer and Roy B. Zuck. Grand Rapids: Baker, 1994.

Potter, G. R., editor. *Huldrych Zwingli: Documents of Modern History.* London: Edward Arnold, 1978.

Powlison, David. *Seeing with New Eyes: Counseling and the Human Condition Through the Lens of Scripture.* Phillipsburg, NJ: P&R, 2003.

_____. *Speaking the Truth in Love: Counsel in Community.* Greensboro, NC: New Growth Press, 2005.

Prime, Derek and Alistair Begg. *On Being a Pastor: Understanding Our Calling and Work.* Chicago: Moody, 2004.

Purefoy, George W. *A History of the Sandy Creek Baptist Association from its Organization in A. D. 1758, to A. D. 1858.* New York: Sheldon & Co., 1859.

Purves, Andrew. *Pastoral Theology in the Classical Tradition*. Louisville: Westminster John Knox Press, 2001.

Ray, Thomas. *Daniel and Abraham Marshall: Pioneer Baptist Evangelists to the South* Springfield, MO: Particular Baptist Press, 2006.

Reid, Alvin L. *Revitalize Your Church through Gospel Recovery*. Amazon Digital Services, 2013.

Reymond, Robert L. *John Calvin: His Life & Influence*. Fearn, Ross-shire, UK: Christian Focus, 2004.

Ridley, Charles R. *How to Select Church Planters*. Pasadena, CA: Fuller Evangelistic Association, 1988.

Roberts, Bob Jr. *The Multiplying Church: The New Math for Starting New Churches*. Grand Rapids: Zondervan, 2008.

Rogers, Matt. "Holistic Pastoral Training: Partnership Between the Seminary and the Local Church in the United States." PhD diss. Southeastern Baptist Theological Seminary, 2015.

Ryken, Philip G. *City on a Hill: Reclaiming the Biblical Pattern for the Church in the 21st Century*. Chicago: Moody, 2003.

Saint Benedict. *The Rule of St. Benedict*. Translated by Boniface Verheyen. Atchison, KS: PlanetMonk Books, 2011. Kindle edition.

Samra, James George. *Being Conformed to Christ in Community: A Study of Maturity, Maturation and the Local Church in the Undisputed Pauline Epistles*. Library of Biblical Studies 320. Edted by Mark Goodacre. London: T & T Clark, 2006.

Sanchez, Daniel R., Ebbie C. Smith, and Curtis E. Watke. *Reproducing Congregations: A Guidebook for Contextual New Church Development*. Cumming, GA: Church Starting Network, 2001.

Sanders, J. Oswald. *Spiritual Leadership*. Chicago: Moody, 1967.

Schnabel, Eckhard J. *Acts*. Evangelical Commentary of the New Testament. Clinton E. Arnold, gen. ed. Grand Rapids: Zondervan, 2012.

_____. *Early Christian Mission*. 2 vols. Downers Grove, IL: IVP, 2004.

_____. *Paul the Missionary: Realities, Strategies and Methods*. Downers Grove, IL: IVP, 2008.

Schreiner, Thomas. *New Testament Theology: Magnifying God in Christ*. Grand Rapids: Baker Academic, 2008.

Schrönherr, Albrecht. "Dietrich Bonhoeffer: The Message of a Life." *Christian Century* (27 November 1985): 1090–1094; cited 4 February 2013, http://www.religion-online.org/showarticle.asp?title=1928.

Shelley, Bruce. *Church History in Plain Language*. 2d ed. Updated. Dallas: Word, 1995.

Sherman, Andrew M. *Historic Morristown, New Jersey: The Story of Its First Century*. Morristown, NJ: The Howard Publishing Co., 1905.

Sibbes, Richard. *The Bruised Reed*. Puritan Paperbacks. Carlisle, PA: Banner of Truth, 1998; from the 1630 edition.

Sills, David. *Reaching and Teaching: A Call to Great Commission Obedience*. Chicago: Moody, 2010.

Sinclair, Daniel. *A Vision of the Possible: Pioneer Church Planting in Teams*. Colorado Springs: Authentic, 2005.

Smith, Glenn. "Models for Raising Up Church Planters: How Churches Become More Effective through Intentional Leadership Development." *Leadership Network* (2007): 1–17.

Snyder, Howard Alan. "Pietism, Moravianism, and Methodism as Renewal Movements: A Comparative and Thematic Study." PhD diss., University of Notre Dame, 1983.

Spencer, David. *The Early Baptists of Philadelphia*. Philadelphia: William Syckelmoore, 1877.

Spener, Philip Jacob. *Pia Desideria*. Translated and edited by Theodore G. Tappert. Minneapolis: Fortress, 1964. Kindle edition.

Spijker, Willem Van't. *Calvin: A Brief Guide to His Life and Thought*. Translated by Lyle D. Bierma. Louisville: Westminster John Knox Press, 2009.

Spurgeon, C. H. *An All-Round Ministry*. Carlisle, PA: Banner of Truth Trust, 1960 from 1900 edition.

_____. *C. H. Spurgeon Autobiography*. 2 vols. Revised and edited by Susannah Spurgeon and Joseph Harrald. Carlisle, PA: Banner of Truth, 1973 reprint. Originally published 1897–1900.

_____. *Lectures to My Students*. Pasadena, TX: Pilgrim Publications, 1990; reprint from 1881 edition.

Sprague, William B. *Annals of the American Baptist Pulpit; or Commemorative Notices of Distinguished Clergymen of the Baptist Denomination in the United States, from the Early Settlement of the Country to the Close of the Year Eighteen Hundred and Fifty-five*. Vol. 6. New York: Robert Carter & Brothers, 1860.

Stackhouse, Max L. *Apologia: Contextualization, Globalization, and Mission in Theological Education*. Grand Rapids: Eerdmans, 1988.

Stanley, Paul D. and J. Robert Clinton. *Connecting: The Mentoring Relationships You Need to Succeed in Life*. Colorado Springs: NavPress, 1992.

Stark, Rodney. *The Triumph of Christianity: How the Jesus Movement Became the World's Largest Religion*. New York: Harper One, 2011.

Stetzer, Ed. "Annotated North American Church Planting Bibliography," cited 25 January 2012, http://www.christianitytoday.com/edstetzer/2009/april/church-planting-bibliography.html.

_____. *Planting Missional Churches: Planting a Church That's Biblically Sound and Reaching People in Culture*. Nashville: B & H Academic, 2006.

_____. "The Impact of the Church Planting Process and Other Selected Factors on the Attendance of Southern Baptist Church Plants." PhD diss., The Southern Baptist Theological Seminary, 2003.

Stetzer, Ed and Warren Bird. "The State of Church Planting in the United States: Research Overview and Qualitative Study of Primary Church Planting Entities," cited 10 July 2012, www.christianitytoday.com/assets/10228.pdf.

_____. *Viral Churches: Helping Church Planters Become Movement Makers*. Leadership Network Series. San Francisco: Jossey-Bassey, 2010.

Stetzer, Ed and Michael Dodson. *Comeback Churches: How 300 Churches Turned Around and Yours Can, Too*. Nashville: B&H, 2007.

Stetzer, Ed and David Putman. *Breaking the Missional Code: Your Church Can Become A Missionary in Your Community*. Nashville: B&H, 2006.

Stiles, J. Mack. *Marks of the Messenger: Knowing, Living and Speaking the Gospel*. Downers Grove, IL: IVP, 2010.

Stott, John. *Between Two Worlds: The Challenge of Preaching Today*. Grand Rapids: Eerdmans, 1982.

_____. *Biblical Preaching Today*. Grand Rapids: Eerdmans, 1961, 1982.

_____. *Christian Mission in the Modern World*. Downers Grove, IL: IVP, 2008

_____. *Guard the Truth: The Message of 1 Timothy & Titus*. Downers Grove, IL: InterVarsity Press, 1996.

_____. *The Message of 2 Timothy*. Bible Speaks Today. Edited by J. A. Motyer and John R. W. Stott. Downers Grove, IL: InterVarsity Press, 1973.

_____. *The Spirit, the Church, and the World*. Downers Grove, IL: IVP, 1990.

Sweet, William Warren. *Religion on the American Frontier: The Baptists 1783–1830, A Collection of Source Material*. New York: Cooper Square Publishers, 1964.

*The Ante-Nicene Fathers*. 10 vols. Edited by Alexander Roberts and James Donaldson. Peabody, MA: Hendrickson, 1994; reprint of 1885–1887 edition.

*The Didache: The Lord's Teaching through the Twelve Apostles to the Nations*. Kindle edition, n.d.

Thomas, Scott and Tom Woods. *Gospel Coach: Shepherding Leaders to Glorify God*. Grand Rapids: Zondervan, 2012.

Tidball, Derek. *Ministry by the Book: New Testament Patterns for Pastoral Leadership.* Downers Grove, IL: IVP Academic, 2008.

Timmis, Stephen, ed. *Multiplying Churches: Reaching Communities through Church Planting.* Hearn, Ross-shire, UK: Christian Focus Publications, 2000.

Towner, Philip H. *The Letters to Timothy and Titus.* New International Commentary on the New Testament. Edited by Ned Stonehouse, F. F. Bruce, and Gordon Fee. Grand Rapids: Eerdmans, 2006.

Underwood, A. C. *A History of the English Baptists.* London: The Carey Kingsgate Press Limited, 1956.

Van Neste, Ray. *Cohesion and Structure in the Pastoral Epistles.* Journal for the Study of The New Testament: Supplement Series 280. Edited by Mark Goodacre. London: T & T Clark International, 2004.

Vaughan, Curtis. *Acts.* Founders Study Guide Commentary. Cape Coral, FL: Founders Press, 2009.

Verner, David C. *The Household of God: The Social World of the Pastoral Epistles.* Society of Biblical Literature Dissertation Series 71. Edited by William Baird. Chico, CA: Scholars Press, 1983.

Walker, Williston. *A History of the Christian Church (1918).* New York: Charles Scribner's Sons, 1918.

_____. *John Calvin: Revolutionary, Theologian, Pastor.* Fern, Ross-shire, UK: Christian Focus, 2005 from 1906 edition.

Walton, Steve. *Leadership and Lifestyle: The Portrait of Paul in the Miletus Speech and 1 Thessalonians.* Society for New Testament Studies Monograph Series. Richard Bauckham, gen. ed. Cambridge: Cambridge University Press, 2000.

Wells, David. *No Place for Truth; Or Whatever Happened to Evangelical Theology?* Grand Rapids: Eerdmans, 1993.

_____. *The Courage to Be Protestants: Truth-lovers, Marketers, and Emergents in the Postmodern World.* Grand Rapids: Eerdmans, 2008.

Witmer, Timothy Z. *The Shepherd Leader: Achieving Effective Shepherding in Your Church.* Phillipsburg, NJ: P&R, 2010.

Wolever, Terry. *The Life and Ministry of John Gano, 1727–1804.* The Philadelphia Association Series, Vol. 1. Springfield, MO: Particular Baptist Press, 1998.

Woodbridge, John D., gen. ed. *Great Leaders of the Christian Church.* Chicago: Moody, 1988.

Wright, Walter C. *Relational Leadership: A Biblical Model for Leadership Service.* Carlisle, Cumbria, UK: Paternoster Press, 2000.

Young, Frances. *The Theology of the Pastoral Letters.* New Testament Theology. Edited by James D. G. Dunn. Cambridge: Cambridge University Press, 1994.

Zachman, Randall C. *John Calvin as Teacher, Pastor, and Theologian: The Shape of His Writings and Thought.* Grand Rapids: Baker Academic, 2006.

Zwingli, Huldrych. *Huldrych Zwingli Writings: In Search of True Religion: Reformation, Pastoral and Eucharistic Writings.* Vol. 2. 500th Anniversary edition. Translated by H. Wayne Pipkin. Eugene, OR: Pickwick Publications, 1984.

# SCRIPTURE INDEX

## JOHN

## ACTS

## ROMANS

## 1 CORINTHIANS

## 2 CORINTHIANS

## GALATIANS

## EPHESIANS

## PHILIPPIANS

# SUBJECT INDEX